PUBLIC FINANCE AND POST-COMMUNIST
PARTY DEVELOPMENT

To Bill and Jeff for setting me on this path

To Ausma, Lucijāns and Veronika, for your care and patience

Public Finance and Post-Communist Party Development

Edited by

STEVEN D. ROPER
Eastern Illinois University, US

JĀNIS IKSTENS
University of Latvia, Latvia

Routledge
Taylor & Francis Group

LONDON AND NEW YORK

First published 2008 by Ashgate Publishing

Published 2016 by Routledge
2 Park Square, Milton Park, Abingdon, Oxfordshire OX14 4RN
711 Third Avenue, New York, NY 10017, USA

First issued in paperback 2016

Routledge is an imprint of the Taylor & Francis Group, an informa business

British Library Cataloguing in Publication Data
Public finance and post-communist party development
  1. Campaign funds - Former communist countries 2. Elections
  - Former communist countries 3. Political parties - Former
  communist countries
  I. Roper, Steven D. II. Ikstens, Jānis
  324.2'1'091717

Library of Congress Cataloging-in-Publication Data
Roper, Steven D.
  Public finance and post-communist party development / by Steven D. Roper and Jānis Ikstens.
    p. cm.
  Includes index.
  ISBN 978-0-7546-7179-4
  1. Campaign funds--Former communist countries. 2. Elections--Former communist countries. 3. Political parties--Former communist countries. I. Ikstens, Jānis. II. Title.

  JN96.A95R65 2008
  324.2'1091717--dc22

                                                                    2008003563

ISBN 13: 978-1-138-27552-2 (pbk)
ISBN 13: 978-0-7546-7179-4 (hbk)

Contents

List of Tables

Notes on Contributors

Vladimir Gel'man is a Professor in the Faculty of Political Science and Sociology at the European University in St. Petersburg, Russia. He is an author and editor of sixteen books in Russian and in English, including *Making and Breaking Democratic Transitions: The Comparative Politics of Russia's Regions* (2003) and *Elites and Democratic Development in Russia* (2003).

Jānis Ikstens is an Associate Professor of Political Science at the University of Latvia. His main research interests are related to party politics and electoral behavior in Eastern Europe.

Gabriella Ilonszki is a Professor at the Institute of Political Science at Corvinus University in Budapest and heads the Centre for Elite Studies. Her research interests include the analysis of political elites, first of all representatives and top government personnel, including women, and their role in maintaining or transforming regimes. Her most recent book is *Parlamenti képviselők Magyarországon* (*Parliamentary Representatives in Hungary*, 2005), and she edited *Women in Decision-making: CEE Experiences* (2004).

Elena Iorga is a Program Coordinator at the Institute for Public Policy in Bucharest, Romania and a researcher on parties and electoral systems. Her major publications include *Your MPs Vote Laws for You: Practical Guide for Using the Nominal Voting Procedure, Registering and Publishing Individual Votes on Bills* (2007) and *How to Lobby Your MP* (2006).

Riho Kangur received his BA from the Department of Political Science at the University of Tartu and is completing his MA thesis. He is an adviser at the Chancellery of the Estonian parliament.

Tatiana Kostadinova is an Assistant Professor of Political Science at Florida International University. Her research focuses on institutional reform and the role of domestic and international institutions in post-communist East European politics. She has published a book on Bulgarian parliamentary elections and articles in the *American Journal of Political Science, Journal of Peace Research, European Journal of Political Research, Electoral Studies, Party Politics* and *Europe-Asia Studies*.

Lukáš Linek is a Junior Researcher at the Institute of Sociology in the Czech Academy of Science and Lecturer in the Department of Sociology at Charles

University in Prague. His interests include party politics, electoral behavior and political attitudes. He has published in the *Journal of Communist Studies and Transitional Politics* and *Journal of Legislative Studies* and is co-author of *Czech Voter 2006* (in Czech). In undertaking this research, the author gratefully acknowledges funding from the Grant Agency of the Czech Republic, grant no. 407/07/1395. E-mail: lukas.linek@soc.cas.cz.

Adrian Moraru is the Deputy Director of the Institute for Public Policy (IPP) in Bucharest, Romania. He has a rich experience in the Romanian NGO sector and has worked as an expert on parties and electoral systems over the past five years. His major publications include *Legislation and Control Mechanism of Political Parties' Funding in the Czech Republic, Poland, Romania and Ukraine* (2005) and *Practical Guide for Political Parties' Financing* (2004).

Ion Osoian is an expert at the Institute for Public Policy in Chisinau, Moldova. He has an MA in European Governance from the University of Kent (UK) and is licensed in Administrative Sciences from the Academy of Public Administration under the Government of the Republic of Moldova. His major research interests and publications relate to public sector reform, regional development, Europeanization, Moldovan and Eastern European affairs.

Jan Outlý is a Senior Lecturer in the Department of Politics at the University of Hradec Kralové. His main fields of interest are electoral and party systems, especially party funding and candidate election. In undertaking this research, the author gratefully acknowledges funding from the Grant Agency of Czech Academy of Sciences, project code KJB712290701. E-mail: jan.outly@uhk.cz.

Oleh Protsyk is a Senior Research Associate at the European Centre for Minority Issues. His research interests include executive-legislative relations, institutional aspects of ethnic conflict regulation and parties. His latest publications include "Nation-Building in Moldova" in *Nation and Nationalism: Political and Historical Studies*, ed. Andrzej Suszycki, and Pawel Karolewski (2007) and "'Real' and 'Virtual' Elements of Power Sharing in the Post-Soviet Space: The Case of Gagauzian Autonomy" (co-authored with Valentina Rigamonti) in the *Journal on Ethnopolitics and Minority Issues in Europe* (2007).

Steven D. Roper is an Associate Professor of Political Science at Eastern Illinois University. His research focuses on constitutional development, conflict resolution and human rights. He is the author of *Romania: The Unfinished Revolution* (2000) and co-author of *Designing Criminal Tribunals: Sovereignty and International Concerns in the Protection of Human Rights* (2006).

Allan Sikk is a Lecturer in Baltic Politics at the School of Slavonic and East European Studies, University College London. His main research interests lie in the field of party system dynamics, electoral behavior and political science methodology. He has earlier published in *European Journal of Political Research* and *Journal of Communist Studies and Transition Politics*.

Ingrida Unikaitė is a Lecturer in the Department of Political Science at Vytautas Magnus University, Lithuania.

Preface

This volume has a rather lengthy and colorful history.

The 1998 parliamentary elections in Latvia saw massive and quite skilful campaigning on a scale not witnessed before. This induced me to look into issues of party and campaign finance, particularly in Eastern Europe. I was very fortunate to enjoy support of the US Fulbright program enabling me to spend a fruitful year at Columbia University exploring trends and problems of political finance in advanced democracies. Scholarly articles on these issues very rarely covered any of post-Communist countries and this gap had to be filled.

I got in touch with Steven Roper whom I had met a few years earlier at the University of Missouri as a PhD student and who had moved to Pace University by that time. We discussed prospects of a comparative analysis of party and campaign finance in post-communist Europe and agreed to follow-up on that. Still residing in New York City, I obtained funding from the Soros Foundation to organize an international conference on party finance in late 2000 in Rīga, Latvia. Michael Pinto-Duschinsky made an unexpected appearance at the conference, and he later put me in touch with Daniel Smilov of the Central European University who had been working on very similar issues. It was Daniel who organized another conference on corruption and party finance in late 2001 to prepare a two-volume comparative project.

However, that project turned out to be complicated enough to materialize in a foreseeable future, which prompted me and Steven to return to a less ambitious plan that we finalized during the 2003 APSA meeting. As we chose to depart from the fashionable linkage between party finance and corruption to consider links between party finance and development of party system, funding for a meeting of potential authors in Rīga became available only in 2005 after a patient fundraising. I would like to thank both the Open Society Institute and the Konrad Adenauer Foundation for their generous support to this event.

The Rīga conference provided us with a very good point of departure but other priorities prompted Steven to leave the project temporarily. Work on the volume intensified upon his return and all country chapters were finalized in the second half of 2007. I thank all authors for their time and energy they devoted to this project and regret that impatience precluded the concluding chapter from being published in this volume.

Tatiana Kostadinova and Steven Roper would like to thank the editor of *Europe-Asia Studies* for allowing them to use ideas from earlier research in their respective chapters.

Steven would also like to thank Mihai Banu, Bogdan Stanciu and Codru Vrabie for their advice and assistance with tracking down documents for the Romania chapter as well as assistance which he has received over the years from outstanding graduate assistants including Chad Cross, Michael Joyce and Arne Romanowski.

I would like to thank Ance Pētersone for her highly diligent help during the 2005 conference and materials on party finance she had gathered for the concluding chapter.

Last not least, I want to thank Kirstin Howgate at Ashgate for support and understanding.

Jānis Ikstens
Rīga, Latvia

List of Abbreviations

AMW	Average Monthly Wage
APR	Agrarian Party of Russia
BPRR	Bloc *Patria-Rodina-Ravnopravie*
BSP	Bulgarian Socialist Party
CDPP	Christian Democratic People's Party
CDR	Democratic Convention of Romania
CEC	Central Electoral Commission
CIS	Commonwealth of Independent States
ČSSD	Czech Social Democratic Party
DEC	District Electoral Council
DPR	Democratic Party of Russia
DSB	Democrats for a Strong Bulgaria
EP	European Parliament
FKGP	Smallholders Party
FSN	National Salvation Front
HSD-SMS	Movement for Autonomous Democracy-Association for Moravia and Silesia
HULC	Homeland Union Lithuanian Conservatives
KDS	Christian Democratic Party
KDU-ČSL	Christian-Democratic Union-Czechoslovak People's Party
KNAB	Anti-Corruption Bureau
KPRF	Communist Party of the Russian Federation
KSČM	Communist Party of Bohemia and Moravia
LChDP	Lithuanian Christian Democratic Party
LDLP	Lithuanian Democratic Labor Party
LDP	Liberal Democrats Party
LDPR	Liberal-Democratic Party of Russia
LLU	Lithuanian Liberal Union
LP	Labor Party
LPP	Lithuanian Peasants Party
LSDP	Lithuanian Social Democratic Party
MDF	Hungarian Democratic Forum
MP	Member of Parliament
MRF	Movement for Rights and Freedoms
MSZP	Hungarian Socialist Party
NAO	National Audit Office
NDR	Nash Dom Rossiya
NEC	National Electoral Commission

NGO	Non-Governmental Organization
NMSII	National Movement Simeon II
NU/SL	New Union/Social Liberal
ODA	Civic Democratic Alliance
ODS	Civic Democratic Party
OF	Civic Forum
OVR	Fatherland-All Russia
PCRM	Party of Communists of the Republic of Moldova
PD	Democratic Party
PDSR	Party of Social Democracy in Romania
PEA	Permanent Electoral Authority
PNL	National Liberal Party
PNTCD	National Peasants Party Christian Democratic
PR	Proportional Representation
PRES	Party of Russian Unity and Accord
PRM	Greater Romania Party
PSD	Social Democratic Party
PU	People's Union
PUR	Humanist Party of Romania
SLP	Social Liberal Party
SMD	Single-Member District
SPS	Union of Right Forces
SRS	State Revenue Service
SZ	Green Party
SZDSZ	Alliance of Free Democrats
UDF	Union of Democratic Forces
UDMR	Hungarian Democratic Union of Romania
UR	United Russia
US-DEU	Union of Freedom

Chapter 1

Introduction:
The Influence of Public Finance
on Post-Communist Party Systems

Steven D. Roper

While it is a worn-out adage that "money is the mother's milk of politics," understanding the influence of money in the political process is more difficult than it might appear. While the general wisdom is that only candidates and parties with access to significant funding have a chance to win, the relationship between money and votes is difficult to empirically study. There are a number of factors which contribute to this complexity including the lack of accurate reporting as well as numerous channels for legal and illegal funding. One would expect that understanding the influence of public finance on parties would be much easier since the funds come from the state treasury which should ensure better reporting and greater ease in empirically isolating the effects of finance as a source of party revenue. However as this volume shows, the provision of public finance does not *replace* private funding but only serves as a *supplement*. Indeed, empirically understanding the relationship among money, voters and parties is made more difficult with the introduction of a system of public finance not easier. However, if the development of individual parties and the party system as a whole is to be properly understood, then an exploration of the role of finance is critical.

While other aspects of the polity such as the system of government and the electoral rules are rarely significantly reformed, public finance systems over the last forty years have typically undergone substantial changes in many countries. These changes have often been motivated by concerns of the corruptive influence of money in the political process. Whether public finance significantly reduces the amount of electoral corruption is high debatable. Indeed, some argue that restrictive public finance laws may actually increase the level of corruption. Other scholars blame the lack of regulatory oversight for the failure of public finance to curb corruption.[1] Most of this prior research focuses on European and Latin American systems of public finance—only recently have post-communist scholars explored themes which

---

1 For excellent discussions on the issue of corruption and public goods see, Susan Rose-Ackerman. 1999. *Corruption and Government: Causes, Consequences, and Reform.* Cambridge: Cambridge University Press; Daniel Smilov, and Jurij Toplak, eds. 2007. *Political Finance and Corruption in Eastern Europe.* Aldershot: Ashgate Publishing.

include the relationship of corruption and finance, and how public finance reflects and influences party competition and development during the initial transition process.

The creation of new post-communist institutions offered the opportunity for parties to exploit the state for private gains. Governing party elites in the early transition period created a set of state administrative structures designed to enrich themselves and their party at the public's expense. Sham privatization deals, loans for shares and pyramid schemes were just some of the most publicized efforts of individuals and party elites to use legislative loopholes and administrative resources to control vast parts of the economy. During this period, the design and the implementation of public finance was part of the general discussion concerning the exploitation of the state by parties and politicians. Grzymała-Busse argues that in post-communist states in which "the opposition parties were clear and plausible governing alternatives and powerful critics, governing parties did not take advantage of the full opportunities for private gain in state reconstruction."[2]

If the opportunity structure influenced the design and the implementation of public finance, then we would expect finance systems to develop first in those post-communist states in which there was less party contestation. Public finance is often regarded as a form of party rent-seeking in which the provision of public finance allows governing parties to extract state resources and access additional funding. However as this volume shows, the introduction of public finance was not necessarily a function of the opportunity costs of party competition. Many post-communist states with limited opposition parties and a fragmented party system did not institute public finance which would have enriched the governing party by extracting further resources from the state. Indeed, some of the states to first adopt a system of public finance, such as Hungary, exhibited some of the most viable opposition parties. This is not to suggest that the adoption of public finance in post-communist states was isolated from the larger issue of party competition. However, party finance as a function of state resource exploitation is a very different phenomenon than other forms of state exploitation because by design, public finance can provide a more level playing field to opposition parties. While the governing parties may extract more finance than other parties, the provision of public finance cannot be completely dominated by these parties in the same way as the use of administrative hirings or local projects.

Moreover as this volume suggests, public finance does not have a determinative effect on party competition. While many post-communist states have witnessed a tremendous increase in the amount of funding available to parties over the past decade, it is difficult to explain electoral outcomes and the development of the party system in these countries simply by looking at the amount of *legal* public funding available. State finance has increased concomitantly with private funding, and the institution of thresholds and changes in party registration requirements have been just as important to the nature of party competition and the development of a stable party system. In short, for those that advocate public funding as a means to consolidate the

---

2   Anna Grzymała-Busse. 2007. *Rebuilding Leviathan: Party Competition and State Exploitation in Post-Communist Democracies.* Cambridge: Cambridge University Press, pp. 3–4.

party system, this volume demonstrates that public finance in isolation has a modest influence on parties and the party system. Instead, the creation of public finance must be considered as part of a larger discussion involving the specific features of finance (for example, the role of private finance, reporting and accounting procedures) as well as party regulation and electoral rules.

Motivations for the Creation of Public Finance

While party and campaign finance are distinct mechanisms for funding parties, the difference between these two forms of finance becomes blurred in practice. Party finance is allocated to parties between elections, and campaign finance is provided to parties competing in a specific election cycle. However as Pinto-Duschinsky argues "since it is hard to draw a distinct line between the campaign costs of party organizations and their routine expenses, party funds may reasonably be considered 'political finance.'"[3] He argues that the public funds for parties, whether campaign-specific or designed for more general party operations, are ultimately used for electioneering purposes. Therefore in this volume, we use the more general term of public finance to include both forms of funding.

While the exact form of party and campaign finance varies among countries, there are some common characteristics associated with public finance. Direct public finance normally includes providing funds to parties (typically the party's central headquarters). Indirect public campaign finance comprises in-kind subsidies including free media time or a tax holiday on the importation of campaign materials. While party and campaign finance legislation varies, the logic behind state subsidies is rather uniform, and the reasons often involve reference to the development of individual parties and the broader party system.

First, public finance has been advocated in many countries in order to create a more level playing field among parties. The increasing importance of mass media has changed the nature of campaigning over the past few decades and placed significant financial burdens on parties. Therefore, public finance is considered a mechanism for creating greater party competition by providing state finance to parties that do not enjoy significant financial resources compared to governing parties. Typically, public finance awards a subsidy based on parliamentary representation, and as the chapters in this volume show, the vast majority of public finance is awarded to governing parties and those with representation in parliament. Rather than stimulating competition, many of the authors in this volume conclude that public finance only serves the interest of the party or parties of power. Indeed, Katz and Mair argue that public finance can produce a cartel party system based on the collusion of parliamentary parties to provide state subsidies in order to prevent the establishment of new parties.[4]

---

3   Michael Pinto-Duschinsky. 2002. "Financing Politics: A Global View." *Journal of Democracy* 13, p. 70.

4   Richard Katz, and Peter Mair. 1995. "Changing Models of Party Organization and Party Democracy." *Party Politics* 1: 5–8.

For example in describing the influence of finance on parties in Hungary, Ilonszki argues that more than ninety percent of public finance has historically gone to the same five parliamentary parties. She concludes, therefore, that the public funding of parties has not assisted smaller, opposition parties or new parties but has entrenched parliamentary parties. Not surprisingly since the founding election, the Hungarian party system has become one of the most stable in Europe. Kostadinova concludes much the same in terms of the effect of finance in Bulgaria and notes that since public finance had to be approved by the major parties, the Bulgarian system of public finance has primarily benefited parliamentary parties, especially ruling parties. The chapters in this volume show that overwhelmingly public finance rewards parliamentary and governing parties at the expense of out-of-parliament parties. Therefore, it is doubtful that public finance has created a more level playing field among parties; rather, public finance has been used by parliamentary parties as a tool to benefit select parties which could stymie party competition.

A second reason why public finance is advocated is to reduce the amount of money in campaigns. Public finance is often introduced to limit party spending and the general costs of campaigning. However, this pre-supposes a specific type of regulatory framework which limits public and private money as well as empowers an oversight body to enforce the law. Several cases have shown that state finance does not decrease the costs of elections. Mendilow reports that in Italy in the mid-1970s, public funding nearly doubled, and in Israel, the major parties after 1988 passed an amendment to the public finance legislation to retroactively increase the expenditure ceiling.[5] In this volume, numerous chapters describe the escalating amounts of finance that have been provided to parties by the state. For example, Sikk and Kangur note in Estonia that public finance has more than doubled in a decade. In addition, many of the country case studies point out that the provision of public finance has not stopped parties from seeking additional private revenue sources. Not surprisingly, Heywood concludes that public finance "was seen as a potential solution to the problem of escalating expenditure, [but it] appears to have little impact on the drive to seek extra funds."[6]

Moreover as the chapters in this volume show, one of the significant problems in designing systems of public finance is the disconnect between legislation and enforcement. While many states have legislation which limits contributions, financial transparency has been murky, and the administrative body tasked to monitor compliance often lacks sanctioning power that could enforce greater financial accountability. Even when the oversight body has robust sanctioning powers, legislative loopholes can thwart transparency. For example, Ikstens notes that even Latvia's highly regarded Anti-Corruption Bureau, which has been very active in uncovering illegal funding, has not been totally successful because of legislative defects in the definition of covert political advertising. Because of the general lack of enforcement recounted in these chapters, not surprisingly, the costs of

---

5   Jonathan Mendilow. 1992. "Public Party Funding and Party Transformation in Multiparty Systems." *Comparative Political Studies* 25, p. 102.

6   Paul Heywood. 1997. "Political Corruption: Problems and Perspectives." *Political Studies* 45, p. 431.

campaigning have not been controlled. Indeed most of these chapters, especially in Estonia, Lithuania and Hungary, note a dramatic increase in the costs of campaigns over the past two decades. As Linek and Outlý point out, the Czech Republic is unique among post-communist countries because the costs of campaigns have remained rather modest (undoubtedly due to the ban on political advertising on television and radio).

The country case studies in this volume highlight the fact that public finance has been used as a supplement not substitute for private money which means that wealthy donors still wield considerable influence within the party organization.[7] In describing Russian parties, Gel'man likens party contributors to major shareholders of firms in which the contributor can take over the party, even through a hostile takeover. He concludes that even with public finance, the influence of wealthy donors affects the policy orientations and the electoral strategies of Russian parties. The question remains whether these donors would have even greater influence within Russian parties if there was no state finance. For example, the case of Moldova shows that in the absence of public finance, wealthy donors play a fundamental role in the internal decision-making of parties. Based on an elite survey, Protsyk and Osoian find that wealthy business patrons are considered to be more important to recruit than rank-and-file members. They argue that the need for finance affects the decision-making of the party and the party's recruitment patterns which concentrates power within the national party headquarters at the expense of local party branches.

Because public finance awards the subsidy to the national party headquarters, the party center gains even greater influence over regional party offices. Indeed, the introduction of public finance can lead to a decreased effort to recruit new party members and a general decline in grassroots activities (as noted by Protsyk and Osoian in Moldova). Moreover, the importance of party elites increases at the expense of rank-and-file members since elites decide how and where the public funds are going to be used. For example, Mendilow argues that all national party headquarters in Israel were strengthened following the first campaign held under public finance.[8] That said, private funding can offset this centrifugal tendency of public finance by providing local party elites an alternative source of funding outside of the party center. As the chapter by Gel'man points out, Russian regional party branches have continued to enjoy a certain amount of autonomy from the central office due to local patrons. Particularly in mixed-member systems such as Lithuania, local party organizations can benefit from candidate-centered elections, and as Unikaitė argues in her chapter, candidates can raise their own funds which benefits the local party.

One of the problems in understanding how public finance affects the broader political system is that finance is just one of the variables that can influence the nature of individual parties and the party system. For political scientists, this is an empirical problem as understanding the impact of public finance requires models

---

7   David Samuels. 2001. "Does Money Matter? Credible Commitments and Campaign Finance in New Democracies: Theory and Evidence from Brazil." *Comparative Politics* 34: 23–42.

8   Mendilow, "Public Party Funding and Party Transformation in Multiparty Systems," p. 101.

which incorporate systemic political variables. The chapter on Bulgaria and Lithuania suggest that the attributes of the electoral system (especially the creation of mixed-member systems) needs to be part of any explanation regarding party system development. Also, the chapter by Roper, Moraru and Iorga note the importance of thresholds and party membership requirements for individual parties as well as the system as a whole. Birnir's research on public finance and party development shows that electoral system variables need to be considered in order to understand the process of post-communist party institutionalization.[9]

Moreover, the direction of the relationship between finance and party development needs to be re-considered. Party competition influences the choice of the electoral system, threshold and party requirements, but of course, these systemic attributes influence the ability of individual parties to compete. Perhaps one of the reasons why many of the authors in this volume find that public finance has not been determinant of the party system is as Grzymała-Busse argues that "party competition is more likely to affect the availability of regulation of public funding than vice versa... it is unlikely that public funding itself determined political party competition."[10] However, this conclusion may also reflect the timing of when public finance was introduced as much as the system itself. The experience of Western Europe in regards to finance and party development is therefore instructive.

Public Finance and Western Party Typologies

One of themes highlighted throughout this volume is that public finance in transitioning regimes may not necessary function in the same manner as in more established democracies. In these democracies, party and campaign finance have a different influence on parties as they transform in response to the possibility of obtaining state financing. For example, Mulé argues that public finance laws changed the character of West European parties from mass to electioneering (catch-all) parties.[11] Before public finance, parties relied on individual members to provide financing which in turn forced parties to develop strong constituency links. However with the advent of public finance, parties no longer relied on financial support from the membership in order to be competitive. Katz and Mair argue that the creation of public finance ultimately transforms parties into cartels which shifted their focus from business to state patronage. Ultimately cartel parties "rely increasingly for their resources on the subventions and other benefits and privileges afforded by the

---

9   Jóhanna Kristín Birnir. 2005. "Public Venture Capital and Party Institutionalization." *Comparative Political Studies* 38: 915–938.

10   Grzymała-Busse, *Rebuilding Leviathan: Party Competition and State Exploitation in Post-Communist Democracies*, p. 200.

11   Rosa Mulé. 1998. "Financial Uncertainties of Party Formation and Consolidation in Britain, Germany and Italy: The Early Years in Theoretical Perspective." In *Funding Democratization*, ed. Peter Burnell, and Alan Ware. Manchester: Manchester University Press, p. 62.

state."[12] The key is that public finance was introduced long after mass parties had been established. These West European parties had developed professional party functionaries, established links with their constituency and created durable party labels which lasted after changes among the party elite.

In contrast to the development of public finance in West Europe, post-communist public finance and parties have developed in tandem. Many post-communist countries instituted public finance during the founding election or shortly thereafter. A decade after the fall of the Berlin Wall, only a few post-communist countries had not created a system of public finance (Latvia and Moldova are the notable exceptions in this volume). Therefore early in the transition process, public finance was a feature of post-communist politics. This has had an influence on post-communist parties because the provision of finance was one of the factors which allowed these parties at inception to be electioneering rather than mass-based. For example, van Biezen notes that the types of parties that have developed in post-communist states have an institutional basis (linkage to the state) rather than societal focus (representation of a specific segment of society).[13] She argues that post-communist parties since inception have placed electioneering as more central than mobilizing and responding to social demands which means that the party in public office (for example, in the parliament and in the government) focuses its activity around electoral competition.

Moreover as the chapter by Gel'man argues, Russian post-communist parties have weak links with the electorate and even their own rank-and-file membership which places electioneering at a premium and also leaves parties open to state or business capture. In their chapter, Protsyk and Osoian argue that most Moldovan parties have not yet developed as professional organizations. They note that in Moldova, the lack of public finance has hindered the development of party functionaries as a distinct professional class and allowed business elites to become important party activists. They note that this dependency on business elites creates risks for the party system by fostering clientelistic rather than programmatic links with voters. Interestingly, Russia and Moldova adopted public finance much later than most other post-communist countries (indeed, Moldova only passed public finance legislation in late 2007). However, their description of party formation does not sound substantially different than other post-communist countries which adopted finance earlier. Whether a system of public finance was instituted immediately after the transition to democracy or a decade later, the one constant was that parties generally had few links with the broader society (aside from the communist successor party). Certainly, pre-war and inter-war parties re-established themselves in the 1990s; however as the case of Romania shows, these parties had difficulty in re-connecting to a constituency after a fifty-year hiatus. Probably, public finance has had less of an overall impact on post-communist party systems because the parties since inception have been primarily geared towards elections rather than rank-and-file members.

---

12 Richard Katz, and Peter Mair, "Changing Models of Party Organization and Party Democracy," p. 20.

13 Ingrid van Biezen. 2000. "On the Internal Balance of Party Power: Party Organizations in New Democracies." *Party Politics* 6: 395–417.

Concluding Thoughts about Public Finance

While much has been made of the lack of post-communist party system institutionalization (especially during the 1990s), one of the conclusions in many of these chapters which is so striking is how stable the party system has become. Even in the case of more fluid systems such as Russia and Moldova, the 2000s have marked a period of greater party consolidation in the creation of parties of power. To what extent public finance has lead to this consolidation is questionable. Moreover, these chapters show that public finance is not a mechanism which provides for the development of viable opposition parties or a panacea against corrupt practices. Perhaps this is why public finance systems have undergone such profound changes in so many post-communist countries. These chapters show that while other attributes of the political system remain relatively stable over time, public finance regimes have been modified, refined and altered in an attempt to fashion finance systems which are more equitable, transparent and enforceable.

For countries such as Latvia, the question is whether public finance provides a tangible benefit to the political process, parties and ultimately the electorate. While the systems recounted in this volume suffer from many regulatory problems, the fact remains that these systems encourage a greater scrutiny of party finances than might otherwise occur. Public finance may not be of great assistance to smaller parties, and it may not reduce the costs of campaigns and elections; however, the provision of public money to parties focuses politicians and the public on better ways in which to regulate the flow of funds into party coffers. As campaign scandals in countries such as Germany, France and the United Kingdom demonstrate, no system of public finance and no system of regulations will alleviate problems of corruption. In addition as countries change threshold requirements and party membership requirements, finance as a tool of party consolidation is less necessary. For those that design finance legislation, one of the lessons from the post-communist experience is that public finance cannot serve as a substitute for private finance and that no matter how well-designed, public finance systems are subject to constant revision as parties, politicians and business elites exploit loopholes which can undermine the integrity of the entire system.

Logic of this Volume

Each of the country case study chapters explores a common set of issues so that we can draw general comparisons and conclusions concerning the role of public finance in party system development. Each author explains the electoral system, including the type of allocation rule, electoral threshold and party registration requirements. The country case study chapters focus on an explanation of the system of public finance (or lack thereof) including the role of public and private money, disclosure and enforcement authority. The chapters provide an explanation of how the system of public finance has influenced individual parties, political strategies and the party system. For country chapters such as Latvia and Moldova, the development of the party system is largely devoid of considerations concerning public finance while in countries such as Hungary, Bulgaria and the Czech Republic, public finance was adopted early in the post-communist transition process.

Part of the strength of the country chapters is the presentation of financial data which is often extremely difficult to obtain. Perhaps the very fact that these data are not readily available highlights the seemingly "private" nature of public funding in post-communist countries. As many of the chapters in this volume point out, public acceptance of state finance is rather low. Part of the transparency problem in public finance is purposeful. Politicians and parties generally shy away from discussions concerning public finance because of voter suspicions that public funds are a form of rent-seeking by parties. However as Grzymała-Busse argues, public finance "by itself is not necessarily an indicator of exploitation or elite collusion."[14] The key, as she notes, is the construction of transparent and regulated systems of finance. Unfortunately, the chapters in this volume show that regulation and enforcement are often difficult to accomplish, and thus public finance generally has a minimal effect on party development as private money and dubious finance practices as well as other features of the electoral system influence party competition.

---

14 Grzymała-Busse, *Rebuilding Leviathan: Party Competition and State Exploitation in Post-Communist Democracies*, p. 220.

Chapter 2

Russia:
Public Offices, Private Money
and Biased Contests

Vladimir Gel'man

Among post-communist countries, Russia demonstrates a rather mixed record of party system development after more than fifteen years since the emergence of competitive electoral politics. Various studies attest to Russia's party system in the 1990s as under-developed, unstable, volatile and highly fragmented without a strong party presence on the ground, especially in regional and local politics.[1] In the 2000s, Russia's party system experienced a pendulum-like swing toward a seemingly successful attempt at building a dominant "party of power" which resulted in the decline of party competition.[2] The democratic quality of elections in Russia is widely questioned, especially in the wake of Organization on Security and Co-operation reports on the 2003 and the 2004 parliamentary and presidential elections which were evaluated as "free but unfair."[3] The focus of this criticism is the nature of electoral competition in Russia, including the systematic encroachment of the state apparatus into electoral politics, the biased coverage of elections in the media, the selective implementation of electoral laws by electoral commissions and

---

1   See for example, Michael McFaul. 2001. "Explaining Party Formation and Non-Formation in Russia: Actors, Institutions, and Change." *Comparative Political Studies* 34: 1159–1187; Grigorii V. Golosov. 2004. *Political Parties in the Regions of Russia: Democracy Unclaimed.* Boulder, CO: Lynne Rienner; Henry E. Hale. 2006. *Why Not Parties in Russia? Democracy, Federalism, and the State.* Cambridge: Cambridge University Press.

2   Regina Smyth. 2002. "Building State Capacity from Inside Out: Parties of Power and the Success of the President's Reform Agenda in Russia." *Politics and Society* 30: 555–578; Regina Smyth. 2004. *Translating State Resources into Political Dominance: The Prospects for the Consolidation of Dominant State Party in Russia.* Unpublished Manuscript; Vladimir Gel'man. 2005. "Political Opposition in Russia: A Dying Species?" *Post-Soviet Affairs* 21: 226–246; Vladimir Gel'man. 2006. "From 'Feckless Pluralism' to 'Dominant Power Politics'? Transformation of Russia's Party System." *Democratization* 13: 545–561.

3   For Organization for Security and Co-operation in Europe reports on Russian elections, see www.osce.org/documents/odihr/2004/01/1947_ru.pdf and www.osce.org/documents/odihr/2004/01/3033_ru.pdf (accessed 10 April 2007).

courts and unequal assess to political finance (including the abuse of public finances for campaign purposes).[4]

Russia's system of political finance (particularly party finance) has been influenced by Russian legal norms and changes in party competition. On the issue of the legal rules, this system initially was oriented towards private donations for electoral campaigns and the under-regulation of political finance. Later, the system of finance became more state-led resulting in the over-regulation of public finance (based on selective implementation). On the issue of its actual practice, the non-transparent system of public finance in Russia greatly contributed not only to the unfairness of electoral politics but also to the organizational development and electoral strategies of parties. This chapter will discuss various aspects of the impact of political finance on Russia's party politics. First, the chapter focuses on the institutional framework of Russia's political finance and its evolution during the post-communist period. Second, it concentrates on the connection of political finance to Russian party development, including the effect of political finance on the relationship among parties, businesses and the state. This chapter also discusses the role of political finance in the organizational development of parties and their electoral, parliamentary and policy strategies. Finally, the chapter concludes by examining the impact of political finance on the development of the Russian party system.

Background: The Institutional Framework of Russian Political Finance

The system of political finance which emerged in Russia in the 1990s was part of a broader electoral reform which led to the formation of the electoral system. A group of liberal experts centered around Viktor Sheinis designed the first draft of the parliamentary election law, and President Boris Yeltsin adopted it in the form of a decree for the 1993 elections to the lower chamber of the parliament (the State Duma). On the basis of this decree, the State Duma in 1994 passed the law "On Basic Guarantees of Electoral Rights of Citizens of the Russian Federation" which defines the framework for all elections in Russia. Within this framework, the law on parliamentary elections was adopted in 1995.[5] During the second sitting of the Duma, both of these electoral laws were amended (in 1997 and in 1999). In 2001, the third sitting of the State Duma adopted the law "On Political Parties in the Russian Federation" proposed by President Vladimir Putin, and in 2002 it passed a new set of

---

4   Vladimir Gel'man. 2004. "The Unrule of Law in the Making: The Politics of Informal Institution Building in Russia." *Europe-Asia Studies* 56: 1021–1040.

5   Steven S. Smith and Thomas F. Remington. 2001. *The Politics of Institutional Choice: The Formation of the Russian State Duma.* Princeton, NJ: Princeton University Press; Robert G. Moser, and Frank C. Thames. 2001. "Compromise Amidst Political Conflict: The Origins of Russia's Mixed-Member System." In *Mixed-Member Electoral System: The Best of Both Worlds?*, ed. Matthew S. Shugart and Martin P. Wattenberg. Oxford: Oxford University Press, pp. 255–275.

amendments to the electoral law. Finally between 2004 and 2006, the electoral law and the law "On Political Parties" were amended again.[6]

Russia's parliamentary electoral system was initially based on a German mixed-member model. In the Duma, 225 out of 450 seats were distributed among individual parties and party coalitions based on nation-wide proportional representation lists (PR). The remaining 225 seats were contested in single-member districts (SMDs) on a plurality basis.[7] Since 2003, a similar electoral system has been extended to regional legislative elections. However, the institutional transfer was incomplete because Russia's parliamentary electoral system did not link the two votes which resulted in Russian voters having little institutional incentive to choose the same party in the PR race and in the SMD election and often splitting their votes. As a result, the electoral system in Russia produced a large number of independent (non-partisan) members of parliament (MPs) from the SMD races. Partisanship was not a major feature of the SMD contests; instead, incumbency and regional administrative support were more important to candidates.[8] However within the parliament, the role of parties was much stronger because of the State Duma's regulations which induced party cohesion and discouraged non-partisanship among MPs.[9] Although party-affiliated SMD MPs tended to be less loyal to their parties than MPs elected under party lists, the overall impact of the institutional arrangement on parliamentary and electoral politics was largely party-centered rather than candidate-oriented.[10]

Based on a proposal by President Putin in 2005, the electoral system was entirely redesigned: since 2007, all State Duma MPs are elected under a nation-wide PR list with a seven percent threshold, and all electoral coalitions (blocs) are prohibited. For the registration of candidates and party lists, there are currently two systems used. Initially, there was only the use of voter signatures for registration (party lists required 100,000 signatures in the 1993 State Duma elections and 200,000 signatures for elections between 1995–2003). However since 1999, State Duma elections have used financial deposits as an alternative option to voter signature registration. The amount of the deposit is rather large (for party lists sixty million rubles or $2,025,000

---

6   Legal texts are available at the official web site of the Central Electoral Commission of the Russian Federation: www.cikrf.ru (accessed 10 April 2007).

7   Thereafter, I use the term parties despite their organizational composition and legal status.

8   Robert G. Moser. 1999. "Independents and Party Formation: Elite Partisanship as an Intervening Variable in Russian Politics." *Comparative Politics* 31: 147–165; Grigorii V. Golosov. 2005. "Political Parties and Independent Candidates in the Duma Election." In *The 1999–2000 National Elections in Russia: Analyses, Documents, and Data*, ed. Vladimir Gel'man, Grigorii V. Golosov, and Elena Meleshkina. Berlin: Edition Sigma, pp. 36–58; Hale, *Why Not Parties in Russia?*.

9   Smith and Remington, *The Politics of Institutional Choice*; Thomas F. Remington. 2001. *The Russian Parliament: Institutional Evolution in a Transitional Regime, 1989–1999*. New Haven: Yale University Press.

10 Grigorii V. Golosov and Iulia Shevchenko. 2005. "Incumbent Re-election Strategies in Duma Elections." In *The 1999–2000 National Elections in Russia: Analyses, Documents, and Data*, ed. Vladimir Gel'man, Grigorii V. Golosov, and Elena Meleshkina. Berlin: Edition Sigma, pp. 166–188.

for the 2003 elections), and this money is returned to the candidate or the party after the election if the candidate or the party list receives more than five percent and three percent of the vote. Since 2003, a similar procedure for the nomination of candidates and party lists has been used in regional legislative elections. Also, most regions use a mixed-member electoral system similar to the system used for State Duma elections before 2007 with a seven percent threshold; although, some regions have adopted a pure PR system.

It should be noted, however, that although parties played a major role in the State Duma, their impact on Russian politics beyond the parliament was fairly limited. The representation of parties in the Russian government is largely ceremonial (even parties of power), and their impact on government politics and policy-making has been negligible.[11] The key actor in Russian politics, the president, has always been above party politics both under Yeltsin and Putin.[12] Russian presidents barely relied upon party support; although, Putin endorsed the party of power (that is, Unity and United Russia or UR) during the 1999 and the 2003 State Duma elections. Thus while parties are a feature of Russian politics, they do not perform well in terms of elite-mass linkages, policy formation and political accountability. In short, even if Russia established some elements of party democracy, it never had a party government. Alongside with many other factors, this led to the ambiguity of the place of particular parties and the party system within Russia's political regime and contributed to the manipulative use of party politics by Kremlin rulers. The system of political finance (both party and campaign finance) was an important (although not major) tool of this manipulative "virtual politics" in Russia.[13]

The institutional framework of campaign finance in Russia was established in 1993–1994, simultaneously with the adoption of the first election law. This framework was initially imported from the American model of political action committees and adapted to local conditions.[14] According to the electoral laws, all parties and candidates at an early stage of the electoral campaign had to open special temporary accounts ("electoral funds") in a bank for the accumulation of campaign donations. The upper-limit of party electoral funds ranged from 10.9 billion rubles ($2.37 million) for the 1995 elections to 250 million rubles (approximately $8.3 million) for the 2003 elections. For individual candidates, the upper-limits for their electoral funds varied from 437 million rubles ($95,000) for the 1995 elections to six million rubles ($200,000) for the 2003 elections. Since 2007, the upper-limit for party electoral funds increased to 400 million rubles (approximately $15.4 million).

All donations to electoral funds were initially divided into four types: (1) State subsidies which are a basic, small lump sum payment from the electoral commission

---

11 Iulia Shevchenko. 2004. *The Central Government of Russia: From Gorbachev to Putin*. Aldershot and Burlington, VT: Ashgate.

12 Lilia Shevtsova. 1999. *Yeltsin's Russia: Myths and Reality*. Washington, DC: Carnegie Endowment for International Peace; Lilia Shevtsova. 2003. *Putin's Russia*. Washington, DC: Carnegie Endowment for International Peace.

13 Andrew Wilson. 2005. *Virtual Politics: Faking Democracy in the Post-Soviet World*. New Haven: Yale University Press.

14 Author's interview with Viktor Sheinis, August 1994.

Table 2.1   Results of the State Duma elections, 1993–2003

Elections	1993			1995			1999			2003		
Parties/Coalitions	Number	Vote,[1] %	Seats, Total (PR+SMD)	Number	Vote, %	Seats, Total (PR+SMD)	Number	Vote, %	Seats, Total (PR+SMD)	Number	Vote, %	Seats, Total (PR+SMD)
Turnout %		54.3			64.7			61.8			55.75	
KPRF		12.4	48 (32+16)		22.3	157 (99+58)		24.3	113 (67+46)		12.6	52 (40+12)
APR		8.0	33 (21+12)		3.8	20 (0+20)					3.6	2 (0+2)
LDPR		22.9	64 (59+5)		11.2	51 (50+1)		6.0	17 (17+0)		11.5	36 (36+0)
Motherland											9.0	37 (29+8)
Women of Russia		8.1	23 (21+2)		4.6	3 (0+3)		2.0	0			
PRES		6.8	19 (18+1)		0.4	1 (0+1)						
DPR		5.5	15 (14+1)								0.2	0
NDR					10.2	55 (45+10)		1.2	7 (0+7)			
Fatherland – All Russia								13.3	68 (37+31)			
Unity								23.3	73 (64+9)			
United Russia											37.6	225 (120+105)
Russia's Choice		15.5	67 (40+27)		3.9	9 (0+9)					4.3	4 (0+4)
Yabloko		7.8	26 (20+6)		6.9	45 (31+14)		5.9	20 (16+4)		4.0	3 (0+3)
Union of Right Forces								8.5	29 (24+5)			
Other parties	5		8 (0+8)	35		32 (0+32)	18		9 (0+9)	15		33 (0+33)
Independent candidates			141 (0+141)			77 (0+77)			105 (0+105)			69 (0+69)
Total	13	94.0		43	95.3		26	94.7		23	94.5	
Over 5% threshold	8	87.0		4	50.5		6	81.2		4	70.7	
Against all lists		2.9			2.8			3.3			4.7	
Invalid votes		1.5			1.9			2.0			0.8	

[1] Represents proportional representation vote.

Source: Michael McFaul. 2005. "Electoral System." In *Developments in Russian Politics* 6th edition, ed. Stephen White, Zvi Gitelman, and Richard Sakwa. Basingstoke: Palgrave Macmillan, p. 69.

Notes: PR stands for proportional lists seats and SMD for single-member district seats.

evenly distributed among all candidates and parties upon the registration of the candidate and/or the party list.[15] (2) The party or candidate's own funds from their institutional (or personal) sources which could comprise up to fifty percent of all donations to their electoral fund. (3) Corporate donations which could not come from state or municipal bodies, state or municipal enterprises or military units, law enforcement agencies, charitable and religious organizations, foreign states or international companies. Anonymous corporate donations were prohibited, and also since 2002, all corporate donors must have a legal registration at least one year prior to the polling date. Each corporate donation cannot exceed a certain limit (for the 2003 elections, fifty percent of the upper-limit of the electoral fund for a candidate and 3.5 percent of the upper-limit of the electoral fund for a party). (4) Individual donations, which could come only from Russian citizens, could not exceed a certain limit (for the 2003 elections, five percent of the upper-limit of the electoral fund for a candidate and 0.07 percent of the upper-limit of the electoral fund for a party). In addition, anonymous individual donations were prohibited. Besides that, parties could also provide donations from their electoral funds to their candidates in the SMD races. These donations could not exceed a certain limit (for the 2003 elections, fifty percent of the upper-limit of the electoral fund for a candidate). Naturally since 2007, this type of donation has become irrelevant for State Duma elections since the change in the electoral system.

After the adoption of the law "On Political Parties," the model of state funding changed. Since 2004, instead of a lump sum payment prior to the elections, direct state subsidies from the federal budget have been provided. According to the law, each party which receives more than three percent of the vote in the previous State Duma election can annually receive a certain amount of funding, depending on the number of votes received. Also each party, whose candidate runs during the presidential election and receives more than three percent of the vote, is eligible for a lump sum payment the year following the election. In 2005, the annual payment to parties was calculated on the basis of 0.5 rubles or $0.01 per vote. Thus for example, the largest party, UR, received almost 11.4 million rubles (approximately $400,000) of state subsidies (a rather small share of its total funding). However according to recent amendments to the election laws and the law "On Political Parties," after the 2007 State Duma elections, the amount of state subsidies should increase at least ten-fold.

According to the electoral law, the list of possible expenditures from electoral funds includes the payment for campaign costs such as payments for activists for the collection of signatures and the cost of the deposit for the registration of candidates and party lists and the costs of pre-electoral media in various forms (including media advertising). The latter item is the most costly, and these expenditures are vitally important for electoral campaigns. According to the electoral rules, all parties and

---

15 Candidates from party lists, which receive more than two percent of the vote, and candidates in single-member districts which receive more than three percent of the vote could claim a reimbursement for travel costs to regions or electoral districts (calculated on a basis of the certain number of trips). Electoral commissions are obliged to cover these costs; although in practice, this norm was rarely applied.

Table 2.2   Electoral funds of major parties and coalitions for election to the State Duma, 1993–2003

Party	State Subsidies	Party's Own Donations	Corporate Donations	Individual Donations	Total
1993					
LDPR	80[1]	0.08			80.08
Russia's Choice	80	1460.96			1540.96
KPRF	80	0			80
APR	80	0			80
Women of Russia	80	0			80
Yabloko	80	224			304
PRES	80	584.12			664.12
DPR	80	0			80
1995					
KPRF	25	202.17	31.63	47.28	306.09
LDPR	25	950	1218.76	216.78	2410.54
NDR	25	950	1795.76	99.13	2869.89
Yabloko	25	950	915.37	1	1891.37
1999					
KPRF	8.3	74.74	1005.23	388.6	1476.87
Unity	8.3	138.27	1139.76	373.7	1660.03
OVR	8.3	620.33	982.81	59.79	1671.23
SPS	8.3	545.59	1072.5	5.6	1631.99
LDPR	8.3	597.91	1057.55	0	1663.76
Yabloko	8.3	0	1436.47	0	1444.77
2003					
UR	N/A	4184.95	3408.7	64.12	7657.77
KPRF	N/A	1569.35	641.24	108	2318.59
LDPR	N/A	3236.58	1468.11	3.37	4708.06
Motherland	N/A	3287.21	1650.35	81	5018.56
Yabloko	N/A	4144.45	1322.98	0.12	5467.55
SPS	N/A	3712.45	3968.95	0	7681.4

[1] Amount in thousand USD, exchange rate 28.50 rubles to $1.

Source: Byulleten'Tsentral'noi izbiratel'noi komissii Rossiiskoi Federatsii. 1994. No. 4; *Vestnik Tsentralnoi izbiratel'noi komissii Rossiiskoi Federatsii.* 1996. No. 6; *Vestnik Tsentralnoi izbiratel'noi komissii Rossiiskoi Federatsii.* 200. No. 12 and *Vestnik Tsentralnoi izbiratel'noi komissii Rossiiskoi Federatsii.* 2004. No. 8. See, www.cikrf.ru (accessed 10 April 2007).

candidates get equal air time and space for free publicity in state-owned and state-sponsored television, radio and newspapers. For the 2003 State Duma elections, the total volume of such airtime on national television channels was limited to thirty minutes per working day during the last month before the polling day (mostly from 8:00 to 21:00). This meant that each of the twenty-three competing parties received altogether about twenty-six minutes of free air time on each television channel. Also, parties and candidates could buy air time and space. The total volume of this air time and space on each state-owned and state-sponsored form of media could be no less than the respective air time and space for free publicity but could not be more than double. As to private television, radio and newspapers, they are allowed to receive unlimited payments for advertising.

According to the election law, all party and candidate expenditures must be paid only from their electoral accounts. All electoral expenditures paid from sources other than electoral funds are strictly prohibited. Also, the election law does not permit independent electoral expenditures. Individuals or organizations not registered as candidates or parties in the election cannot incur electoral expenditures other than through donations to respective electoral accounts. Finally, the electoral law requires that parties and candidates must report all their revenues and expenditures both during the campaign (at least twice) and after the election to the electoral commission. Parties must file with the Central Electoral Commission (CEC), and this commission, with the Federal Tax Inspection Service, is responsible for the enforcement of campaign finance rules. The CEC is also in charge of publishing reports in the media and on their web site.[16] Since 1999, these reports must include the list of all corporate and individual donors, but after the 2003 elections, such lists were limited to those donors whose contributions to a party or a candidate exceeded a certain limit.[17] Also since 1999, all candidates from party lists and SMDs must declare their personal income and assets before the campaign (for example, apartments, houses, land plots, cars, bank accounts and company shares). The local-level electoral commissions are responsible for making this information available to voters. In addition since 2002, parties are legally obliged to submit annual (since 2006, quarterly) financial reports of their revenues, expenditures and assets (beyond electoral funds). These reports must contain data on corporate and individual donors for parties, and the CEC publishes these reports on its web site.[18]

Overall, the institutional framework of public finance in Russia has gradually evolved since 1993 into a clearer, more detailed and comprehensive system. The changes in the legal rules were oriented toward the greater transparency of public finance and toward the shift from pre-dominantly corporate funding to an increase

---

16 For financial reports of parties during the 1993, the 1995, the 1999 and the 2003 State Duma elections see, *Byulleten' Tsentral'noi izbiratel'noi komissii Rossiskoi Federatsii*. 1994. No.4; *Vestnik Tsentralnoi izbiratel'noi komissii Rossiiskoi Federatsii*. 1996. No. 6 (as well as the issue for 2000, No. 12 and 2004, No. 8); see also www.cikrf.ru (accessed 10 April 2007).

17 For example, the amount was 800,000 rubles ($27,000) for corporate donations to a party and 200,000 rubles ($6,750) to a candidate, and 20,000 rubles ($675) for an individual donation to a party.

18 For the 2005 annual financial reports of the twenty-five officially registered Russian parties, see http://www.cikrf.ru/cikrf/politparty (accessed 7 April 2007).

Table 2.3   Officially reported revenues of major parties, 2005

Party/ Income Source	Membership (Fees)	Corporate Donations	Individual Donations	Business Profits	State Subsidies	Total[1]
UR	1354.3[2]	32185.1	220.3	4.7	399.7	35335.6
KPRF	1029.9	312.9	490.8	81.3	134.2	2165.4
LDPR	3.2	3128.6	5.4	3.6	121.8	3271.4
SPS	0.8	1282.4	219.1	–	42.2	1580.5
Yabloko	–	1028.7	147.8	–	45.8	1233.2

[1]As reported on the Central Electoral Commission web site (not exactly the sum of the previous column amount).
[2]Amount in thousand USD, exchange rate for 28.50 rubles to $1.

Source: Available at the web site of the Central Electoral Commission of the Russian Federation, see http://www.cikrf.ru/cikrf/politparty (accessed 7 April 2007).

in the role of the state for funding political finance. An increase in the legal amount of campaign spending is obvious as well. However, this more transparent legal framework poorly corresponds with the realities of Russian party politics.

Beyond the Tip of the Iceberg: The Practices of Russian Political Finance

Russia's system of political finance has been previously compared to an iceberg with a small visible amount above-water and a much bigger invisible portion underneath.[19] Although it is difficult to estimate the amount of finance (assumed to be rather substantial) that went beyond official electoral funds and party budgets, several trends can be observed.[20] First, the system of political finance encouraged the large-scale involvement of business leaders in party politics; although more recently, state officials have replaced business elites. Second, the legal regulations of public finance are rather vague while the implementation of these rules and their enforcement is very selective. Third, the combination of these features with more general anti-democratic trends in Russian politics produced a set of inverse incentives for the development of parties.[21]

---

19 Vladimir Gel'man. 1998. "The Iceberg of Russian Political Finance." In *Funding Democratization*, ed. Peter Burnell and Alan Ware. Manchester: Manchester University Press, pp. 158–179.

20 For some descriptions, see Wilson, *Virtual Politics*. See also Chrystia Freeland. 2000. *Sale of the Century: The Inside Story of the Second Russian Revolution*. Boston: Little, Brown; David Hoffmann. 2002. *Oligarchs: The Wealth and Power in the New Russia*. New York: Public Affairs Books.

21 Among the vast literature on this subject, see for example, Shevtsova, *Putin's Russia*; Michael McFaul, Nikolai Petrov, and Andrei Ryabov. 2004. *Between Dictatorship*

The liberals' priority for corporate donations in Russia's campaign finance system led to a model of public funding which was different from the system in Hungary or in the Czech Republic where state funding was the priority and private and corporate funding was limited if not outright prohibited.[22] The reason for this choice was ideological. As Sheinis argues "[i]t is not quite so bad that some rich people buy votes and come to power. It is state-owned redistribution that does the most harm to Russian democracy."[23] This ideology coincided with the interests of Russian liberals who desired legitimization in the new political and economic order and hoped for financial support from Russian businesses. In the context of the formation of Russian capitalism in the 1990s, this choice eventually led not only to the non-transparency of public finance but also to multiple problems for parties.

Russian businesses were active in funding parties; even though officially, large donations from companies to parties in their campaign finance reports were rare.[24] Instead, companies used liaison organizations for these purposes, and parties in their turn, established special "pocket" non-governmental organizations (NGOs) or foundations for the accumulation of contributions.[25] The major part of corporate funding was often covert. Svetlana Barsukova, who analyzed various practices of "shadow politics" in Russia, argues that no more than between thirty and fifty percent of campaign expenditures for all parties were legal, and the transparency of campaigns remained merely on paper.[26] The same was true for the funding of day-to-day party activities: most of these activities remained unreported or apparently misreported.[27] Also, despite the liberals' hopes that they would become the major beneficiary of corporate donations, the largest share of funds went to the various

---

and Democracy: Russian Post-Communist Political Reform. Washington, DC: Carnegie Endowment for International Peace.

22 Paul Lewis. 1998. "Party Funding in Post-Communist East-Central Europe." In *Funding Democratization,* ed. Peter Burnell and Alan Ware. Manchester: Manchester University Press, pp. 137–157; see also chapters in this volume.

23 Interview with the author, August 1994; see also Gel'man, "The Unrule of Law in the Making," p. 1033.

24 For example in 1999, Lukoil, Russia's oil giant, invested 2.8 million rubles ($104,633) to the electoral fund of the prospective party of power Fatherland-All Russia (OVR). This was approximately 10.6 percent of all the party's corporate donations. However when the Kremlin launched its electoral venture, Unity, Lukoil switched to a new party of power and ceased funding OVR. Timothy J. Colton and Michael McFaul. 2003. *Popular Choice and Managed Democracy: The Russian Elections of 1999 and 2000.* Washington, DC: Brookings Institution Press, p. 93.

25 For example, the Union of Right Forces during the 2003 elections received almost all of its corporate donations from fifteen organizations designed to channel funding to the party including the Foundation of Democratic Initiatives, the Foundation of Assistance to Reforms, and the Foundation for Support of Democratic Unity just to name a few.

26 For in-depth analysis, see Svetlana Baruskova. 2006. *Tenevaia ekonomika i tenevaia politika: mekhanizm srashchivaniia.* Moscow: State University–Higher School of Economics, p. 26.

27 For example, the Liberal Democratic Party of Russia officially reported that the costs of its annual national party conference in 2005 were approximately 14,000 rubles (less than $500) which is undoubtedly below any real expenditures, see: http://www.cikrf.ru/cikrf/

parties of power. In fact, all major Russian parties enjoyed big business support (State Duma incumbency was certainly an advantage for fundraising), but they have had to pay a high price for this funding.

The emerging Russian business class considered these political investments as a sort of enterprise, and because parties were not regarded as reliable partners, entrepreneurs soon went into electoral politics. Early attempts to establish so-called "business parties" during the 1993 and the 1995 State Duma elections totally failed, and business elites soon turned to the infiltration of established party lists. They bought not only seats but powerful positions in the parliament. The first obvious example was Mikhail Gutseriev, an entrepreneur from Ingushetia, who became well-known due to an offshore project in his region which was a notorious black hole in the federal budget.[28] In 1995, Gutseriev was seventh on the party list of the Liberal-Democratic Party of Russia (LDPR) which combined nationalist, populist rhetoric with loyalty to the Kremlin. Between 1996–1999, Gutseriev served as deputy chair of the State Duma on behalf of that party, and the LDPR, in its turn, actively lobbied on behalf of his business projects.[29] In a similar way in 1995, another businessman, Mikhail Yur'ev, was eighth on the list of the liberal party, Yabloko, and later was promoted to deputy chair of the State Duma. After the end of his parliamentary term, he left Yabloko and became a vocal Russian nationalist. After the 1999 parliamentary election, one observer noted that "big business came to the State Duma in various forms, ranging from key managers (but not CEOs) of large holdings to independent company owners."[30] These business elites obtained key positions on most of the party lists and on major parliamentary committees. Before the 2003 elections, large companies were able to diversify their party portfolio. The oil giant Yukos, then led by Mikhail Khodorkovskii, not only put four of their representatives on key positions on the Yabloko party list but were also represented on the party list of the UR.[31] In addition, two of Khodorkovskii's allies occupied key positions on the party list of the Communist Party of the Russian Federation (KPRF).[32]

The consequence of this party-business cohabitation was two-fold: first, business sponsors decisively affected some party policy decisions. For example Yabloko, thanks to its close links to Yukos, passionately promoted in the State Duma bills on production sharing agreements which reflected the interests of large oil producers.[33] Also between 2001 and 2003, Yukos' lobbyists in the parliament (from various

---

politparty (accessed 7 April 2007). See also Barsukova, *Tenevaia ekonomika i tenevaia politika*, p. 39.

28 Freeland, *Sale of the Century*.

29 Gel'man, "The Iceberg of Russian Political Finance" p. 170; Wilson, *Virtual Politics*, pp. 206–207.

30 Yakov Pappe. 2001. "Gosudarstvo i krupnyi biznes: chto ostalos' starogo v ikh otnosheniyakh (2000 g. – nachalo 2001 g.)?" In *Kto i kuda stremitsya vesti Rossiyu? Aktory makro-, mezo- i mikrourovnei sovremennogo transformatsionnogo protsessa*, ed. Tat'yana Zaslavskaya. Moscow: Moscow School of Social and Economic Science, p. 211.

31 After the arrest of Khodorkovskii in the course of electoral campaign, representatives of Yukos were expelled from the list of the party of power.

32 Wilson, *Virtual Politics*, pp. 109 and 259.

33 Colton and McFaul, *Popular Choice and Managed Democracy*, p.148.

parties) effectively blocked several attempts of the government to increase the tax share of oil companies and minimize legal loopholes for tax evasion.[34] Second and more importantly, business links affected not only parties in the parliament but also party organization leadership and the party on the ground. Unlike companies, Russian parties were often unable to diversify their business portfolio, and thus could be easily captured by oligarchs. This is especially true for local party branches which tended to receive little financial support from their central party office so that they had to secure their own funds (especially for regional legislative elections). In some regions, the labels of various parties were used as smokescreens for the promotion of local (or national) interest groups.[35] Sometimes, even an entire party was the project of one oligarch. To some extent, this was the case for the Union of Right Forces (SPS). The shadow leader of the party was Anatolii Chubais, chief executive officer of the nation-wide state-owned electricity holding RAO UES and former Russian deputy prime minister in 1990s.[36] He initially influenced the SPS through his financial support and having his associates in key party positions. Chubais' former deputy in RAO UES, Leonid Gozman, serves as a deputy chair of the executive committee of SPS. During the 2003 elections, Chubais was third on the party list, and he soon replaced all SPS party and campaign staff. His long-term ally, Alfred Kokh, was appointed chief campaign manager.[37] Several local branches of RAO UES were also actively involved in the party campaign (in certain regions, electricity tariffs were lowered before the polling date). After the electoral failure of SPS, Chubais remains the only major party sponsor. He strongly insisted that Gozman should be elected as the new party leader, but he was unacceptable to many of the party activists. After some bargaining in 2005, Gozman became a first deputy chair of the SPS while Chubais retained his control over the party.[38]

The Russian state became a major counterweight to businesses—key state officials extended patronage to parties and often replaced business leaders in this respect.[39] For building parties of power, the Kremlin has regularly used resources of the state. Its infrastructure, apparatus, media and money provides campaigning for the Kremlin's electoral vehicles. The direct or indirect bribery of voters was also a great help for the Kremlin in achieving desirable election outcomes.[40] This

---

34 Vadim Volkov. 2003. "The Yukos Affair: Terminating the Implicit Contract." *PONARS Policy Memos*. No. 307, www.csis.org/rusera/ponars/policymemos/pm_0307.pdf (accessed 10 April 2007).

35 Golosov, *Political Parties in the Regions of Russia*.

36 On the background of Chubais, see Janine Wedel. 1998. *Collision and Collusion: The Strange Case of Western Aid to Eastern Europe, 1989–1998*. New York: St. Martin's Press, pp.121–158; Hoffmann, *Oligarchs*, pp. 78–99.

37 On the role of Kokh in Russia's privatization in the 1990s, see Freeland, *Sale of the Century*.

38 Andrei Ryabov. 2005. "Iskusstvennoe vzrashchivanie i estestvennyi otbor." *Gazeta*. 29 May, http://www.carnegie.ru/ru/pubs/media/72658.htm (accessed 10 April 2007).

39 See Andrei Yakovlev. 2006. "The Evolution of Business-State Interaction in Russia: From State Capture to Business Capture?" *Europe-Asia Studies* 56: 1033–1056.

40 See Daniel Treisman. 1998. "Dollars and Democratization: The Role of Power and Money in Russia's Transitional Elections." *Comparative Politics* 31: 1–21.

led to an increase in the financial asymmetry between the party of power (which received generous official and unofficial funding and also state resources) and the rest of Russia's party politics.[41] Financial leverages also played a role in Kremlin politics towards other parties. Loyal parties were bought (for example, those parties, which endorsed Yeltsin during the 1996 presidential election campaign received covert funding).[42] Disloyal parties and their sponsors experienced state-led pressure in various forms (for example, the threatening of the leading financier of the KPRF, Viktor Vidmanov, with prosecution).[43]

The Yukos affair and the subsequent imprisonment of Khodorkovskii in 2003 (his involvement in politics considered one of the possible reasons for his arrest) served as a turning point in the party-business-state relationship. Although the degree of business activism in party funding probably did not decrease after this event, the ability of business activism in party funding became possible only with the Kremlin's support. On the one hand, Russian businesses were forced to contribute to the UR's campaign (for example, Vladimir Ryzhkov, an independent MP, called this practice UR's "extra tax").[44] However, the Kremlin also provided certain benefits, including places on the UR party list to some large donors.[45] The Yukos affair was a clear sign to Russian businesses that the Kremlin would no longer tolerate uncontrolled sponsorship of the "wrong" parties. No wonder that after the 2003 State Duma elections, most opposition parties in Russia faced major problems with political funding.[46] The uneven access to party and to campaign funding and informal state barriers to the sponsorship of the opposition combined with the new formal regulations to deliberately shrink party competition. For example during March 2007, legislative elections in several regions required an enormous increase in the amount of deposits for the registration of party lists (some increased to ninety million rubles or approximately $3.5 million).[47] Those opposition parties, which were unable to raise money for the overwhelming costs of regional campaigns, were forced to rely upon the (less costly) collection of voters' signatures. In some regions, these signatures were disqualified for groundless reasons and party lists denied registration (this was the case of Yabloko in St. Petersburg).[48]

Given the "color revolutions" in Georgia, Ukraine and Kyrgyzstan between 2003 and 2005, the Kremlin considered external donations to political opposition (both

---

41 Barsukova, *Tenevaia ekonomika i tenevaia politika*, pp. 37–40.

42 Gel'man, "The Iceberg of Russian Political Finance" p. 175.

43 Wilson, *Virtual Politics*, p. 113 and 233.

44 Natalia Gladysheva. 2003. "Vladimir Ryzhkov: Ne zhdite kharakiri." *Delo.* 22 December, http://www.idelo.ru/307/1.html (accessed 10 April 2007).

45 Wilson, *Virtual Politics*, p. 108.

46 Jim Stanton. 2005. "It's Ruble Trouble for Opposition in Russia." *Scotsman.* 7 July; also Russian translation: Jim Stanton. 2005. "Oppozitsiya v Rossii ispytyvaet denezhnye zatrudneniya." http://www.inopressa.ru/scotsman/2005/07/08/16:23:33/opposit (accessed 10 April 2007).

47 Parliamentary parties, which are currently represented in the State Duma, do not pay deposits for the nomination of their lists for national and regional elections.

48 The Russian non-governmental organization Golos presented detail coverage of these, and other, unfair electoral practices, see www.golos.org (accessed 10 April 2007).

to parties and to NGOs) as a major threat to its dominance, and President Putin unequivocally announced that the Russian state would not permit any international funding of political activism in the country.[49] In sum, top Kremlin officials seem to be the only gatekeepers who are allowed to decide which Russian parties will be funded and to what extent. The Kremlin's domination over party finance led to a paradox: the day-to-day activities of parties of power were more open and legal than those activities of non-Kremlin (and especially opposition) parties which funded their routine activities outside legal channels.[50]

The systematic encroachment of Russian state officials into campaign and party finance has also another vital dimension. Although the legal regulation of campaign and party finance gradually improved over time, the model of public finance implemented in the electoral law and the law "On Political Parties" was full of loopholes and deliberate omissions. The institutional vacuum in this area opened many opportunities for various subversive informal practices. In fact, this was a pattern of the regulation of electoral governance as a whole, but in the area of political finance, it led to many unfair consequences because of the non-transparent nature of Russia's public finance and difficulties with implementation of legal regulations in this area.[51] Most legal norms of Russian political finance were by-products of "fuzzy legality" which includes a sweeping delegation of power to electoral commissions and courts, selective enforcement of the rules and dead-letter law.[52] Most regulations of public finance were little more than a "declaration of good intentions."[53] In other words, electoral commissions and courts, the bodies in charge of the implementation and the oversight of the electoral law, have insufficient capacities for monitoring political finance. At best, they close their eyes to violations in this area.[54] Moreover, some legal regulations were inefficient. For example, the mandatory disclosure of income and assets of candidates (which was introduced before the 1999 State Duma elections) often has nothing to do with the real financial status of these candidates or their parties. At the same time, a misreporting of income and assets was the legal reason for electoral commissions to refuse the registration of candidates and party lists. Only in 2002 did the State Duma abolish this dubious legal sanction; although, electoral commissions have yet to inform voters about cases of misreporting.

In the worse case scenario, the broad discretion of power to electoral commissions and courts creates ample opportunities for the arbitrary use of the law governing

---

49 See, for example, "Putin zapretil oppozistii brat' den'gi u inostrantsev." available at: http://www.polit.ru/news/2005/07/20/inostr.html (accessed 10 April 2007).

50 Personal communication with Svetlana Barsukova, April 2007.

51 Gel'man, "The Unrule of Law in the Making."

52 Margrit Cohn. 2001. "Fuzzy Legality in Regulation: The Legislative Mandate Revisited." *Law and Policy* 23, p. 474.

53 Stephen White, Richard Rose, and Ian McAllister. 1997. *How Russia Votes*. Chatham, NJ: Chatham House Publishers, p. 213.

54 Since 1995, the Central Electoral Commission established its special audit service (*kontrol'no-revizionnaya sluzhba*) which is a working group including representatives of the Ministry of Interior, Federal Tax Inspection Service and other law enforcement agencies. This service was in charge of the control over legal issues related to political finance, but none if its activities have been reported or disclosed as of yet.

public finance as a weapon of selective use to sanction opposition parties and candidates. According to the election law, local electoral commissions can refuse to register candidates and party lists or revoke their registration in the case of violation of public finance laws. Due to such violations, even election results can be annulled (courts have to make the final decision in this kind of dispute). The major problem is that the legal definition of these violations is rather vague, and the enforcement of the rules is fully in hands of local electoral commissions and courts. Given the fact that most parties and candidates violate the rules of public finance, no one is protected from this arbitrary rule (except for the parties of power and loyal pro-governmental candidates).

Electoral commissions, the major organizers of elections in Russia, were appointed by Russian authorities, and thus enjoyed little political independence. The president, the State Duma, and the Federation Council (the upper chamber of the parliament) appoint fifteen members of the CEC (five members each) while members of regional and local electoral commissions have to be evenly appointed by respective executive and legislative bodies. In a number of cases, these regional bodies demonstrated a bias toward pro-government candidates; although, courts were much more objective in this respect.[55]

Several cases of selective sanctions became widely known because of their blatant unfairness. A typical example was the revoking of the registration of Albert Makashov during the 1999 State Duma elections. Makashov, a retired general, established a nation-wide, hard-line Stalinist and anti-Semitic reputation. He had a good chance to secure a landslide victory in his SMD (Number 152). Before the polling day, however, he was accused of violating the electoral law because the printing of his electoral leaflets was pre-paid in cash rather than from his electoral fund. Most candidates did exactly the same, but only Makashov lost his registration as a candidate and was removed from the ballot (a female candidate from SPS, endorsed by the regional governor, won the seat). Two months after the election, the Supreme Court overturned the decision of the regional court in revoking Makashov's registration, but the election result in the district was not annulled so he lost the race.[56] The mayoral election in Nizhnii Novgorod in March 1998 was even more notorious. When populist outsider Andrei Kliment'ev, an entrepreneur with a criminal background, surprisingly won, the electoral commission declared the election invalid because during campaign he promised to raise pensions and wages. This was considered an act of "bribery."[57] On similar grounds, one could denounce the results of any Russian election. During the 2003 State Duma election campaign, the registration of several promising candidates in SMDs was revoked

55 For a quantitative analysis, see Maria Popova. 2006. "Watchdogs or Attack Dogs: The Role of the Courts and the Central Election Commission in Resolution of Electoral Disputes in Russia." *Europe-Asia Studies* 58: 391–414.

56 On details of the case, see Dmitrii Badovskii. 2000. "Samarskaya Oblast." In *Rossiya v izbiratel'nom tsikle 1999–2000 godov*, Michael McFaul, Nikolai Petrov, and Andrei Ryabov. Moscow: Gendal'f, pp. 346–347.

57 See Vladimir Gel'man, Sergei Ryzhenkov, and Michael Brie. 2003. *Making and Breaking Democratic Transitions: The Comparative Politics of Russia's Regions*. Lanham, MD: Rowman and Littlefield, p. 121.

due to violations of financial rules without presenting any proof (the only "violation" was that they had a good chance to beat pro-government candidates).[58] However during the 1996 presidential election, the CEC paid no attention to the arrest of two of Yeltsin's campaign staff who were carrying $538,000 in cash, taken from a government office earmarked for election purposes.[59]

One may conclude that the practice of Russian political finance by the mid-2000s was a non-democratic form of state-led corporatism.[60] While state officials rewarded loyal parties and candidates with generous funding both from faithful businesses and from the state, they also punished disloyal parties and businesses through various means. The question remains to what extent this emerging state-led corporatism could become a model for the Russian party system in general and for Russian political finance in particular.

Concluding Remarks: Public Finance and Russian Party Politics

Speaking about public finance, one might rightly compare parties with companies in a political market. Like firms for successful market competition, parties need to borrow money from the state, businesses or individuals. Like firms, they face multiple challenges in the political market. On the one hand, the financial dependence of Russia's parties contributes to the increase of their cohesiveness at the parliamentary and the electoral level. Also despite recent efforts toward a greater centralization of the Russian party system, regional branches of parties enjoy a certain degree of organizational autonomy from their central offices due to the existence of autonomous sources of funding.[61] The trend towards state-led corporatism in the Russian party system might stabilize the system of campaign and party finance. The problem is that such stabilization could be achieved at the expense of real party competition in Russia's political market.

On the other hand, the dependence of Russian parties on their donors affects not only their policy orientations, parliamentary and electoral strategies but also their governance and leadership. Like some major stakeholders of firms, external donors to parties could take over a party, even through a hostile takeover. Donors could buy the party label or trademark and also replace party leaders, staff, regional branches,

---

58 For a detail and in-depth description of unfair electoral practices in Putin's Russia, see Vladimir Pribylovskii. 2004. "Upravlyaemye vybory: degradatsiya instituta vyborov pri Putine." In *Rossiya Putina: istoriya bolezni*, ed. Grigorii Belonuchkin. Moscow: Panorama, pp. 6–85.

59 Gel'man, "The Iceberg of Russian Political Finance," pp. 158–159.

60 On the state-led corporatism in Russia, see David Lane. 2000. "What Kind of Capitalism for Russia? A Comparative Analysis." *Communist and Post-Communist Studies* 33: 485–504.

61 See Golosov, *Political Parties in the Regions of Russia*; Grigorii V. Golosov. 2004. "What Went Wrong? Regional Electoral Politics and Impediments to State Centralization in Russia, 2003–2004." *PONARS Policy Memos*, No.337, see http://www.csis.org/media/csis/pubs/pm_0337.pdf (accessed 10 April 2007).

if not the party electorate.[62] In developed political markets of well-established democracies, the institutional infrastructure as well as the very mechanism of party competition prevents such developments. In emerging political markets, parties could easily be captured by the state or by businesses. In Russia, these scenarios are typical not only for the parties of power and their associates (which are puppets of the Kremlin) but also for some independent political entities (as the experience of the SPS suggests). Trends towards the monopolization of Russia's political market would make possible not only the prospect of party capture but also the prospect of a state-led capture of the party system. Thinking in more general terms, the nature of public finance in Russia depends upon the overall development of party competition and the rule of law in the country. At present, both of these areas are very far from democratic ideals so the arbitrary use of private money and public offices in biased electoral contestation are merely by-products of these more basic developments. However, the current trend in Russian party politics and political finance deserves to be viewed not only as a temporary "halfway house" state of affairs but also as a possible long-term principal feature of Russia's political regime.

---

62 See Wilson, *Virtual Politics*.

Chapter 3

Lithuania:
Political Finance Regulations as a Tool
of Political Manipulation

Ingrida Unikaitė

Lithuania is a post-communist state which has experienced numerous changes since independence in 1990. The period since independence has marked a transition from communism and its legal rules legacy to new Western democratic laws and practices. This chapter examines the changes in the area of party and campaign finance rules and practices and looks at the continual development of the Lithuanian campaign finance and party system by discussing the electoral system, the legislative framework in which finance occurs, practices in the area of campaign finance and the effect of the system on the development of individual parties and the party system as a whole. This analysis of the development of parties focuses on the number of parties gaining representation in the parliament and the consistency of voter partisanship.

The long-term competition of parties has three basic pillars: organization, volunteer work and finance. Political finance is important due to its effect on election results and on parties which are the dominant political actors and as a means to secure the everyday activities of parties which try to establish links with different social groups. This activity demands a lot of financial resources. The importance of money has grown especially during the last decade as election campaign costs have dramatically increased due to the changes in development of election communication and the transformation of campaign organizations (for example, the growth of spin doctors and political consultants, strategic news management, the decline of traditional forms of party campaigning and the growing use of indirect channels of communication such as different types of mass media).[1] Lithuania is no exception—an analysis of Lithuanian election campaign spending indicates that the importance of campaigning started to grow during the 1996 parliamentary elections and the tendency continues today.

Party finance sources are as follows: public subsidies, membership dues, individual and corporate donations and income from party property. Corporate and individual donations usually dominate party funds. During the last decade, a debate among politicians as well as among political scientists continues on how much the

---

1 Karl-Heinz Nassmacher. 2001. "Comparative Political Finance in Established Democracies." In *Foundations for Democracy: Approaches to Comparative Political Finance*, ed. Karl-Heinz Nassmacher. Baden-Baden: Nomos Verlagsgesellschaft, p. 21.

public subsidy should form party resources. One group advocates an increase in public subsidies and stricter rules for campaigning in order to make campaigns less expensive and more transparent. As Nassmacher argues, public funding makes party competition clearer and fairer.[2] Another group opposes these changes arguing that the government has no resources to support all the parties. This creates unequal opportunities for different political players. Moreover, the public finance of parties is unpopular among citizens. There is also a disagreement about the effect of public finance on parties and party system development. The Lithuanian case provides an interesting example because the state introduced legislation regulating parties and campaign finance rather late, experiencing many modifications in these regulations and yet still has a rather stable multi-party system. This chapter analyzes the development of the party and campaign financing mechanism in Lithuania and its effect on the broader political system.

The Electoral System and Elections in Lithuania

The electoral system is a very important factor determining party system development as well as political finance regulations. Lithuania has a semi-presidential political system. The president is directly elected, and the elected president must constitutionally resign their party membership. Therefore, parties do not play a major role in the presidency. Parties may help a candidate run for election, but they are not allowed to influence the activities of the president. Moreover, the president is free to choose his/her advisory team. Thus, parliamentary and local government elections are much more important for parties in Lithuania. The 1990 founding parliamentary election in Lithuania was based on the inherited Soviet majoritarian system of representation. In 1992, the debate over a new electoral system was contentious and controversial. Politicians from the Movement for Independent Lithuania, *Sąjūdis*, which represents the right in Lithuanian politics, argued for a majority (two-round) system while the left advocated a proportional list (PR) system. Both groups believed that the different electoral systems promoted by them would allow their party to secure a larger share of parliamentary seats and would restrict political fragmentation in the parliament.[3] Each of the two groups, especially the left, did not understand the characteristics of electoral systems and expected that small, extra-parliamentary parties would have difficulty entering the parliament.

The first post-communist election law was passed by the parliament in July 1992. A mixed-member proportional electoral system was introduced in Lithuania. This decision was an outcome of political compromise. Nevertheless, the mixed electoral system was one of the best options available to provide balance between representation and fragmentation in the parliament (the *Seimas*). The "Law on Elections to the *Seimas*" states that seventy-one members would be elected in single-member districts (SMDs), and seventy members would be elected by PR. All parties

---

2   Ibid., p. 16.

3   Giedrius Žvaliauskas, and Algis Krupavičius. 2002. "Party Organizations: Case of Lithuania." Paper prepared for Workshop Party Organization Development in Eastern Europe, Kaunas, Lithuania.

needed four percent of the vote to enter the *Seimas*. The only exception was political organizations representing ethnic minorities. They had a special threshold of two percent. In June 1996, amendments to the law were introduced: the threshold was increased to five percent for a single party and to seven percent for a party coalition. The special threshold for minority ethnic parties was abolished. These changes were made by efforts of the three strongest parties including the Lithuanian Democratic Labor Party (LDLP), the Homeland Union Lithuanian Conservatives (HULC) and the Lithuanian Christian Democratic Party (LChDP) which desired to restrict electoral competition to a small set of competitors. By increasing the price of pre-election party coalitions, the law eliminated most opportunities for smaller parties to compete against larger competitors.

The outcome of the 1992 and the 1996 parliamentary elections largely disappointed the major parties. The expectations of *Sajūdis* failed because the two-round system allocated seats to thirteen parties in 1992 and fourteen in 1996 (see Table 3.1).[4] With the exception of the Lithuanian Social Democratic Party (LSDP), the moderates failed to get into the parliament in 1992 on the PR list. In both elections, only five parties were able to enter the *Seimas* through the PR system while the two-round system produced party fragmentation—many members of parliament (MPs) in the SMDs represented different, not well-known parties. Before the 2000 *Seimas* elections, the two-round formula in the SMDs was changed to plurality. However, this change had no major effect on the distribution of party seats in the 2000 parliamentary elections (see Table 3.1). Some changes were introduced before 2004 *Seimas* elections. The governing parties brought back the majority, two-round formula in the SMDs. This produced no significant changes in the distribution of seats. It seems that citizens have learned to split their votes, and thus changes in the electoral formula have had no major influence in Lithuania.[5]

All the above mentioned changes in the electoral system were initiated by the governing parties to create a system more beneficial to them. According to the "Law on Elections to the *Seimas*," candidates are nominated no earlier than sixty-five days prior to the elections. Parties and political organizations have a right to nominate candidates in both SMDs and PR lists. Individuals only have a right to be nominated in the SMD when they collect at least 1,000 signatures within that particular district. The registration of candidates has additional requirements. The cash deposit for one candidate registration in a SMD is equal to one average monthly wage (AMW).[6] The registration of one party candidate list requires twenty AMWs. These deposits are reimbursed forty days after election results are announced if the results of the party or the candidate are successful.

---

4   In Table 3.1, there are eight parties, but I count thirteen because the *Sajūdis* coalition had members from five different parties.

5   See Mindaugas Jurkynas, and Ainė Ramonaitė. 2004. "Kairė ir dešinė Lietuvoje: ekspertų ir elektorato nesusikalbėjimas." In *Lietuva po Seimo rinkimų*, ed. A. Jankauskas. Vilnius: Naujasis lankas.

6   In 2004, the average monthly wage (AMW) was equal to 1,200 LTL ($429). In 2007, the AMW was equal to 1,731 LTL or $666.

Table 3.1   1992–2004 Parliamentary election results

Party	1992 Vote, %	1992 Seats	1996 Vote, %	1996 Seats	2000 Vote, %	2000 Seats	2004 Vote, %	2004 Seats
Democratic Labor Party	44.0	73	10.0	12	–	–	–	–
Sajudis Coalition	21.2	30	–	–	–	–	–	–
Christian Democratic Party	12.6	18	10.4	16	–	–	–	–
Social Democratic Party	6.0	8	6.9	12	–	–	–	–
Coalition United Lithuania	3.6	1	–	–	–	–	–	–
Center Union	2.5	2	8.7	14	2.9	2	–	–
Lithuania's Poles	2.1	4	3.1	2	1.9	2	3.8	2
National Union	2.0	4	2.2	3	–	–	–	–
Homeland Union			31.3	70	8.6	9	14.6	25
Young Lithuania			4.0	1	1.2	1	–	–
Women's Party			3.9	1	–		–	–
Christian Democratic Union			3.2	1	4.2	1	–	–
Liberal Union			1.9	1	17.3	34	–	–
Peasants Party			1.7	1	4.1	4	–	–
Political Prisoners and Deportees			1.6	1	–		–	–
A. Brazauskas Social Democratic Coalition					31.1	51[1]	–	–
New Union/Social Liberals					19.6	29	–	–
Moderate Conservative Union					2.0	1	–	–
Liberty Union					1.3	1	–	–
Labor Party							28.6	39
Working for Lithuania (Brazauskas, Paulauskas)							20.7	31[2]
For Order and Justice (Paksas)							11.4	11[3]
Liberal and Center Union							9.1	18[4]
Peasants and New Democrats							6.6	10
Others		1		4		4		5
Total	**100**	**141**	**100**	**139[5]**	**100**	**141**	**100**	**141**

[1] A. Brazauskas Social Democratic Coalition includes the Social Democratic Party and the Democratic Labor Party which were united into the Social Democratic Party.
[2] Includes the Lithuanian Social Democratic Party (twenty seats) and the New Union/Social Liberals (eleven seats).
[3] Includes the Liberal Democratic Party (ten seats).
[4] The Liberal Union was united with the Center Union.
[5] Excludes two vacant seats.

Source: Central Electoral Committee, 1992–2004.

Notes: Party votes in bold mark parties that entered the Seimas through proportional representation lists.

The mixed-member proportional electoral system determines a similar electoral campaign format in both single and multi-mandate districts. Parties are the central players in electoral campaigns, but individual candidates are equally important, especially when competing in the SMDs. Lithuanians are more likely to trust leaders and personalities instead of parties. This tendency is noticeable from the results of public opinion polls and SMD election results. It is very common to vote for one party in the PR list system but in the SMD, to vote for a candidate from another party or independent candidate. In such situations, parties play a supporting role. An analysis of interviews with party leaders indicates that the major party organizations are closely coordinated at the central level by political leaders and advised by professional consultants such as opinion pollsters.[7] The leadership of the party forms the common strategy, allocates resources, prepares the means for the election campaign and at the same time, allows some independence for individuals running in the election. The party allows them to adjust the campaign to local settings. For example, individual candidates use the same poster templates, but they may use their own slogans. In addition, the party prepares a common agenda for the candidate meetings with electors, but each candidate picks the most important topics for their region. In sum, the Lithuanian mixed-member electoral system introduces two types of electoral campaigns, and accordingly, it demands huge sums of money. Parties cannot rely on their own campaigns when their members compete in SMDs.

The Campaign and Party Finance Model

By August 2004, a number of legislative acts regulated campaign finance in Lithuania. From 1990 to 1997, campaign finance was regulated by the election laws including the "Law on Presidential Elections," the "Law on Elections to the *Seimas*" and the "Law on Elections to Local Government Councils of the Republic of Lithuania."[8] In 1998, the special "Law on the Control of the Funding of Political Campaigns of the Republic of Lithuania" was introduced which has brought some new elements to the regime of campaign finance. It also explained in detail the right to collect donations and gifts, which donations are prohibited, laid out the rules governing the use of finance and how to present financial campaign reports. Party activities and finance were regulated by the "Law of Political Parties" which was enacted in 1990. The "Law of the Funding of Political Parties and Political Organizations" was enacted only in 1999.[9] For the first time, it provided direct state subsidies to

---

7   Interviews with twenty party leaders were conducted by the author before 2004 parliamentary elections. The majority of questions were concerned with election campaign content, advertisement, party programs and campaign financing.

8   Central Electoral Committee of Republic of Lithuania. "Law on Presidential Elections; the Law on Elections to the *Seimas*; the Law on Elections to Local Government Councils of the Republic of Lithuania" available at: http://www.vrk.lt/index.eng.html (accessed 15 October 2005).

9   Ibid. Central Electoral Committee of Republic of Lithuania. "Law of the Funding of Political Parties and Political Organizations" available at: http://www.vrk.lt/index.eng.html (accessed 15 October 2005).

parties. The idea of public subsidies for parties was initiated by Jonas Šimenas, a member of the LChDP in 1997. With the agreement of all parties, a working group of party representatives was established in order to create a pilot project on the state funding of parties. The major argument for the necessity to introduce direct subsidies to parties was the need to strengthen them and to promote the transparency of party funding. Also, there was the belief that the subsidies would further the democratization of the Lithuanian political system. Some parties held the opinion that public funding should not be introduced until 1998 because of the economic crisis in Russia which negatively affected the Lithuanian economy. However, parties were in great need for resources for the upcoming parliamentary elections in 2000, and the law introducing state subsidies was enacted as soon as possible after the agreed limits on 12 January 1999.

According to the law, parties that have amassed no less than three percent of votes in parliamentary and municipal elections (since 2004 in European parliamentary elections as well) are eligible for a state subsidy. The subsidy to all the parties cannot exceed 0.1 percent of the state budget. This law states that even those parties that were unsuccessful in the elections are eligible for a state subsidy.[10] In August 2004, a new "Law of the Funding and Funding Control of Political Parties, Political Organizations and Political Campaigns" was enacted.[11] It is the most important law regulating a rather strict regime of campaign finance in Lithuania. It provides a new mechanism to control the process of finance. Some of the above mentioned laws (for example, the "Law on the Control of the Funding of Political Campaigns of the Republic of Lithuania" and the "Law of the Funding of Political Parties and Political Organizations") are now inoperative.

The present campaign system provides that campaigning shall be financed from the funds received from parties or candidates which are accumulated in a special election account opened according to a certificate issued by the Central Electoral Committee (CEC). The maximum amount of money permitted in the special election account is fifty AMWs for a candidate in a SMD, and 1,000 AMWs for a list of candidates in a multi-member constituency.[12] If the amount of money transferred to the appropriate account exceeds the established sum, the surplus shall be transferred by the bank to the state budget.

Campaign money can be deposited to the special account from the following sources: the financial resources of parties (the state subsidy as well), personal funds of the candidates, donations from natural persons and legal persons. The law does not set a limit on the amount of a donation from natural persons. The only requirement is that all the donations of natural and legal persons that exceed the amount of 100 Lithuanian litas (LTL) should be made public and registered on donation lists. Thus, only contributors of a sum which is less than 100 LTL have a right to be anonymous. A legal person is allowed to give to a party per year a donation which amounts to

---

10 The authors of this law used the experience of Canada.

11 Central Electoral Committee of Republic of Lithuania. "Law of the Funding and Funding Control of Political Parties, Political Organizations and Political Campaigns."

12 In 2004, the average monthly wage (AMW) was equal to 1,200 LTL. In 2007, the AMW was equal to 1,731 LTL or $666.

no more than 625,000 LTL. If elections are held the same year, a legal person has a right to give an additional 37,500 LTL to a party or candidate. Parties and candidates are prohibited from accepting financial resources from state or municipal institutions and organizations in which the state or municipality owns more than fifty percent of the shares. They are forbidden from receiving money from foreign sources unless the natural or the legal person is a citizen of Lithuania, a person of Lithuanian origin, a branch of a Lithuanian party founded in an area populated by Lithuanians or an international organization which includes Lithuanian parties.

The major problem which still remains is the transparency of the donations of natural persons. During the last parliamentary election, numerous natural persons donated only small amounts of money to parties (they donated less than 100 LTL in order to remain anonymous), but the total amount of their donations was impressive. This sum casts suspicions about the transparency of natural person donations. The reporting of these "special sums" leads one to suspect that the people who were donating were being used as fronts. Institutions controlling campaign finance have discovered that some donors had a very low income, and it is unusual for poor people to donate money to parties. A common violation of donor laws is the use of dummy organizations. An analysis of financial reports shows one or another of these organizations in the list of violations in every election.

As previously mentioned since 2000, parties which amass three percent of the vote in the previous election receive afterwards a state subsidy every year until the next election. The state allocated subsidies in the amount of 980,000 LTL ($245,000) for all Lithuanian parties in 2000 (see Table 3.2). That year, the largest part of the allocation of the state subsidy was received by two right-wing parties which initiated the introduction of these subsidies, the HULC (384,700 LTL) and the LChDP (143,200 LTL). It is important to note that the state subsidy was not a significant resource for any party with exception of the LChDP (thirty-eight percent). In 2001, the state allocated a smaller amount of money to parties (approximately 400,000 LTL). The biggest subsidy was received by three parties, the LSDP, the New Union/ Social Liberal (NU/SL) and the Lithuanian Liberal Union (LLU).[13] The next year in 2002, the state subsidy was reduced. Again, the three above mentioned parties were successful in receiving the largest share of the state subsidy (ninety-six percent). In 2003, parties received approximately the same sum, but this sum was larger due to changes in the exchange rate. Only in 2004 did the state decide to give a larger subsidy (one million LTL). Also before parliamentary elections, the governing parties decided to make some changes in the state budget, and allocate an additional 5.5 million LTL to parties. In total, parties received $1,937,143 of state subsidies. All these funds were transferred by the parties to their 2004 election campaign accounts. In 2005, the sum was three times larger than in 2004. Parties also received compensation for election campaign expenditures. The largest subsidy was received by the Labor Party or LP (approximately $117,857). The LSDP and the HULC received $91,786 and $86,428 respectively. In 2006, the state gave $3,571,428 to seven parties. It was expected that parties would use this money for the 2007 municipal elections.

---

13 These parties were the winners of 2000 parliamentary elections, see Table 3.1.

Table 3.2   State subsidies for Lithuanian parties, 2000–2005

Party name	2000	2001	2002	2003	2004	2005
LLU	8099[1] (3.3)[3]	26200 (25.3)	27600 (20)	17242 (2.6)	_[2]	
LCU	25000 (10.2)	10400 (10.1)	10972 (8)	23483 (3.5)	_[2]	
LChDP	35800 (14.5)	7450 (7.2)	7886 (5.7)	10966 (1.6)	16000 (0.9)	6429 (0.6)
HU(LC)	96175 (39.3)	14350 (13.9)	15086 (10.9)	62874 (9.4)	20250 (1.1)	172856 (16.2)
NU/ SL	7000 (2.9)	28300 (27.3)	29829 (21.6)	67543 (10.1)	432750 (24.1)	72858 (6.8)
LSDP	22225 (9.1)	16804 (16.2)	35258 (25.6)	477361 (71.3)	588750 (32.9)	183572 (17.4)
LDLP	33800 (13.8)	_[4]	–	–	–	–
VNDP	–	–	6273 (4.5)	10035 (1.5)	131107 (7.3)	84286 (7.8)
LLCU	–	–	–	–	604285 (33.7)	100000 (9.4)
LP	–	–	–	–	–	235714 (22)
Others	16901 (6.9)	–	5098 (3.7)	–	–	214286 (20)
Total	245.000 (100)	103.504 (100)	138.000 (100)	669.502 (100)	1.937.143 (100)	1.071.429 (100)

[1] Amounts listed in USD. Currency calculated according to the following: In 2000 and 2001 the rate of $1 = 4 LTL, in 2002 $1 = 3.5 LTL, in 2003 $1 = 2.9 LTL and in 2004 $1 = 2.8 LTL.
[2] In 2004, the LCU and the LLU merged into one party.
[3] Subsidy as a percent of total party revenue.
[4] In 2001, the LDLP and the LSDP merged into one party.

Source: Prepared by the author according to party official financial declarations.

Notes: Abbreviations of party names: HULC-Homeland Union (Lithuanian Conservatives), LChDP-Lithuanian Christian Democratic Party, LCU-Lithuanian Center Union, LDLP-Lithuanian Democratic Labor Party, LDP-Lithuanian Democratic Party, LFP-Lithuanian Farmers' Party, LLU-Lithuanian Liberal Union, LPP- Lithuanian Peasant's Party, LSDP-Lithuanian Social Democratic Party, NP 'Y.L'-National Party Young Lithuania, NU/SL-New Union/Social Liberals, LP-Labor Party, LDU-Liberal Democratic Union, LPA-Lithuanian Poles Action, LLCU-Lithuanian Liberal Center Union.

The allocation of state subsidies to parties continues to grow each year, and unfortunately, violations also continue to increase. For example in 2006, the LP did not hand in the compulsory financial declaration to the CEC on time and was denied the second part of the state subsidy.[14] Furthermore, the party and its former leader, Victor Uspaskich, have been accused of financial impropriety and withholding eight million LTL. As Table 3.3 indicates, the percentage of state subsidies for all Lithuanian party budgets varies from six percent in 2002 to thirty-eight percent in 2004. According to these data, state subsidies for parties have a tendency to comprise a bigger share of party funds each year. Despite this fact, the largest part of party funds continues to comprise individual and corporate donations. Also, the majority of subsidies have been received by governing parties. Thus, this public support is beneficial for the incumbent parties. All the new and smaller parties remain in a disadvantaged position. According to the "Law of the Funding of Political Parties and Political Organizations," the state has a right to allocate a much larger sum from the budget to parties (up to the 0.1 percent of the state budget). However, no government has allocated the full amount to parties. There is now a situation in which the state does not allocate enough subsidies for parties, and parties must find donors.

Table 3.3   Party income for the period 1995–2004 (in USD and as a percentage)

Year	Income Total	State Subsidy	Individual and Corporate Donations	Membership Dues	Other Income	Expense Total
1996	1,385,192 (100)	–	950,243 (68.6)	69,681 (5)	365,268 (26.4)	–
2000	1,736,537 (100)	245,000 (14.1)	666,029 (38.3)	77,933 (4.5)	700,606 (43.1)	
2001	562,493 (100)	103,504 (18.4)	221,655 (39.4)	133,918 (23.8)	103,416 (18.4)	
2002	2,201,843 (100)	138,000 (6.3)	900,566 (40.9)	171,681 (7.8)	991,596 (45)	1,460,800
2003	1,932,071 (100)	669,502 (34.7)	729,260 (37.8)	204,235 (10.5)	329,075 (17)	1,520,938
2004	5,110,961 (100)	1,937,143 (37.9)	2,629,155 (51.4)	307,243 (6)	237,420 (4.7)	4,655,176

Source: Prepared by the author according to party financial reports.

---

14 The Central Electoral Committee is responsible for the distribution of allocated state subsidies in Lithuania. It has the right to prevent the release of subsidies to a party which violates the law.

Campaigning is also financed from state funds. According to the "Law on Elections to the *Seimas*," a candidate or a party does not pay for the time allotted to them on state or municipal radio and television. Every party list has a right to one free hour of television and radio time to present their political platforms. Candidates on party lists participate in debates with one another. Also, every candidate in an SMD receives five minutes of free radio time, and candidate debates are sponsored on radio programs. The state also funds the printing of campaign posters for a candidate in an SMD, publishing an election program and lists of candidates in newspapers. This state funding is included to the maximum amount permitted in the special election account. Candidates have the possibility to buy air time for advertisements in the private and the national media for their campaign without limitation. During the last election to the *Seimas*, the legislation on advertising did not require equal price policy for all campaign participants in media. However, amendments to the election law were passed by the parliament in 2006 that provide such a requirement. The important requirement of the law is to mark and clearly distinguish between political advertisements from other published or aired information.

A new type of public funding was introduced in 2004. Parties which receive at least three percent of the vote in parliamentary elections and do not violate the laws regarding reports to state institutions may ask the state to compensate up to twenty-five percent of their election campaign expenditures. In 2005, the state allocated $571,428 to parties for these expenditures. All electoral expenditures are defined in the law. Campaign finance expenditures are as follows: the cost of producing and distributing political advertisements or other agitation material, staging of campaign events as well as services aimed at influencing voters, the salary of the campaign treasurer, payment for transportation and the costs of campaign volunteers and observers.

The electoral expenditure limits are not set in legislation, but they exist *de facto*. The amount of expenditures cannot exceed the limit of the special election account. It is prohibited to cover these expenditures from other sources. Those who desire to support a list of candidates or a candidate must do this by transferring funds to this special election account. The mass media which have no state or municipal capital can indicate which list (lists) of candidates or which candidate (candidates) they support and thereafter provide media free of charge. In this event, the costs of mass media may not be remunerated.

The use of funds allocated for campaigning is controlled by the state tax inspector and the CEC which are accountable to the *Seimas*. The CEC's chairman is appointed by the chair of the parliament. The fourteen members of the CEC are appointed by different institutions including the Ministry of Justice (four), the Association of Lawyers (four) and parties having seats in the parliament (eight). The CEC is elected for a four-year period. Ten days before the elections, parties and candidates are required to make a preliminary report to the CEC concerning their donations received and their use. Parties must file with the CEC reports on the source of funds and their use for campaigning no later than twenty-five days following the announcement of the final election results, and candidates of SMDs must report no later than within fifteen days following the announcement. Parties and candidates have to submit lists with the names and the addresses of their donors. The CEC publishes these reports in the *Valstybes Zinios* (the official gazette), and these data are later published on the CEC Internet site. If registered campaign participants fail to file their report, they are required to pay a double deposit to submit candidates for registration in the next election. When the state tax inspector reviews the reports and identifies violations, some administrative penalty is prescribed. The party's campaign treasurer is primarily responsible for violations by the party. More serious sanctions against violators of campaign finance are not provided. In 2006, a new report on the declaration of public information was introduced into law. The organizer of public information must declare all advertisements published or announced during the election campaign period, indicate the costs of these advertisements, the time of announcements and the person who paid. These declarations should be submitted to the CEC. They are reviewed and compared with the results of reports of election campaign monitoring presented by the auditors.

Trends in Party and Campaign Funding

Since independence, party and campaign funding have been hotly debated among politicians, political scientists and the public. Campaign costs have increased dramatically, and in each election, the costs of political advisers and mass media air time have increased. Since 1996, when the first professional campaigns started, parties each year have attempted to collect more financial resources. During the 2000 parliamentary elections, fifteen parties reportedly spent $875,000, and none of them had a debt. In the 2004 parliamentary elections, parties spent a total of $7,357,142. However, a new tendency is noticeable among some election participants during the last presidential and parliamentary elections, namely the accumulation of election debts. During the 2004 parliamentary elections, some parties were unable to avoid debts. According to the "Law of the Funding and Funding Control of Political Parties, Political Organizations and Political Campaigns," the debt should be re-paid six months after the elections.

Overall, Lithuania's system of party finance has consisted of two periods: first from 1990 to 1999 and the second since 2000. The first period is considered dominated by individual and corporate donations which constituted about seventy percent of all party income. The second period is associated with the growing importance of public subsidies which comprise about fifty percent of party income. This public finance system enjoys legitimacy among parties, but is unpopular with voters. Citizens are hostile to public subsidies for parties because of general low support of parties as institutions. In Lithuania, parties have the lowest ratings among all institutions. A 2006–2007 public opinion poll indicates that approximately only five percent of respondents trust parties.[15]

State subsidies form a rather large part of parliamentary party funds. The parliamentary parties receive the biggest share of public subsidies. Only four to eight percent of direct state subsidies are allocated to non-parliamentary parties. Lithuanian

---

15 Data provided by the Market and Opinion Research Center Vilmorus. The polls were conducted in February and March. See, *Didziausias pasitikejimas Sodra*, available at: http://www.bernardinai.lt/index.php?url=articles/59493.

laws do not fix the amount of public support (only the ceiling which has never been allocated); therefore, state subsidies for parties vary each year. Despite the fact that Lithuania introduced state subsidies for parties, the importance of individual and corporate, donations continues. It seems that state subsidies do not stop parties from raising money from other resources. Usually, a special group consisting of between five to ten party members is appointed to be in charge of fundraising. Such groups are in the central office as well as in local branches. Also, every candidate has the responsibility to secure money for the SMD race. The candidates are not expected to cover their campaign expenses fully. The parties usually cover some expenses for candidates, but the contribution is very small. It also depends on the candidate's popularity rating. Only some parties fully cover campaign expenses for top leaders. For instance, the LSDP had such a practice during the 2004 election campaign. In raising money from individual and private donations and having the possibility to receive state subsidies, parliamentary parties enjoy a huge advantage. This is because donors are likely to support major parties already having power. Small and extra-parliamentary parties have difficulty in competing with parliamentary parties. Party members generally establish close relationships with business leaders to secure money for their party.[16] Parties try to conceal their connections with businesses and corrupt practices continue with recent scandals involving fundraising.

Several factors should be taken into consideration when analyzing the trends in campaign funding in Lithuania. Party financial reports indicate that in every election, parties are financed by a number of organizations. Some companies and corporations have a tradition of donating to a number of parties. Companies such as Achema and Clasko allocate donations to as many as five different parties. Lithuanian companies do not support one party but try to support numerous parties. Also, membership dues are not a large percentage of total party income. They comprise about five to ten percent of party income. This is because Lithuanian party membership is very low. Only three parties have a membership of more than 10,000. All the other parties have a membership from 400 to 5,000 individuals.[17] Not every party has compulsory membership fees, and some of these fees are rather symbolic. For example, the LP has 13,848 members, but ordinary members pay just twelve LTL per year.[18]

In terms of spending, every candidate in an SMD has the possibility to spend their own money as well as money from the party for campaigning purposes. These candidates spent around 2,000,000 LTL. Having information about the mandates that parties received and the amount of expenditures, it is possible to determine the cost of a seat. The 2004 election estimates show that the most expensive seat was for the LCU (see Table 3.4). The HULC spent their money the most effectively as their mandates were the most inexpensive. However, the aforementioned costs are unreliable because the whole system of party financial reports is distrusted.

The area most prone to manipulation was the charge for political advertisements. The 2004 "Law of the Funding and Funding Control of Political Parties, Political Organizations and Political Campaigns" provides a mechanism for controlling

---

16 See, "Laiko ženklai." 2004. *Lietuvos rytas.* 21 July.

17 Information provided by party financial reports.

18 See official site of the party: http://www.darbopartija.lt/index.asp?DL=E&TopicID=7.

Table 3.4   The cost of a parliamentary mandate in 2004

Party	Seats in the Parliament	The Cost of the Mandate (LTL)
Labor Party	39	94934
Homeland Union (Lithuanian Conservatives)	25	36401
Lithuanian Social Democratic Party	20	100883
Liberal and Center Union	18	149745
New Union/Social Liberals	11	125964
Peasants and New Democrats	10	98220
Liberal Democrats Party	9	45544
Lithuanian Poles Action	2	50066

Source: These data from the Central Electoral Committee.

expenditures for political advertisements in the mass media. Independent experts compare the real costs of advertisements with those declared by parties. However, parties explained the differences between the size of their advertisement and the real costs due to the fact that television channels offered them a system of flexible discounts. The other parties said that donors helped them to get inexpensive advertisements. Outdoor political advertising was legally limited during the 2004 election campaign. Parties could only place their posters in specially designated spaces by the municipality. This is why hidden political advertising became popular in a variety of forms. So-called "de-politicized" articles about candidates to the *Seimas* were published by newspapers and magazines. According to Makaraityte, the monitoring of hidden political advertising shows that the LP and the LCU were especially adept at using it.[19] In the case of the ruling LSDP and the NU, there is also the suspicion that significant public administrative resources have been used for campaigning. For example, positive developments in the social sphere have been advertised as the personal achievement of the incumbent minister of social affairs, a candidate to the *Seimas*. The signs show that this tendency of hidden advertisement and the use of administrative resources will continue.

Party finance is not transparent and is open to illegal money. However for a long time, parties were not very keen to stop the growing importance of money by

---

19 Indre Makaraityte. 2004. "Lithuania after the *Seimas* Election 2004." Paper delivered at the LPA Conference.

prohibiting paid advertisement or corporate donations. However in 2006 under an initiative of some MPs, a new amendment to the "Law of the Funding and Funding Control of Political Parties, Political Organizations and Political Campaigns" was introduced which would create a more transparent system.[20] The Lithuanian government in January 2007 approved the amendment which provides three major changes. First, it prohibits the financing of parties and campaigns by legal persons (one of the main sources of party financing). Second, instead of legal persons donating, a new source of party financing is provided which comprises a civic income tax (two percent).[21] Third, the Lithuanian government approved the proposal to forbid political advertisements on television. According to a Lithuanian government press release, the amendment seeks to create an effective a reliable finance control system as well as increase transparency.

Transparency International's Lithuanian branch director Rytis Juozapavičius approved the decision of the Lithuanian government.[22] He states that the Lithuanian government seeks to lower party electoral budgets which each election are higher and reduce the level of political corruption. According to Juozapavičius, the amendment would be a small step forward. The only comment he mentioned was that prohibition of political advertisements should not deprive politicians the right to free speech. The Chair of the CEC, Zenonas Vaigauskas, is uncertain whether it is necessary to prohibit political advertising on television but thinks that paid political advertising should be prohibited.[23] It is evident that, regardless all the different opinions, changes in party and campaign financing are necessary. They would contribute more transparency to the party financing system and would create more equal opportunities for all the Lithuanian parties.

Development of Parties and the Party System

The votes received by parties in elections directly affect their standing. Results from different Lithuanian elections show that the party system is based on a volatile electorate. As Krupavičius and Lukošaitis argue, the increasing passivity of voters and constant changes in party choice affects the permanent fluctuation of governing parties in Lithuania.[24] Though there were approximately forty registered parties during the period from 1990 to 2000, some kind of bipolar party system emerged. Voters have chosen between the right and the left or sometimes between governing

---

20 "Nutarimas dėl LR Politinių Partijų ir Politinių Kampanijų finansavimo bei finansavimo kontrolės įstatymo." 2, 7, 8, 10, 12, 16 ir 18 straipsnių pakeitimo, available at: http://www.litlex.lt/scripts/sarasas2.dll?Tekstas=1&Id=100918 (accessed 20 January 2007).

21 At the moment, the law allows citizens to give two percent of their income tax to non-governmental organizations as charity. The amendment allows citizens to provide the two percent to parties.

22 "Partiju finansavimo pakeitimai – tai zingsnelis i prieki," available at: http://www.delfi.lt.

23 Ibid.

24 Algis Krupavičius, and Alvydas Lukošaitis. 2004. *Lietuvos Politinė Sistema*. Kaunas: Poligrafija ir informatika, p. 211.

and opposition parties. Since the 2000 elections, each parliamentary election has produced political "newcomers" in the Lithuanian government. Party politics has slowly become more multi-polar, and ruling coalitions are broader than during the first period. In Lithuania, party system development and funding are inter-related. The bipolar party system period overlaps with the lack of public finance. The second stage of a multi-party system is concurrent with the funding regime introducing state subsidies. Though it is difficult to demonstrate that there is a causal relationship, there is a relationship which needs to be analyzed.

It seems that the unwillingness to introduce state subsidies for parties was aimed to provide the same chances for every party to stabilize their donors and electorate without blaming each other that some parties received state subsidies. However once created, the Lithuanian party and campaign finance system contributed more to governing parliamentary parties than to extra-parliamentary ones. This makes them stronger and creates unequal conditions for party competition. Major parties themselves argue that this is a fair system. Parties which do not have enough public confidence cannot be supported by the state. However, this is a circular argument in which extra-parliamentary parties have difficulty in fundraising because of a lack of access to state support. Corporations are more likely to donate to major parties which have a greater chance to be elected and especially to form government. This tendency is clear from the analysis of reported party donors. Thus, smaller or extra-parliamentary parties have fewer chances to become visible and to gain public confidence. They have fewer chances to create a well-organized party with a good team of paid personal unlike major parliamentary parties which receive subsidies.

Some right-wing politicians before introducing state subsidies argued that the Lithuanian finance system would stabilize the party system; however, there has been no stabilization of electoral choice and party identification in Lithuania. In the 2004 elections, new parties such as the LP, the Lithuanian Peasant's Party (LPP) and Liberal Democratic Party (LDP) won altogether sixty seats in the parliament. Some extra-parliamentary parties somehow still manage to secure public confidence and attract financial resources, and one of their means is the promotion of a famous and powerful party leader. Only those newcomers who have popular leaders earn the confidence of corporate and individual donors. In the 2000 parliamentary elections, the NU was among these parties. In the 2004 parliamentary elections, the LP entered parliament, and their financial funds were unusually large and collected only from private donations. Private donors trust famous leaders and are very generous. The previously mentioned parties manage to enter the parliament without direct public subsidies, but of course, they put all their efforts to entering the parliament knowing that later they will be able to receive subsidies.

In Lithuania, governing parties tend to appoint individuals friendly to them to state-owned television and radio channels in order to be able to control the public media. This problem was eliminated because of changes in the laws regulating the mass media; however, the speculation is that public television is ironically now more favorable to opposition parties. This public channel sometimes serves as the "headquarters of conservatives" because a lot of programs invite some particular people very often. There is uncertainty over the future direction of public media neutrality. The private media unsuccessfully try to be neutral. Some of the channels are bought by big corporations which have links to certain political groups. This becomes especially evident during electoral campaigns. Also, the systematic inter-relationship between political and economic elites is visible in Lithuanian politics. Some rich Lithuanian companies are likely to support all major parties. While relations between parties and economic elite at the moment seem strong, they may be weakened after new amendments prohibiting legal persons from donating are passed.

Conclusions

The examination of the development of party and campaign financing in Lithuania shows different modifications from the first introduction of party and campaign regulations in 1990–1992, and it is still under development. Due to different violations, MPs have initiated amendments to the laws almost every year. The financing mechanism has changed from unrestrictive to a rather strict regime, having numerous bans and enforcement regulations. This analysis of election results and financial regulations shows that though regulations are changing, the party system changes slowly. Major parties are represented in the parliament after every election; although, some newcomers enter the parliament. However, the number of parties represented in the *Seimas* is more or less the same.

The data provided by party financial reports indicate that Lithuanian parties attract more and more money to their accounts each year which is inter-related to the growing expenses of electoral campaigns. Campaigns demand a lot of money for mass media advertising, and Lithuanian parties, due to the mixed electoral system and volatile electorate, organize two types of campaigns. One is more party-centered and another one is candidate-centered. There is a very visible relationship between parties and candidates. They help each other to gain votes during the campaigns. In the regions where the party is not popular, a famous leader becomes the candidate in the SMD. Famous candidates help to attract votes for the party in the PR contest. Though candidates raise money for their campaign, parties finance their candidates as well. Consequently, there is a close relationship between the party on the ground, in the central office and in the public office. The question about the impact of party and campaign regulations on party development in Lithuania has no clear answer. At the moment, it is possible to claim that some indirect relationship exists. Regulations are one of the factors influencing party system development. Stricter regimes help to stabilize the party system, and public subsidies bring more transparency to party competition and make parties stronger.

Chapter 4

Latvia:
Disclosure yet Abuse,
Volatility yet Stability

Jānis Ikstens

Latvia based its struggle for re-gaining independence on the principle of the legal continuity of the republic. This approach was crucial for adopting a parliamentary system that closely resembled the institutional arrangement before the 1934 coup. The *Saeima*, a unicameral parliament, is solely entrusted with law-making while the cabinet depends on the confidence of the parliament. The president and all judges are chosen by the parliament. Although the role of the *Saeima* as a law-making body has been notably diminishing, its powers of appointment make it a key political institution.[1] Consequently, parliamentary elections are regarded as the most important political event during the four-year electoral cycle.

Parliamentary elections are based on a party-list proportional representation system. Only registered parties and their alliances may field candidates for the lists. A party can be officially established if it has the support of at least 200 adult Latvian citizens and if the party's program is not against the principles of the constitution. Once registered, a party does not have to offer a party list or receive votes to maintain its legal status. A party or alliance has to deposit 1,000 lats ($1,960[2]) for its list to be registered for parliamentary elections. This fee is refunded to parties that clear the nation-wide electoral threshold of five percent.

Seats are allocated in accordance with the Saint-Laguë formula. All calculations are made by the Central Election Commission which is entrusted with the general administration of parliamentary elections. What makes the calculation more complex is the system of flexible lists. Voters are allowed to indicate their personal preferences by crossing out any number of candidates on their preferred slate or giving a "plus" to their favorites on the same slate. Thus, the final rank-order of candidates depends on voter's preferences not just the negotiated party list.

Although the system of flexible lists is often seen as conducive to intra-party competition, it has not created major rifts in Latvian parties. The election campaigns

---

1   Jānis Ikstens. N.d. "Political System of Latvia: Adjustment to Regained Independence." In *European Democracies*, ed. Jean-Michel de Waele, and Paul Magnette. Brussels: Free University of Brussels. Forthcoming.

2   All currency conversions are made at the exchange rate set by the Bank of Latvia on the day of adoption of a law or the amendment or the day of the election.

of major parties are typically conducted in a centralized manner. Separate campaigns of individual candidates to receive "pluses" from voters are rarely seen.[3] It is the leading figures of each party that make such efforts, and they are difficult to distinguish from the party campaign that often puts an emphasis on its leader's ability to attract broader public support. Second-tier candidates rarely conduct noteworthy individual campaigns.

A majority of Latvia's citizens seem to under-estimate the power of the system of flexible lists and believe that the current electoral system should be replaced by one which provides a closer link between voters and elected officials as well as fosters greater accountability of parties and members of parliament (MPs). An opinion poll in March 2006 showed that only twenty-six percent of residents of Latvia were satisfied with the current electoral system. Moreover, thirty-seven percent of respondents favored a first-past-the-post system, and another fifteen percent preferred a mixed-member system.[4]

Municipal elections are held every four years under a similar system of flexible party lists. However, unregistered associations of citizens may field candidates in municipalities with less than 5,000 residents. With the expected completion of territorial reform by 2009, these smaller municipalities will largely become extinct, and thus parties will also dominate at the municipal government level. Campaigning for municipal elections is less centralized but the election to the Riga City Council involves substantial political advertising on national radio and television and, thus, carries a spill-over effect to other municipalities. Elections to the European Parliament (EP) are based on flexible candidate lists submitted exclusively by registered political organizations. The very limited experience with the first EP elections in Latvia in 2004 revealed short, centralized and sparingly-funded campaigns.

Legal Framework of Public Finance

Owing to public pressure, the model of party finance in Latvia has evolved from a notably liberal one to a considerably regulated and transparent system, but one in which direct subsidies do not occur. The "Law on Public Organizations" adopted in late 1992 established the guidelines for the organizational structure and registration procedure of political organizations. Nevertheless, the law was vague on the issue of party funding. The 1995 "Law on Party Financing" and the 1995 "Law on Parliamentary Pre-Election Campaigns" established more detailed regulations. The 1995 "Law on Party Financing" introduced a number of important limitations on the generally unregulated field of political finance. The law stipulated that campaigning expenses are to be covered from party accounts. According to the law, the legal sources of income for a party were membership dues, donations (by both natural and legal persons), profit from party enterprises and other income not prohibited by the legislation.

---

3   Jānis Ikstens. 2006. "Patronage as Party Building Tool: Case of Latvia." Paper presented at the EJPR Joint Sessions of Workshops. Nicosia, Cyprus.

4   The poll of 1,023 residents of Latvia was commissioned by ELJA 50, a non-governmental organization of Latvian expatriates and carried out by SKDS Public Opinion Research Center.

A donor was not allowed to contribute more than 25,000 lats (approximately $47,980) per year, per party. Furthermore, parties were prohibited from receiving donations from enterprises where the state or a municipality holds at least fifty percent of shares, from state or municipal institutions, from religious organizations, from non-citizens as well as from any foreign or anonymous source. If an anonymous donation was received, it had to be transferred to a separate fund controlled by the Ministry of Justice which subsequently re-distributed the donation in equal parts to all registered parties. The legislation specifically prohibited setting-up foundations for the purpose of financing a party.

Donations to individual candidates were not explicitly regulated but the controlling authority, the State Revenue Service (SRS), could regard such donations as an act of mediation, in which the party would benefit, which is a criminal offense. Furthermore, the 2002 "Law on the Eradication of the Conflict of Interests" sets restrictions on accepting donations for public officials and stipulates that all officials (including MPs and municipal deputies) have to file annual declarations indicating any income.

The "Law on Parliamentary Pre-Election Campaigns" laid out the basic rules regulating the use of advertising in the media during parliamentary elections. Most importantly, it stipulated that a limited amount of free air time on national television and radio was to be equally allocated to all lists registered for the election. The law explicitly strived for equalizing opportunities and minimizing unfair campaign practices by means of demanding an adequate compensation to other lists if one of the lists had been given free air time on public or commercial channels in addition to the amounts specified in the law. Another form of indirect state support was a free-of-charge publication of the political platforms of parties running for election.

It should be stressed that there were no limits on the total campaign spending or income as long as the party complied with the limitation for individual donations. Also, parties were not obliged to submit additional pre- or post-campaign financial declarations. Advertising was *de facto* unlimited, and the legislation did not require equal price policy for all contenders in either state or private media. However since 1995, all registered parties had to submit annual financial declarations to the Ministry of Justice and the SRS containing detailed information about the amount and the sources of income as well as aggregate data on spending. These declarations were freely accessible after they were published in *Latvijas Vēstnesis* (the official gazette). Failure to submit the declaration on time could result in dissolving the party by a court order. The Ministry of Justice was the foremost institution entrusted with enforcing party financial regulations. The National Council of Television and Radio supervised allocation of free air time on public radio and television and also observed the election campaign in the media.

The sanctions against violations were weak and primarily administrative in nature. The penal code of Latvia did not contain sanctions against violations of party finance legislation until 2004. However, parties could be held responsible for violations of accounting procedures or similar minor offenses. However, the enforcement mechanism was far from complete. It is important to note that the 1995 law did not provide for any direct state subsidies to parties. Moreover, parties did not enjoy any taxation privileges or exemptions; although, they (just like other non-profit organizations) did not pay income tax. Similarly, donations to parties were not tax-exempt.

At the time of the parliamentary debates on the 1995 "Law on Party Financing," the issue of introducing direct state subsidies was never substantially discussed. Jānis Lagzdiņš, Chairman of the Public Administration and Local Government Committee and the chief author of this law, dismissed the idea of state subsidies for two reasons: the lack of money in the state budget,[5] and the failure of parties to fulfill their education and information functions.[6] More than a decade later, Lagzdiņš admitted that this law was too important and that he did not want to jeopardize its chances of being adopted by including the provision of state subsidies. Many politicians at that time hoped that the law would be implemented formally and would not substantially affect party competition.[7]

Although parties have subsequently made attempts to introduce direct public subsidies on the grounds of fighting corruption, making parties more autonomous and educating voters, they faced a clearly negative public attitude.[8] It has been shown that the amounts proposed by politicians would hardly cover routine administrative costs of major parties let alone the hefty campaign expenses.[9] Furthermore, the general public has a very low trust in parties.[10] They are frequently seen as extensions of certain business groups further under-cutting their legitimacy.[11]

Public pressure after the 1998 parliamentary elections and record high spending levels in the 2002 parliamentary elections, however, led to several revisions of the existing party finance regime. In June 2002, the parliament agreed to cut the maximum amount of a donation per party, per year to 10,000 lats ($16,130). Public institutions and companies where the state or municipality is the shareholder were completely prohibited from donating money to parties. Establishing subsidiaries for financial purposes and funding political organizations through third parties (for example, foundations and companies) was explicitly prohibited. In a move to increase transparency and to strengthen the enforcement of party finance legislation, the parliament ruled that all parties would be required to submit their annual financial declarations to the Anti-Corruption Bureau (KNAB) which was entrusted

---

5   These debates were taking place in March 1995 when the banking crisis in Latvia was developing.

6   Minutes of the 5th *Saeima* plenary meeting, 2 March 1995, http://www.saeima.lv/steno/st_955/st0203htm (accessed 23 April 2007).

7   Author's interview with Jānis Lagzdiņš, 6 August 2007.

8   According to surveys with representative sample of Latvian residents conducted by the SKDS Public Opinion Research Center, eighty-seven percent of respondents in July 1998, seventy-eight percent in August 2000 and seventy-two percent in August 2001 opposed the introduction of direct state subsidies to parties.

9   Jānis Ikstens. 2003. "Partiju finansēšana Latvijā: problēmas un alternatīvas." In *Partiju finansēšana: Latvijas pieredze pasaules kontekstā,* ed. Jānis Ikstens. Riga: Baltijas Sociālo zinātņu institūts.

10   Eurobarometer surveys in 2004–2006 found that only between six and seventeen percent of respondents said they trusted parties. The New Baltic Barometer conducted under by Richard Rose in 1993–2004 registered a slight decline in the trust of parties, from fourteen percent in 1993 and 1996 to seven percent in 2001 and ten percent in 2004.

11   Jānis Ikstens. 2000. "Party Finance in Latvia: Preliminary Observations." Paper presented at the 16th Conference on Baltic Studies. Washington, DC.

with controlling party financing. Moreover, parties were required to disclose on the Internet any donation within ten days of receipt. Separate pre- and post-election financial declarations were introduced.

In 2004, further limitations were introduced: corporate donations were prohibited altogether while individuals could only donate money from their taxable income of the last three years. Also, the maximum amount of membership fees per year was limited so that combined membership fees and donations for individual did not exceed 10,000 lats a year. Limits on campaign spending were introduced for the first time, and they were set at .20 lats (38 cents) per registered voter in a given election district. Campaign spending could start 270 days before the election day, and include any party expenses apart from routine administrative expenses. Harsher sanctions against the violation of party finance legislation were introduced providing an opportunity to bring criminal charges against those individuals serving as conduits of finance to parties. However, key areas of so-called "independent campaigning" by third parties (for example, non-governmental organizations or NGOs) and hidden advertising in breach of ethical standards of journalists remained largely unaddressed. A few parties used legislative loopholes in 2006 to wage capital-intensive campaigns before the parliamentary elections. This re-ignited public discussions about the regulatory framework of party and campaign finance and prompted Prime Minister Aigars Kalvītis to ask the KNAB to produce a policy paper on further reforms by 2007.

Trends in Latvian Party Funding

While the Latvian legislation allows for a variety of funding sources, donations have been the primary source of income for parties since 1995 when annual financial declarations were introduced. As Table 4.1 shows, within a single election cycle, most of the funds were raised in national election years (for example, 1995, 1998, 2002 and 2006) while years of municipal elections (for example, 1997, 2001 and 2005) saw less incoming funding. The 2004 amendments to the party finance legislation have significantly reduced the total official income of parties. Since 1995, party income during parliamentary election years doubled on an election-to-election basis. In 2006, the trend was reversed and party aggregate income dropped by nearly two thirds compared to 2002. Also, the income gap between parliamentary election years and municipal election years has diminished dramatically since 2004.

On average, more than seventy-five percent of funding comes from donations; however, the pattern of donations has changed. Corporate donations outweighed donations by individuals in the 1990s. The trend reversed in the 2000s, and individual donations have become the dominant source of party income (this was facilitated by a prohibition of corporate donations in 2004). It would be premature to conclude that the general public has developed a greater trust in parties. Donations by private persons appear to have become a dominant way of channeling corporate money into party accounts. Indeed, major parties that have parliamentary representation appear to rely heavily on large contributions. As shown in Table 4.1, large donations (more than $6,000) constituted eighty percent of corporate contributions, and donations of more than $1,200 cover almost seventy-five percent of income from private donations.

Table 4.1. Party income in 1995–2006, %

	1995	1996	1997	1998	1999	2000	2001	2002	2003	2004	2005	2006
Donations by individuals	42.2	16.6	29.3	41.2	58.2	40.0	41.1	62.0	66.2	70.5	83.6	75.7
Donations by legal persons	47.3	61.8	61.9	42.3	30.3	31.8	54.0	27.9	22.3	5.3	n/a	n/a
Membership dues	2.2	20.5	7.1	3.2	9.0	3.4	3.3	3.6	10.3	18.7	14.5	23.4
Entrepreneurship	5.5	0.04	0.5	0.3	0.4	0	0.3	1.6	0.4	4.9	1.0	0.8
Other	2.8	1.1	1.2	12.9	2.1	24.8	1.3	4.9	0.9	0.5	0.9	0.1
Total	100	100	100	100	100	100	100	100	100	100	100	100
Total in Thousands of Lats	1,122.3	485.4	548.5	3,029.7	756.5	1,677.3	1,808.2	6,455.0	907.4	1,421.2	2,423.4	2,746.6
Total in Thousands USD	2,089.9	873.0	929.7	5,324.6	1,296.7	2,736.2	2,834.2	10,867.0	1,677.3	2,754.3	4,086.7	5,124.3

Source: Annual financial declarations of Latvian parties.

Membership dues did not normally constitute a considerable source of income until 2003; although, the amount of membership dues was unrestricted until 2004. More than a third of all registered parties declared no income from membership dues between 1995 and 2006. A significant increase in collected membership dues can be observed since 2003 which coincides with the introduction of new restrictions on the amounts and the types of donations.

One would expect that leftist parties, which traditionally have better developed organizational structures, would turn to membership dues as a significant source of income. It is true that for many of them, the dues have been a major source of income in off-election years. However, the collected totals are less than impressive. Instead, it is some of the right-of-center parties that have developed reasonably strong organizations, consistently collecting significant amounts of membership dues. Parties tend to avoid entrepreneurship in order to fund their political activities. However, 1998 saw the first use of bank loans as a source of financing. However, amendments to the legislation in 2004 put an end to this kind of party funding. Indeed, the stream of income appears to be fairly focused. The five wealthiest parties within a single election cycle tend to collect seventy-five to eighty-five percent of the total party income. This pattern is also observed in election years. It appears that the list of the best-funded parties changes only insignificantly during a full election cycle, but the top five do change between election cycles. On the other hand, the number of parties that claim to have no income has increased from six in 1995 to thirteen in 1998 and to sixteen in 2002 (but dropped to eight in 2006).

One can observe that donations are targeted towards a narrow circle of parties. On average, five to seven parties collect more than ninety percent of all donations. The wealthiest parties appear to be members of governing coalitions or control important municipal offices (as was the case of the Social Democratic Workers' Party of Latvia in 2002 and 2005 which controlled the mayoral office in Riga). Patronage appointments are used to facilitate fundraising for party's political purposes.[12] However, the size of their factions in parliament seems to matter less for their financial well-being.

This money-for-influence thesis is further strengthened by the fact that the ideological positions of parties appear to have low salience for party financing. Aggregate data indicate that both left-of-the-center and right-of-the-center parties receive donations in proportions comparable to their parliamentary strength while the left's incomes have been lower than those of the right in absolute figures. Curiously, major parties advocating the interests of various Slavic minorities (for example, Russians, Ukrainians and Belarussians) appear to have far less financial resources than their Latvian counterparts. However, this cannot be taken as an indication of the economic weakness of these minorities.[13] Rather, this situation supports the money-for-influence thesis in which out-of-government parties do less well. Also, these minority parties have been reported to receive support from Russia which is not

---

12 Jānis Ikstens, "Patronage as Party Building Tool: Case of Latvia."

13 Artis Pabriks. 2002. *Ethnic Proportions, Employment and Discrimination in Latvia.* Rīga: Nordik.

Table 4.2   Party spending in 1995–2006, %

	1995	1996	1997	1998	1999	2000	2001	2002	2003	2004	2005	2006
Expenses to attain programmatic goals	71.2	49.8	63.8	78.7	26.1	19.4	72.3					
Entrepreneurship expenses	1.9	0.2	0.3	1.7	1.1	0	0.01					
Administrative expenses	5.2	14.9	4.7	4.2	10.2	11.6	12.9					
Salaries and wages	16.7	29.6	27.3	8.3	17.2	9.7	7.0	3.4	25.0	12.4	3.9	3.8
Services								56.3	37.1	52.9	61.6	55.0
Purchase of property								0.6	3.0	0.2	0.4	0.2
Printing expenses								4.4	4.4	6.9	5.5	6.7
Public events								1.0	4.2	8.2	9.5	11.9
Charity								3.6	5.5	2.6	2.0	3.3
Returned donations								0.1	2.9	3.3	1.6	2.1
Taxes								0.6	0.1	4.7	2.8	1.8
Payments to the state budget								0.1	1.6	3.8	4.7	1.1
Other expenses	5	5.5	3.8	7	45.4	59.2	7.7	30.1	16.4	5.1	7.8	14.2
Total	100	100	100	100	100	100	100	100	100	100	100	100
Total in Thousands of Lats	1,474.7	329.8	514.6	3,111.4	346.3	1,486.5	1,818.8	6,475.9	832.0	1,312.0	2,349.9	2,853.0
Total in Thousands of USD	2,746.2	593.2	872.2	5,468.2	594.0	2,425.0	2,850.8	10,902.2	1,537.9	2,552.5	3,962.7	5,322.8

Source: Annual financial declarations of Latvian parties.

Note: Template for annual financial declarations changed in 2002.

officially reported.[14] Given the strictly ethnic pattern of political mobilization among Slavs and the joint party list of the three major Slavic parties in 1998 and 2002, ethnic Slavic parties did not experience fierce electoral competition, and thus their funding needs were lower.[15] The increased income and spending by the main Slavic contenders in 2006, following a break-up of the joint party lists in 2004 through 2006, confirms the role of competition for party funding.

The expenditure side of the balance sheet reveals that most of the money of parties is spent on what used to be loosely termed "expenses to attain the goals defined in the party program." A new template for party financial reports was introduced in 2002 providing more detailed information about party spending. It is now clear that parties spend more than half of their election year budgets on purchasing campaign-related services including air time on television and radio as well as space in newspapers and on billboards. Printing of leaflets, brochures and the like consumes five to six percent of the budget while the holding of public events uses ten percent of total spending. After a surge in the first half of the 2000s, the spending on staff salaries has returned to six to seven percent of the budget (characteristic of the latter part of the 1990s). A close examination of party balance sheets raises a number of questions that cannot be answered without using qualitative research. Therefore interviews with top representatives of the eleven major parties were conducted in 1999.[16] These interviews shed some light on various mechanisms of party financing in Latvia. It emerged that political fundraising is a highly concentrated process. An absolute majority of party representatives admitted that, on average, two to four persons were involved in raising money for their respective party. Additionally, three to five persons were extensively informed about fundraising efforts on a regular basis.

The national election campaign is the most capital-intensive event for any party. The time allotted for campaign fundraising varies between two months and two years. During the fundraising efforts, it appears that party leaders tend to approach companies or wealthy individuals that have indicated at least some ideological proximity to a given party. It seems that right-of-center parties frequently rely on their well-to-do members while leftist parties cite shared goals and ideology as their basis for approaching potential donors. At the same time, the personal contacts and the experience of leaders from previous campaigns also plays an important role in planning fundraising activities.

Party representatives were highly skeptical about approaching an average person with a request to donate to a party. Virtually all of them believed that such efforts would be a waste of time since the general income level is low as is the public's trust in parties and party politics. All parties denied support from multi-national corporations. Five parties indicated they have received assistance from parties abroad in the form of staff training and campaign consultations. However, the majority of party leaders confirmed the assumption that sponsors seek certain "interests" from

---

14 For details, see Aleksandrs Šabanovs. 2004. "Štābs." *Sestdiena* 21 February.

15 Jānis Ikstens. 2005. "FHRUL Bloc: Leftist Parties or Parties or Russian-Speaking People?" *Acta Universitatis Latviensis* 680: 152–161.

16 Major parties were defined as organizations that have or have had parliamentary representation since 1993.

their investments in parties. Eight out of eleven respondents admitted that potential sponsors frequently put forward suggestions or even demands of a political and/or economic character. However, party leaders stressed their selectivity in accepting these demands. While a few representatives claimed that their parties never yielded to those demands, most admitted "occasional" acceptance. Moreover, three representatives conceded that, at times, their parties had to give up their ideological principles in order to satisfy their financial supporters.

All parties seem to agree that it is much easier to solicit donations for a party that participates in a governing coalition since that position gives additional political leverage. In the meantime, representatives of only two parties admitted the existence of "kick-backs" or donations from companies that have received contracts or licenses from state or municipal agencies controlled by representatives of the respective party. The interviews revealed that almost all major parties do not account for some of their campaign expenses. Some parties are said to leave more than half of their expenses unregistered which means that these expenses are paid in cash or covered by a company or directly by individual without involving the party. On average, the unregistered share of the party expenses is said to amount to between five and twenty percent of the total campaign budget. While all major Latvian parties claim not to use offshore companies for campaign financing purposes, another questionable mechanism is employed. Nine out of eleven parties admitted that they use private donations as a way of funneling corporate money into the party's accounts. Some organizations use membership dues for that purpose as well.

Follow-up interviews with select party representatives in 2006–2007 indicated that certain aspects of party finance have changed since 1999. Although the process of fundraising remains a highly restricted area of party management, the role of patronage positions and kick-backs in party funding is said to have increased. Taking the activities of law enforcement agencies into account, parties manage the flow of private donations much more carefully, but unofficial payments to campaign consultants, advertising agencies and the media have grown in view of the recent spending restrictions. More sophisticated methods of campaign funding are now implemented. In sum, Latvia's parties rely heavily on private donations and exploit public resources since direct state subsidies have not been introduced. A gradual increase in the importance of individual donations was accelerated after a ban on corporate donations was introduced in 2004. However, it is highly plausible that donations by private persons (as well as membership dues) are used to channel corporate money into party accounts. On par with the large amounts of single donations, this is an indication of the plutocratic financing of parties.[17] There are vast differences between parties represented in the parliament and parties outside in their ability to attract financial resources.

A sizeable share of campaign spending is unaccounted. The exact origins of corporate money and unaccounted funds are unclear, but one of the sources could be Russia that has allegedly supported one of the pro-Moscow political organizations in Latvia. Also, investigation of money laundering charges against Aivars Lembergs,

---

17 This term denoting large donations by wealthy individuals was coined by Gullan Gidlund.

the long-standing Mayor of Ventspils, has led to the belief that some 5 million lats (nearly $9.5 million) have been illegally disbursed to Latvian politicians and parties between 1995 and 2006. In reaction to the near-doubling of campaign spending for parliamentary elections every four years, campaign spending limits were introduced in 2004 which drastically reduced the spending figures reported officially. However, more sophisticated (and not necessarily legal) forms of covering electioneering expenses emerged.

Disclosure and Enforcement

Latvia introduced annual financial declarations for parties as early as 1995. The SRS, responsible for the collection of taxes, was entrusted with the task of controlling the annual declarations. Although parties were submitting their declarations rather diligently, the SRS conducted merely formal inspections of declarations which led to sharp criticisms of the SRS and accusations of bias and superficiality. To improve the enforcement of party finance legislation, the parliament since 2002 has entrusted the KNAB with the task of collecting and verifying the declarations. The KNAB was established specifically as an institution to fight corruption, and its director is appointed by the parliament. Although the Bureau is placed under the supervision of the prime minister, the KNAB enjoys a high degree of autonomy as stipulated in the relevant legislation.

The KNAB not only collects all party financial declarations and makes them publicly available on its website but also maintains an up-to-date database on all donations to parties since 2001. The publicly available part of the database contains the names of the donor as well as the date and the amount of each donation. Parties have to disclose this information within ten days of receipt of a donation. Since 2004, parties additionally have to submit to the KNAB declarations about the projected campaign spending no less than thirty days before the elections. Within thirty days after each election, parties have to file post-election financial reports indicating all income and spending as well as outstanding financial obligations. Repeated failure to submit any of the mentioned declarations may lead to the closure of a party by court order.

The KNAB also draws on its investigative capacities to scrutinize party declarations. Between January 2003 and June 2007, the KNAB examined 2,308 donors and their financial capacity to give money to parties. As a consequence, the SRS was asked to audit 155 natural persons which led to the collection of an additional 589,840 lats ($1,072,430) in revenue. The KNAB has issued 135 decisions with party fines and has collected 33,070 lats ($60,000) in administrative fines. In addition, the Bureau has discovered sixty-six cases of illegal funding totaling 380,116.90 lats ($691,100) of which 263,645 lats ($479,360) has been transferred to the state budget. Importantly, both the number of cases and the total amount of illegal funding have sharply diminished within this four-year period. The courts have ruled to close down seven political organizations due to non-compliance with financial reporting requirements.[18] While the transfer of enforcement responsibility from the SRS to the KNAB has produced palpable results and has made parties more accountable to the public and cautious about their funding schemes, legislative loopholes and the politically sensitive character of inquiries have an effect on aspects of implementation.

The National Radio and Television Council supervises both private and public broadcasters and is entrusted with the enforcement of certain parts of the "Law on Pre-Election Agitation." The nine-member Council is elected by the parliament, funded from the state budget and consists of political appointees. It has been criticized for excessive politicization, inefficiency and slowness which are a major problem during an election campaign when swift and resolute actions are necessary.[19] However, the Council finally relied on an NGO carrying out its own media monitoring with the aim of discovering cases of hidden advertising after 2000. Although the methodology used in these efforts was not perfect, the Council grudgingly endorsed the findings that the presence of hidden advertising in electronic media was substantial.[20]

The use of the court system was unimportant in terms of party finance up until 2002 as a court decision was only necessary to close a registered political organization if it repeatedly failed to submit its annual financial declaration. As tighter restrictions were placed on donations and the KNAB was given the task of scrutinizing party financial declarations, courts emerged as an important arena for settling party and campaign finance disputes as parties began to contest the KNAB decisions on the legality of particular donations. However as previously mentioned, the KNAB has won most of the court cases. The courts have played an important role in shaping finance rules for independent campaigning. As noted above, financial limits on campaign expenses were set in 2004 but the 2005 municipal campaign saw no significant independent advertising. Although an NGO modestly endorsed municipal candidates of the People's Party, the KNAB took no action. On the other hand, the KNAB added the campaign expenses incurred by individual party members to the overall spending limit of the party which presumably caused the party to violate the limit.

In 2006, party operatives set up two NGOs with the aim of promoting the People's Party and the First Party of Latvia in the parliamentary elections. According to press reports and court transcripts, the Society for the Freedom of Speech spent approximately 500,000 lats ($904,160) to support the People's Party while the Pa Saulei Endowment spent some 300,000 lats ($542,500) to support the First Party of

---

18 This information was provided to the author by Diāna Kurpniece, Head of the KNAB Public Relations and Education Department, August 2007.

19 For example, it took several weeks for the Board to penalize Radio PIK for gross violations of campaign legislation during the 2005 municipal elections and the penalty itself was closure of the station for three days after the election.

20 "Iespējamo slēptās reklāmas gadījumu analīze medijos pirms 2005.gada pašvaldību vēlēšanām." http://www.politika.lv/index.php?f=554 (accessed 1 August 2007); "Iespējamās slēptās reklāmas gadījumu analīze medijos pirms 8.Saeimas vēlēšanām." http://www.politika. lv/index.php?f=106 (accessed 1 August 2007); Rihards Bērugs et. al. "Slēptās reklāmas monitorings Latvijas televīzijas kanālos." http://www.politika.lv/index.php?f=100 (accessed 1 August 2007).

Latvia. Both NGOs claimed that they were exercising the right to free speech and their campaigns and spending had nothing to do with those two parties. Several minor parties contested the parliamentary election results in the court on the grounds that the two parties had exceeded the financial limits of campaigning (set at 279,631 lats or $505,660). Although the Senate of the Supreme Court did not order new elections, it ruled that the campaign expenses incurred by both NGOs were to be added to the spending by the People's Party and the First Party of Latvia. This cleared the way for the KNAB to rule that both parties had not only received donations from legal persons but also substantially exceeded campaign spending limits. Both parties faced fines of several hundred thousands lats and have contested the KNAB decisions in court. If the courts uphold the KNAB decisions, the Senate of the Supreme Court will have substantially narrowed the use of independent campaigning, a rather unregulated area so far.

Party Finance and the Development of Parties

As outlined above, Latvia's legislation provides a rather liberal institutional framework for the development of parties, and the number of registered parties has increased.[21] However, only a fraction of these parties have managed to enter the parliament. Data for the last four parliamentary elections show that parties with a larger war chest have a better chance to gain parliamentary representation. Although, two examples of wealthy parties failing to clear the threshold are widely known (for example, Democratic Party Saimnieks in 1998 and Latvia's Way in 2002), and the only systematic exception is represented by parties claiming to represent Slavic minorities. The ethnic Slavic parties have traditionally taken advantage of their "eternal opposition" status and their favorable coverage by Russian-language media.

A simple analysis of the correlation between campaign spending and the number of votes confirms a noteworthy relationship between the two variables. These figures demonstrate that funding is an important factor affecting the electoral fortunes of parties and clearly separating realistic contenders from bystanders. This appears to affect party cohesion and intra-party relations. Successful fundraisers (for example, charismatic leaders, key ministers and holders of important patronage positions) tend to exercise a disproportionately large influence on a wide array of party decisions regardless of their formal position within an organization. Particularly at the outset of a new party, these persons largely control the recruitment of party members and manage the selection of candidates for the upcoming elections. While the process of party institutionalization may increase the importance of other segments of the party elites, the fundraisers tend to retain their say in policy matters.

A very narrow circle of a party elites is involved in raising sizeable funds. Therefore, the funding of the organization is highly centralized and depends largely on the "party in public office" including primarily government ministers which only enhances their role within the party. Successful revolts against the leadership are rare.

---

21 The number of registered parties has grown from twenty-seven in 1993 to forty-seven in 1999 to sixty-four in 2005 and seventy-two in 2007.

Table 4.3   Correlation between campaign spending and votes obtained

Year	1995	1998	2002	2006	2006[1]
Spearman's *R*, all parties running in the *Saeima* elections	0.736***	0.714***	0.699***	0.884***	0.914***
Spearman's *R*, parties receiving at least one percent of total vote	0.691***	0.442	0.409	0.564	0.718**

[1] Data include the campaign spending of two non-governmental organizations in favor of the People's Party and the First Party of Latvia.

Source: Data from party financial declarations and the Central Election Commission.

Notes: $*p < .10$, $**p < .05$ and $***p < .01$.

In the case of a serious disagreement, however, "dissidents" often choose a strategy of exiting and using fund raising in order to set up a new political organization. Therefore, the regime of party funding cannot be regarded as one that serves as a deterrent to potential defectors.

Given the centralized nature of campaigning and the high value party decision-makers apparently attach to it, local branches of parties in Latvia tend to be under-developed and little effort is invested in building party organizations outside major cities.[22] Furthermore, parties make no effort to collect membership fees from all members in a regular manner. Consequently, membership fees constitute an insignificant source of income, and they are often insufficient to fund a local office or local activities. Although local branches are typically encouraged to seek local funding for municipal elections, the bulk of the expenses are covered from funds raised centrally. All these factors raise questions about how level the playing field is, and how equal is the access of parties to financial resources.

Indeed, the availability of financial resources appears to depend on several factors. First of all, incumbency counts. Parties of the governing coalition in the parliament or in the Riga City Council (by far the largest and wealthiest municipality in the country) tend to be more successful in attracting funding. Coalition parties seem to draw on patronage appointments in the top management of public companies to raise funds for political activities.[23] At the same time, the politicization of the senior ranks of public servants appears to be rather low.[24] Second, the personal wealth of party leaders is of clear importance to provide "seed money" for further fundraising or even a lion's share of the party's expenditure. Third, charismatic and promising leaders can also serve as centers of gravity for noteworthy financial resources.

---

22 Party members constitute one percent of eligible voters. For details see, Daunis Auers, and Jānis Ikstens. 2005. "The Democratic Role of Political Parties." In *How Democratic is Latvia: Audit of Democracy*. ed. Juris Rozenvalds. Riga: University of Latvia Press.

23 Jānis Ikstens, "Patronage as Party Building Tool: Case of Latvia."

24 Iveta Reinholde. 2003. "Role and Role Perceptions of Senior Officials in Latvia." Paper presented at the 11th annual NISPACEE Conference. Bucharest, Romania.

State support to parties plays little (if any) role in this equation. Twenty minutes of free air time given in two, ten minute segments to each registered list on public television cannot off-set the massive advertising campaigns designed by media professionals for the wealthiest parties. Similarly, the concise political platforms of all parties running in parliamentary elections that are printed in black and white and distributed by the government free of charge cannot substitute for colorful billboards and half-page print advertisements placed by the financially better-off parties.

Moreover, the use of administrative resources available to incumbent parties may have grown over the years. The 2005 municipal elections are to be noted for the unprecedented scale of discussions and complaints about the use of these resources in a number of cities.[25] While state subsidies are often favorably biased towards large parties with parliamentary representation regardless of their position and opposition status, an absence of the subsidies in Latvia highlights the importance of being part of the governing coalition for considerations of political fund-raising. This clearly makes the playing field of parties less level.

Direct state subsidies to parties are regarded as entrenching the existing party system.[26] The case of Latvia indicates that a lack of such subsidies in combination with unrestricted spending opens-up the party system for competition and also instability. Latvia has seen a high degree of electoral volatility[27] and a notable turnover of parties at the parliamentary level.[28] The finance regime appears to have contributed to the frequent emergence of political newcomers to the *Saeima*. It is tempting to attribute the decrease in both volatility and turnover to the campaign limits introduced before the 2006 parliament elections. However, both the number of observations and the gross violations of campaign legislation by the two leading parties render such a conclusion premature. On the other hand, the impact of the party finance regime at the systemic level is more difficult to detect as the system has been rather stable.

The number of lists elected to the parliament has shown a tendency towards a decrease (due to greater party coalition-building) while the number of parties represented in the *Saeima* and the effective number of parties have slightly increased (see Table 4.4). This is an indication of increasing political competition as parties pool their resources together to clear the five percent threshold. Thus, the generally competitive relations between parties have persisted. The principal axis of political

---

25 "Administratīvo resursu izmantošanas novērošana pirms 2005.gada pašvaldību vēlēšanām." www.politika.lv/polit_real/files/lv/AR_galazinojums.pdf (accessed 15 October 2005).

26 Richard S. Katz, and Peter Mair. 1995. "Changing Models of Party Organization and Party Democracy: The Emergence of the Cartel Party." *Party Politics* 1: 5–28.

27 The value of the Pedersen's Index of Volatility (calculated for seats obtained) for the period between 1993–1995 is sixty-one percent, for the period between 1995–1998 fifty-five percent, between 1998–2002 fifty-seven percent and between 2002–2006 twenty-seven percent.

28 As a result of the 1995 *Saeima* elections, three new parties entered the parliament while one party lost its representation. In 1998, there were three newcomers and four parties lost their parliamentary presence. In 2002, three new parties cleared the electoral threshold while two previous parliamentary parties failed to do so. In 2006, one new party entered the parliament.

Table 4.4   Quantitative attributes of Latvia's party system, 1993–2006

Year	1993	1995	1998	2002	2006
Number of lists above the electoral threshold	8	9	6	6	7
Number of parties in the parliament	8	11	8	9	11
Effective number of parliamentary parties	5.1	7.2	5.5	5.0	6.0

Source: Central Election Commission.

Note: Calculated using the Laakso-Taagepera Effective Number of Parties Index on the basis of share of mandates by each list (not each party).

competition between right-of-center Latvian parties, on the one hand, and the left-of-center Slavic parties, on the other, remains strong. However, the ideological positions of some parties may have been modified due to considerations of party prospects and the availability of funding. Two cases exemplify such a feature.

The Farmers' Union of Latvia lost its parliamentary representation in 1998 but maintained its presence in a number of municipalities (mainly rural) on the basis of its historical appeal to rural voters. The Green Party of Latvia also failed to clear the electoral threshold in 1998 but drew support from urban segments that held the party's environmental program in high esteem. These two parties of quite contradictory political orientations joined forces to set up the Union of Greens and Farmers that subsequently attracted rather generous financial support from a group of entrepreneurs headed by Aivars Lembergs, the Mayor of the city of Ventspils. The two parties not only had to reconcile their rhetoric but also move towards a more moderate position on issues of ethnic policy.

A similar mechanism was at work when the once-influential Latvia's Way joined forces with the First Party of Latvia. Latvia's Way is known as a free-market, liberal political organization supporting the country's integration into the European Union. The First Party of Latvia had positioned itself as a Christian conservative organization advocating traditional values and fiercely opposing same-sex marriage. The two parties also had divergent views on a number of foreign policy issues with Latvian-Russian relations among them. However, programmatic differences did not prevent them from establishing a joint party list for the 2006 elections so as to gain access to the financial resources of Ainārs Šlesers, a wealthy businessman and politician and to the political expertise of individuals in Latvia's Way.

If larger shifts in party political orientations related to a perceived necessity to acquire funding are infrequent, tactical maneuvering on policy issues is more commonplace. The *ad hoc* shifts may be related to the tacit influence of the entrepreneurial elite and those are greatly facilitated by the closed character of Latvia's policy-making process.[29] Preliminary observations suggest that government instability in the latter part of the 1990s may have been related to the interests of major donors in the governing parties.

---

29 For details see, United Nations Development Program. 2001. *Human Development Report. Latvia 2000/2001: Public Policy Process* Riga: UN Development Program.

Table 4.5　　Parliamentary election results, 1993–2006

	1993		1995		1998		2002		2006	
	Seats	Votes %	Seats	Votes %	Seats	Votes %	Seats	Votes %	Seats	Votes %
Latvia's Way	36	32.4	17	14.6	21	18.1	0	4.9	10	8.6
First Party of Latvia	–	–	–	–	–	–	10	9.5		
New Party	–	–	–	–	8	7.3	–	–	–	–
Christian Democratic Union	6	5	8	6.3	0	2.3	–	–	–	–
Farmers' Union of Latvia	12	10.7			0	2.5	12	9.4	18	16.7
Green Party of Latvia	0	1.2	8	6.3	0					
LNNK	15	13.4			17	14.7	7	5.4	8	7.0
For Fatherland and Freedom	6	5.4	14	11.9						
Harmony for Latvia, Rebirth of the Economy	13	12	–	–	–	–	–	–	–	–
National Harmony Party	–	–	6	5.6	16	14.1	25	19.0	17	14.4
Socialist Party of Latvia	–	–	5	5.6						
Equal Rights	7	5.8	–	–					6	6
Democratic Centre Party	5	4.8	–	–	–	–	–	–	–	–
Democratic Party "Master"	–	–	18	15.2	0	1.6	–	–	–	–
People's Movement "For Latvia"	–	–	16	14.9	0	1.7	–	–	–	–
Unity Party of Latvia	–	–	8	7.1	0	0.5	–	–	–	–
People's Party	–	–	–	–	24	21.2	20	16.6	23	19.6
Social Democratic Union of Latvia	–	–	–	–	14	12.8	0	4.0	0	3.5
New Era	–	–	–	–	–	–	26	23.9	18	16.4
Other	0	9.3	0	12.5	0	3.2	0	7.3	0	7.8
Total	100	100	100	100	100	100	100	100	100	100

Source: Central Election Commission.

Conclusions

The regulatory framework of party finance in Latvia has been evolving towards increased regulation and transparency. The increased sophistication of relevant legislation has not obstructed its implementation. On the contrary, the KNAB has been notably successful in uncovering illegal funding cases and enforcing campaign spending limits. However, a further increase in transparency and improvement in law enforcement appears less likely. Neither direct state subsidies nor a ban on paid political advertising has been introduced in Latvia in order to off-set the rapidly growing campaign expenses. Consequently, parties are likely to use increasingly sophisticated (and capital-intensive) campaign methods.

The analysis of campaign expenses and election results in Latvia reveals an important correlation, highlighting a key role of the war chest in electoral competition. In combination with the regulatory framework of party finance, this has led to a plutocratic funding of parties in combination with heavy exploitation of public resources, the centralization of internal decision-making, the pre-eminence of a narrow circle of political fundraisers within parties and the neglect of party organization-building and recruitment of new rank-and-file members. However, this regime has not contributed to the cohesion of parties as "dissidents" have often opted to leave and establish their own organizations with the help of major donors. The role of money has also facilitated electoral volatility and the turnover of parties at the parliamentary level. However, the resultant electoral competition has only slightly contributed to changes at the systemic level as features of the party system in Latvia have changed little.

Chapter 5

Estonia:
The Increasing Costs and Weak
Oversight of Party Finance

Allan Sikk and Riho Kangur

The evolution of the Estonian party finance system shares similarities with processes in other East European countries. Campaign costs have been rising while parties rely increasingly on state subsidies. The Estonian legal system establishes few limits on financing—the most noteworthy of which is a ban on corporate donations. Overall, the main concern regarding party finance in Estonia is the lack of transparency. Although parties have to submit declarations concerning campaign costs and donations, there is no effective system to scrutinize the truthfulness of the declarations. This chapter will address these issues, and how finance influences party system development in Estonia.

Since re-gaining independence in 1992, Estonia has used a proportional representation (PR) electoral system for elections to the national parliament (*Riigikogu*) with a five percent national threshold. The system is comprised of two tiers: the lower-level constituencies (eleven or twelve depending on the time period) and a nation-wide tier for distributing compensational seats. Until 2003, the compensational seats accounted for between forty-five and sixty percent of all the seats, decreasing to twenty-six percent in 2007 due to slight changes in the electoral system.

The system of PR has brought with it a rather fragmented party system (see Table 5.1). However, the number of parties entering the parliament has decreased somewhat over the years. The effective number of parliamentary parties was 5.9 in 1992 and 4.4 in 2007, and the frequency of splits and mergers has declined to some extent.[1] Party systems in European post-communist countries have usually been regarded as unstable and, if at all, showing only slight signs of stabilization and consolidation. Using the traditional measures of party system stability (for example, electoral volatility, partisan loyalty, programmatic clarity and the persistence of party programs) the Estonian party system is partially consolidated at best. However in national elections, the "menu" of viable parties has changed surprisingly little from the first post-independence elections in 1992 to 2007. The vote shares of individual

---

1   The number of parliamentary parties appears to be lowest in 1995 (see Table 5.1). However, the electoral coalition of the Coalition Party and the Rural People's Union formed three factions in the parliament after the elections.

Table 5.1   Estonia: *Riigikogu* elections 1992–2007

	1992		1995		1997		2003		2007	
	V%	S%	V%	S%	V%	S%	V%	S%	V%	S%
Reform Party	–	–	16.2	18.8	15.9	17.8	17.7	18.8	27.8	30.8
Center Party	12.2	14.9	14.2	15.8	23.4	27.7	25.4	27.7	26.1	28.7
Union of *Pro Patria* and *Res Publica*	–	–	–	–	–	–	–	–	17.9	18.8
Moderates/Social Democrats	9.7	11.9	6.0	5.9	15.2	16.8	7	5.9	10.6	9.9
Country People's Party/ People's Union[1]	–	–	–[1]	–[1]	7.3	6.9	13	12.9	7.1	5.9
Greens	–	–	–	–	–	–	–	–	7.1	5.9
Res Publica	–	–	–	–	–	–	24.6	27.7	–	–
Pro Patria	22.0	28.7	7.9	7.9	16.1	17.8	7.3	6.9	–	–
Coalition Party	13.6	16.8	32.2	40.6	7.6	6.9	–	–	–	–
United People's Party[2]	–	–	5.9	5.9	6.1	5.9	2.2	0	1	0
National Independence Party	8.8	9.9	–	–	–	–	0.2	0	0.2	0
Independent Royalists	7.1	7.9	0.8	0	–	–	–	-	–	–
Estonian Citizen/Better Estonia	6.9	7.9	3.6	0	–	–	–	–	–	–
Others	19.7	2.0	13.2	0	6.4	0	2.6	0	3.2	–
Total	100	100	100	100	100	100	100	100	100	100

[1] In 1995, these parties where in coalition with the Coalition Party.
[2] In 1995, the electoral coalition with twenty-one under the name "Our Home is Estonia."

Source: Data compiled by the authors.

parties have swung dramatically at times, but for the most part, the votes simply shift direction in the next election. Also, the programmatic stance of parties has changed to some extent, and yet the ranks of key politicians and parties remain to a large extent consistent throughout the past two decades.

The general context of party competition in Estonia is similar to developed Western democracies: electoral campaigns have been professional, dominated by the mass media and focused on leaders and also a system of public party financing has been well-established. However, the parliamentary elections of 2003 brought with it the impressive rise of a genuinely new party, *Res Publica*, which seems to undermine the prior relative persistence of the party system. However after the initial success and formation of the government after the 2003 parliamentary elections, scandals quickly undermined the party's popularity. In 2005, *Res Publica* struggled to maintain five percent popularity in public opinion polls. Finally in 2006, it merged with *Pro Patria* to form the *Pro Patria* and *Res Publica* Union.

While the focus of electoral competition has been mostly on the party at the constituency level (with open lists), the closed lists at the national level have also played a significant role. Much of the actual campaigning has usually been conducted nationally, even with regard to local elections. This has been strengthened by the fact that Estonia is a small country, with less than a million eligible voters, and the national media are much more important compared to local media. Campaign coverage on national television and newspapers accounts for the bulk of party campaign expenditures. While parties have been the central actors, some candidates, especially the more wealthy ones, run independent campaigns. Increasingly, parties are concentrating their campaign on particular candidates, usually those on top of the constituency list. This is perhaps also because voters cannot give a "blank" party vote but are required to vote for a particular candidate.

There is no special petition requirement for contesting elections. All parties officially registered in Estonia can run. However, the principal requirement for registration is a minimum of 1,000 members. Such a criterion is effectively stricter than would be a petition requirement of equal size as the members are more or less permanent while signatures are one-off only. Since 1999, parties are not allowed to form electoral coalitions, and the lists are strictly party-based.[2] However, they can include non-members and even members from other parties. Especially in 1999 shortly after the introduction of the ban on coalitions, there were some *de facto* electoral coalitions under the name of the major partner.

The cash deposits for contesting elections are set at the level of two minimum wages per candidate (whether they are individual candidates running in party lists). As of 2007, this amounts to $611. This deposit is returned to all party candidates if their party passes the national electoral threshold or to an independent candidate if they receive at least 0.5 percent of the quota's worth of votes in a constituency. Both the membership criterion and cash deposits are rather high considering the small size of the country and the level of economic development. For instance if a party wishes to run a full list of candidates for parliamentary elections, the total cash deposit would be $61,791 which is more than three times *per capita* GDP. However, these figures are greatly overshadowed by the campaign expenditures of parties as will be discussed below.

The Campaign Finance Model

The restrictions on campaign financing in Estonia stem from the "Political Parties Act" as there are no specific restrictions regarding campaign financing. The accepted sources of donations are quite limited: only membership fees, proceeds from party property, donations from the state budget and contributions from private persons are allowed. Anonymous donations are banned, and corporate and organization donations have been explicitly banned since 2004. At the same time, parties are allowed to borrow money from banks. There are no limitations regarding the nationality of private persons, and parties have received support from European party organizations in connection with Estonia's accession into the European Union.

Estonia has an advanced system for the public financing of parties. All parties which obtain at least five percent of the vote in a national election receive funds

---

2   This only applies to national elections. Electoral coalitions are still possible in local elections despite attempts by the parliament to ban them as the attempts have been blocked by the Supreme Court on two occasions.

from the state budget in proportion to the number of seats won in the parliament. In 2004, financing for extra-parliamentary parties was introduced. At least one percent of the vote in a parliamentary election guarantees a party 150,000 Estonian kroons or EEK annually ($12,775) and up to four percent guarantees a party 250,000 EEK annually ($26,600). The total amount of public funding for parliamentary parties is decided each year in the state budget. The small support for extra-parliamentary parties is set in the "Political Parties Act." In contrast to some other countries, the support for parties is a lump sum payment to the party headquarters. Thus, there are no provisions regarding the distribution of support to sub-national party units and no special reimbursement of electoral campaign expenditures. Also, there is no indirect support for electoral campaign activities.[3]

In periods between elections, public funding has accounted for the bulk of parliamentary party income. During campaigns, party expenditures have been remarkably higher than donations from the state budget, and parties have relied substantially on private funding. Still, the actual difference is likely lessened by the fact that some of the money used in campaigning was probably accumulated during the preceding electoral term and the money borrowed from banks is later re-paid with the help of state subsidies.

Access to the Media

Most of the air time used by parties in the electronic media is predominantly television (during electoral campaigns it is in the form of paid advertisements on commercial channels). Private media advertisements are only limited by the amount of money parties are willing to pay for purchasing air time. Since July 2002, there are no advertisements, either political or non-political, on public television. The state-run channel only broadcasts pre-election debates. There, the air time has usually been distributed equally among the parties represented in the parliament or as was the case in 2003 with the rising new party *Res Publica* and in 2007 with the Greens (including particularly strong extra-parliamentary contenders), smaller extra-parliamentary parties and individual candidates have received some coverage in these debates but significantly less than parliamentary parties. In some cases, they have been disregarded completely (for example, before the local elections in 2005). This has caused discontent among the smaller parties relying on support of less than one percent of the electorate.

Party Expenditures

The definition of a campaign expenditure covers a wide array of items: advertising (for example, printing, advertisements on television, radio and in the print media), public relations expenditures, expenditures for transportation, rents, campaign events and mailing. Thus, there are no effective restrictions on what can and cannot

---

3　The parties enjoying the benefits of political office are in all likelihood using some state resources or at least transferring some of their routine tasks to offices paid by the state (for example, those with a parliamentary faction).

be classified as an electoral expenditure. This is logical given that there is neither any ceiling on electoral campaign expenditures nor any restriction on particular types of expenditures. After the 2003 parliamentary elections, ideas on expenditure ceilings were put forward, but at the time of this writing, they are not actively debated. The proposed limits have been at a very high level, even exceeding the most costly parliamentary campaigns. The only real limitation in Estonia has been the complete ban on outdoor advertising six weeks prior to elections which was introduced in 2005. While the rule came into force before the 2005 local elections, it has been challenged legally by the chancellor of justice and in practice by some of the parties (see below). Before the 2007 parliamentary elections, all the major parties ran rather extensive outdoor campaigns (but more than six weeks before the election day). During the final six weeks, the focus shifted from the streets to vigorous campaigns on television, newspapers and the direct posting of leaflets promoting candidates.

Individual candidates face the same restrictions on expenditures as parties. The only significant difference is in regards to the source of campaign funds. In contrast to parties, individual candidates are not barred from receiving donations from companies or other organizations, as this restriction comes from the "Political Parties Act." Also, they can use their own money. At the same time, these provisions do not extend to candidates on party lists. While the latter can, and sometimes do, run their personal campaigns in addition to and independently from party campaigns, they are faced with the same restrictions as parties.

Disclosure and Reporting

All parties and individual candidates running in elections are required to present a report of revenues and expenditures no later than one month after the election (this requirement began in 1992). The reports were initially submitted to the National Electoral Commission (NEC) and made public over the Internet. Since 2004, the reports have been submitted to the Parliamentary Select Committee on the Application of the Anti-Corruption Act. Additionally since 1999, parties are required to present quarterly and annual reports covering their income and expenditures to a special party register at the central commercial registry. These are made public over the Internet (until 2004 at the register's web site and since then on the party's web site). Names and identity codes of all donors are disclosed by parties which are required to keep a public registry of donations on their web pages. Candidates are not required to present any declarations concerning their economic interests. In Estonia, this is only required from members of parliament, the president, cabinet ministers and certain officials as dictated by the "Anti-Corruption Act." The reports on campaign financing have been submitted virtually without any problems, but other disclosure requirements have been largely overlooked by parties because of the lack of sanctions. Only since 2003 have parties which failed to present declarations or violate the "Political Parties Act" in other ways faced a fine. The declarations for most parliamentary parties are only available since 2002 on their web site.

Enforcement

The enforcement of campaign rules in Estonia is the responsibility of the NEC. The seven members of the NEC are appointed by different institutions: the chief justice (2), the chancellor of justice (1), the state auditor (1), the state prosecutor (1), the director of the chancellery of the Estonian parliament (1) and the state secretary (1). The NEC is not a permanent organization, and its members have full-time jobs elsewhere.[4] Its work and daily management is assisted and organized by the elections department of the chancellery of the parliament. The NEC is funded directly by the state budget. Most of the budget is used for organizing elections, in particular, for staffing the county and the local election commissions.

Both the "Political Parties Act" and "*Riigikogu* Elections Act" include a fine for violating the rules on the disclosure of donations and failing to file the economic activity reports. It is differentiated according to who is responsible for the violation in question. The standard fine is $1,600, but if a violation is committed by legal persons, it is increased to $4,250. While the declarations on campaign spending and donations have been routinely submitted, no government body audits the accuracy of the total amounts, sources of income or the reported expenditures. By far, most parties have failed to submit their annual financial declarations to the *Riigi Teataja* (the official gazette) while they have been more compliant with the requirement to publicize them on their web pages. However, locating the declarations on some party web pages is impossible as links to them are impossible to find.

The lack of transparency and absence of effective control over party financing, together with the unequal treatment of parties, has been severely criticized by the Estonian chancellor of justice. In his report submitted to the parliament in 2006, the argument was made that the legislation regulating party financing violates the principles of democracy and equal treatment as stipulated in the constitution. Following the report, the constitutional committee of the *Riigikogu* proposed a draft act significantly amending the finance principles. The proposal included setting a maximum limit on cash donations (approximately $850 per month) and establishing a permanent, neutral body which would check and investigate the financial matters of parties (members appointed by the chancellor of justice, the state prosecutor, the state auditor and the chief justice). However, the parliament failed to pass the law before the 2007 parliamentary elections, and the draft sparked criticism from the two largest parties at the time (for example, the Center Party and the Reform Party). The chancellor of justice submitted a petition to the Supreme Court for declaring the present system of party financing to be in breach of the constitution, but the ruling has not been announced at the time of this writing.

---

4   In fact, they are required to be working as judges or officials in the bodies under the abovementioned officials. The chairman of the NEC at the time of writing was Heiki Sibul, the Director of the Chancellery of the *Riigikogu*.

Trends in Party and Campaign Funding

The main developments in regards to party and campaign funding have been the increasing cost of campaigning and the rise in the public financing of parties. State finance was introduced in Estonia in 1994 in the first "Political Parties Act." It has been in effect since 1996, and since the introduction, the total level of subsidies has increased more than tenfold (see Table 5.2). The sharpest increase came in 2004 when the public financing of parties was increased threefold together with the introduction of new restrictions on private financing.

Until 2004, public party financing was exclusively targeted to parliamentary parties. Since then, tiny subsidies are also provided to parties receiving more than one percent of the vote in national elections (0.15 million EEK per year), and only slightly larger subsidies for parties with at least four percent of support (0.25 million EEK per year). These subsidies are not only minuscule, but also very disproportionate compared to subsidies provided to parliamentary parties. The two parties with the highest number of seats in the parliament (for example, the Center Party and *Res Publica*) received about 130 EEK (slightly over $10) for each vote in the election— the smallest of the parliamentary parties (for example, the Social Democrats) received 100 EEK (over $8) per vote. The only two parties not represented in the parliament but eligible for public subsidies (for example, the United People's Party and the Christian People's Party) received between $1 and $3 per vote. Moreover, the support for extra-parliamentary parties is fixed in "Political Parties Act" and is not subject to annual changes in the state budget that sets the amount of total financing for parliamentary parties.

The restrictions on private donations to parties were modest until 2003. Until then, the law only banned donations from state and local governments, whether Estonian or foreign, and companies in their ownership. In 2003, an annual 10,000 EEK ($850) limit for private persons was introduced that superseded the ineffective ban on one-time cash donations in excess of 1,000 EEK. Since 2004, the only legitimate sources of party income are limited to membership fees, public subsidies, donations from private persons and proceeds from party property. Donations from business companies or other organizations have been banned altogether. This has led at times to parliamentary parties becoming almost exclusively reliant on public

Table 5.2   Public subsidies to Estonian parties, 1996–2004

	1996	1997	1998	1999	2000	2001	2002	2003	2004	2005	2006	2007
Million USD	0.42	0.72	0.91	0.56	1.08	1.08	1.27	1.47	4.79	4.57	4.81	5.23
$ per registered voter[1]	0.51	0.91	1.15	0.65	1.14	1.26	1.48	1.71	5.57	5.31	5.59	5.83

[1] In 1995, 1999, 2003 and 2007.

Source: Sven Mikser. 2001. "Eesti kogemus erakondade rahastamisel." *Riigikogu Toimetised* 4:22–26; State Budget Law 2003–2007.

subsidies according to their account statements.[5] In 2004, the average share of public subsidies in parliamentary party income was eighty-two percent, a dramatic rise from forty-three percent during the second half of 2003.[6]

The reporting of campaign income and expenditures has been obligatory since 1995. Quarterly and annual reports on all financial activities were introduced in 1999. However, there is no effective control over the validity of these reports. Despite that, most parties have submitted the reports on electoral campaigns. There have been some allegations concerning the authenticity of reports, mostly concerning the sources of income rather than the overall level of expenditures. In several cases reported by the Estonian media, parties have been supported by shell companies. One of the most prominent cases was in 1999, when the Reform Party reported receiving forty-two percent of its campaign resources from an obscure company, R-Hooldus, that was established by some of its leaders and had almost no turnover, but the cases are not limited to that.[7] At times, members of parties in the parliament have donated sums likely in excess of their financial capacity. The most notable case was the Estonian Country People's Party in 1999 when nine of their top national candidates donated 100,000 EEK each, approximately twenty times the average monthly wage at that time. In some cases, doubts have been cast over the genuine sources of private donations. Besides the abovementioned example, some of the Center Party's candidates donated 999 EEK in cash several days before the local election campaign in 2002 (at the time it was forbidden to receive donations in cash exceeding 1,000 EEK).

While the Estonian media has made accusations regarding party financing from time to time, the inaccuracy of donation registries is very difficult to verify. Also while most major parties have seen some adverse coverage of their financial practices, the accusations have not significantly damaged their relative popularity. The incentive to lie about the overall costs of campaigns is low as there have been no ceilings on expenditures. The fact that some of the electoral campaigns have been highly expensive has been evident. Electoral campaign costs in Estonia have increased substantially from 1995 to 2007, on average more than doubling after each electoral term (see Table 5.3). The figures for the 2003 election can be considered lower than normal because they took place just few a months after local elections (which was also a rather costly campaign). Total self-reported spending in parliamentary elections from 1995 to 2007 has increased more than tenfold.

A problem is posed for the calculation of the share of public financing in the total party income by the fact that reporting on routine income has until recently been inaccurate, and the share of public subsidies in campaign finance reports

---

5   "Suuremat lisaraha korjas annetajatelt vaid Reformierakond." 2004. *Äripäev* 13 April.

6   Parliamentary elections took place in March 2003. Therefore, the two first quarters are excluded for the sake of comparability. The figures are from Ülle Madise, and Allan Sikk. N.d. "Die Institution der politischen Partei in Estland," In *Parteienrecht im europäischen Vergleich*, ed. Martin Morlok. Baden-Baden: Nomos. Forthcoming.

7   Jaanus Piirsalu. 1999. "Reformierakonda suurrahastas tundmatu firma." *Eesti Päevaleht*. 14 April.

Table 5.3   Self-reported expenditures on electoral campaign, Estonia

Party	1995	1999	2003	2007
Center Party	0.09	0.52	1.50	3.62
Res Publica	–	–	1.34	1.73[1]
Reform Party	0.21	0.34	1.26	2.84
Country People's Party / People's Union	–	0.19	0.49	1.17
Coalition Party	0.13	0.25	–	–
Pro Patria Union	0.11	0.31	0.31	–[1]
The Moderates/Social Democrats	0.08	0.24	0.21	0.69
The Right Wingers	0.11	–	–	–
Our Home is Estonia / United People's Party/ Constitution Party	0.05	0.07	0.08	0.05
Estonian Christian Democrats	–	–	–	0.23
Greens	–	–	–	0.21
Total[2]	**0.88**	**2.01**	**5.24**	**10.54**
Per registered voter (USD)	**0.88**	**2.15**	**5.65**	**11.79**

[1] *Pro Patria* and *Res Publica* Union.
[2] Includes parties and individual candidates not listed here.

Source: The expenditures from 1995–2003 are from the Estonian National Electoral Commission (http://www.vvk.ee) and the expenditures from 2007 from *Kokkuvõte 2007. aasta Riigikogu valimistel osalenud erakondade ja üksikkandidaatide valimiskampaania rahastamise aruannetest*: http://www.riigikogu.ee/public/Riigikogu/Korruptsioon/kokkuv_ te_RKval2007.pdf. The exchange rate from Bank of Estonia: www.eestipank.info/frontpage/ et (accessed 17 June 2007).

has been very low. Indeed, some parliamentary parties have not listed the state budget as a source of income at all. Thus, the post-election financial reports do not reflect the extent of public donations very well. Therefore, the rise in public subsidies and the increase in reported campaign spending have been markedly higher than increases in GDP (which increased only 2.3 times between 1996 and 2006).[8] During the first electoral cycle after the introduction of public subsidies, campaign expenditures grew at approximately the same rate as public subsidies to parties. Even though the campaign expenditures in 1999 were higher compared to "year zero" than public donations, campaign activities started in 1998 when public donations were exceptionally high (elections always take place in early March). By 2003, the growth in campaign expenditures had clearly surpassed the increase in public subsidies. This is partly the consequence of the emergence of a new, big spending party, *Res Publica*, which was at the same time excluded from receiving subsidies from the state budget. The trend seemed to reverse itself after the 2003 election, as the public funding of parties surged. However after the 2007

---

8   Eurostat, http://epp.eurostat.ec.europa.eu (accessed 18 June 2007).

parliamentary election, it was clear that campaign expenditures had kept pace even though they had been comparatively high already earlier.[9]

More information regarding the breakdown of party income has been available since 2002 when routine reporting became more regular. After 2004, there was a slight increase in overall party income compared to earlier periods without national elections. This increase is basically due to the sharp rise in public subsidies for parties. Donations from other sources actually declined for most of the parliamentary parties compared to 2002. For some quarters in 2004, several parties reported less than $1,500 of income from sources other than the state budget. It is notable that in the 4th quarter of 2003, subsidies for parties increased sharply from the previous quarters. This was likely because of the inflow of corporate donations that became outlawed from the beginning of 2004. The increase in the total as well as non-public income in 2005 and in 2006 can be explained by local and national elections, but income from other than public sources remained less than two times what was reported in 2002.

Development of Parties and the Party System

Given the high level of public funding almost exclusively targeted to parliamentary parties, the existence of a level playing field for extra-parliamentary (including potential new) parties can to some extent be called into question. However as the Greens proved in 2007, even a very modest campaign can still be an option for small, new parties occupying a niche on the political spectrum. Apart from that, the discrepancy among major parties is also rather large and to some extent visible in the campaign before the 2005 local elections. As corporate donations by far outweighed support from individuals in campaign income until 2003, the ban on all donations from legal persons introduced in 2004 has contributed to difficulties in fundraising for extra-parliamentary parties. The effectiveness of that legal provision in restricting political corruption can be questioned as illegal transfers of money do not necessarily take place from companies and party bank accounts. Instead, they can flow from owners to powerful party leaders. The provision that possibly balances the playing field between parties is the possibility to borrow money from banks. Thus, a party can meet expenses if it can convince a bank that it will gain access to budget funds after a successful election. This was a strategy partly used by *Res Publica* in

---

9   It is difficult to compare party expenditures cross-nationally, as both population size and the level of economic development need to be taken into account. However, when comparing the level of spending in Estonia to Western democracies based on the approach used by Hiltrud and Karl-Heinz Nassmacher, Estonia appears among the top spenders based on the 2003 and the 2007 elections. See, Karl-Heinz Nassmacher. 2001. "Major Impacts of Political Finance Regimes." In *Foundations for Democracy: Approaches to Comparative Political Finance*, ed. Karl-Heinz Nassmacher. Baden-Baden: Nomos Verlagsgesellschaft, pp. 181–196; Allan Sikk. *Highways to Power: New Party Success in Three Young Democracies*. Dissertationes Rerum Politicarum Universitatis Tartuensis, 1. Tartu: Tartu University Press, p. 100.

2003 as a notable share of its campaign expenditures was covered by loans. In 2007, borrowing was used by the Center Party and the Social Democrats.[10]

The 1,000 membership requirement has certainly contributed to more organized parties. The stability of the party system has been enhanced by other regulations as well. First, the party financing regime is rather restrictive, currently even more so than before the 2003 elections. Second, it is not possible to form electoral coalitions or form a splinter faction in the parliament or change factions. Thus, the costs of changing allegiances are rather high for politicians. Notably if a completely new party were to form within the parliament, it would be barred from forming a faction and excluded from receiving subsidies from the state. When seven members left the Center Party fraction in 2004, the share of the party's public financing remained the same (based on its number of seats after the 2003 election). While these factors have not prevented changes completely, the likelihood of a new party forming is reduced.

While the equality of opportunity among parties may have declined with regard to the financing of campaigns, the playing field regarding media has likely become more level. There is some evidence, although somewhat impressionistic, that the public media have grown more independent during the last decade. While in the mid-1990s journalists were often concerned about being politically "incorrect," this is increasingly less the case. Estonia has not seen attempts at controlling the state media on the scale of the Czech Republic. Although, there have always been some concerns over the appointment of successive heads of public television, none of them has actually been too strongly linked to any party. There are some recent cases of appointments of politicians to high non-political offices, but once selected, they have attempted to keep a low and non-partisan profile.[11]

The private media have presented more controversies as some of the major media outlets (primarily newspapers and radio) have been linked to specific parties. In February 2005, all parties represented in the parliament, except for one, wrote an open letter to the Norwegian owner of Estonia's biggest non-tabloid daily, *Postimees*, accusing the editors of being biased in favor of the Reform Party. The Party also has links to a major private radio group (*Trio*). In general, however, the Estonian media landscape remains basically free and quite heterogeneous. At the same time, there are no guarantees that future appointees to public media stations will remain politically neutral.

While connections between political and economic elites have not been as problematic as those reported in neighboring Baltic states, there have been cases of supposed corruption. Some of the most prominent examples include the financial support from companies successfully participating in the privatization of Estonian

---

10 Holger Roonemaa. 2007. "Odavaimalt riigikokku pääsenud roheliste koht maksis 0,42 miljonit." *Eesti Päevaleht*. 7 April. The practice of borrowing from ambiguous sources, as a potential way of circumventing the ban on corporate donations, was among the issues criticized by the chancellor of justice in his report to the parliament in 2006.

11 In 2004, the former minister of justice was appointed the new chief justice, and the former minister of culture was appointed the director general of *Eesti Raadio* (Estonian public radio broadcasting).

Railways to all the parties represented in the governing coalition at that time. Also notable has been the generous support of Oliver Kruuda (the managing director of chocolate producer *Kalev*) to the Center Party. *Res Publica*, the new party that emerged in 2003, was strongly supported by Olari Taal and Tõnis Palts, wealthy Estonian businessmen. They were, however, also prominent politicians. In addition, *Res Publica* initially tried to follow a principle that no sponsor could contribute in excess of ten percent of the total party income, attempting to limit the potential negative impact of sponsors on the party and underline its image as a transparent and honest party.[12]

A common occurrence in parliamentary elections has been the support to all major parties by some rich companies. Examples of this include Urmas Sõõrumaa (the managing director of security company *Falck* and the former owner of its Estonian branch), some construction, oil transit and shipping companies. Even though the relationship between parties and their sponsors has sometimes raised doubts about corrupt practices and the sources of party income have not always been clear, the links have not been very explicit or oligarchic. The latter implies that despite problems in party financing, none of the parties could reasonably be considered to be "pocket parties" (a term sometimes used for instance in Latvia) of businessmen or groups.

It should be noted, however, that party financing has not been a subject of meticulous public scrutiny in Estonia. There are no non-governmental organizations or government bodies actively engaged in analyzing party financing. For example in Estonia, there is no institution similar to the Latvian Anti-Corruption Bureau which analyzes the accuracy of financial declarations. Neither has any significant independent analysis been conducted on campaign expenditures or party finance practices which has been extensively done in Latvia assisted by the Soros Foundation. It is difficult to say whether less scrutiny has been a cause or an effect of relatively less problematic party financing. The level of corruption in Estonia may be lower than in some of its neighboring countries, or in contrast, the perception of problems in party financing could be less because relatively little public attention has been devoted to this issue. State finance has been brought up in media reports during elections, and more recently by the chancellor of justice, but there have not been full-scale scandals. On the other hand, a public body analyzing the accuracy of party financing declarations and evaluating financing practices is probably needed. Otherwise, the declarations required from parties will remain unreliable.

Until 2004, party declarations were submitted to the NEC. Since then, they have been submitted to the Parliamentary Select Committee on the Application of the Anti-Corruption Act. While the submission of declarations of economic interests by civil servants to a parliamentary committee is reasonable, designating a committee as the recipient of electoral campaign declarations is a more contentious issue. In national elections, this effectively means that parties end up being on both sides of the reporting process. On the other hand, the NEC was never effective when inspecting the accuracy of financial reports.

---

12 Rein Taagepera. 2004. "Meteoric Rise: *Res Publica* In Estonia, 2001–2004." Paper prepared at the ECPR Joint Sessions of Workshops. 13–18 April. Uppsala, Sweden.

Conclusions

During the fifteen years since independence, Estonian party financing has developed into a high-spending system with considerable state subsidies and few restrictions except for the ban on corporate donations. Scandals related to party financing have been modest compared to most Central and East European countries, but the system has been neither transparent nor thoroughly fair. While parties have been rather law-abiding in submitting declarations required by the legislation, no effective scrutiny of their truthfulness has ever taken place. It is also doubtful whether a parliamentary select committee is an appropriate body for the adequate oversight of party financing. The sharp increase in overall campaign costs raises doubts regarding the evenness of the electoral playing field. Even though both in 2003 and in 2007 new parties managed to be elected to parliament, the advertising by a few of the largest parties has easily overshadowed the rest.

Chapter 6

Czech Republic:
Is it Possible to Buy Political Stability?

Lukáš Linek and Jan Outlý

This chapter describes the main features of the public finance model in the Czech Republic, analyzes the level and the structure of the income and the expenditures of major parties and indicates the effect of party finance on Czech parties and the party system. Before addressing issues related specifically to party finance, the first two parts of the chapter are devoted to an introduction to the Czech political system, including a discussion of the major parties, party system and electoral system. Later, the chapter describes the party finance model and its main components: private donations, state subsidies and indirect funding. We also report on disclosure measures, and we examine trends in party finance which indicate an increased level of state funding that has caused party finance to become a significant part of total income for all main parties. In the last section, we suggest three main effects of public finance on the development of parties and the party system in the Czech Republic.

Introduction to the Czech Political and Party System

The Czech political system is a bi-cameral parliamentary democracy (the Chamber of Deputies contains 200 deputies and the Senate eighty-one senators). Institutionally, the role of the parliament in the Czech political system is crucial because it is involved in legislative activities, approves international treaties and also has a voice in the formation of other political institutions, mainly the cabinet. In addition, the parliament elects the president, selects and appoints important state officials and constitutional judges.[1] Parties are the only organizations that may run for election to the Chamber of Deputies. Thus, they provide the main vehicle for mass-elite linkages. Moreover, they are embedded in state institutions, and since 1990, they have been operating under a specific legal regulation (the "Law on Political Parties") and have been receiving state subsidies.

The development and transformation of the Czech party system were brought about by elections, re-alignments between elections and processes of intra-party

---

1 For more on the role of the Czech Parliament see, Lukáš Linek and Zdenka Mansfeldová. 2007. "The Parliament of the Czech Republic, 1993–2004." *Journal of Legislative Studies* 13: 12–37.

fission and inter-party co-operation.[2] Before the first democratic elections in June 1990, almost a hundred new parties emerged. The dominant position was played by the Civic Forum (OF) which in the 1990 elections secured almost a majority of votes and seats in the Federal Assembly and the Czech parliament.[3] There were other parties that secured seats in the Czech parliament—two of them existed during the communist period (the Communist Party of Bohemia and Moravia or KSČM and the Czechoslovak People's Party which was later re-named in 1992 the Christian-Democratic Union–Czechoslovak People's Party or KDU-ČSL). The last party in the parliament was the regionally-based Movement for Autonomous Democracy–Association for Moravia and Silesia or HSD-SMS (for election results, see Table 6.1). At the beginning, the Czech cabinet was supported by the OF, the KDU-ČSL and the HSD-SMS, but eventually the two smaller parties withdrew their backing.

In the period before the 1992 elections, a process of a gradual establishment of a left-right party spectrum started, and the future main right-wing parties emerged. The split of the Civic Forum resulted in the establishment of the liberal-conservative Civic Democratic Party (ODS) under the leadership of Václav Klaus and the social-liberal Civic Movement which had the support of President Václav Havel (it did not succeed in the 1992 elections). Another right-wing party, the conservative Civic Democratic Alliance (ODA) left the Civic Forum at the time of its dissolution. On the left, the KSČM went through discussions and factional fights over the democratization of the party, but in the end by 1993, the communist faction became dominant within the party. Even without re-naming the party and instituting only a minor change in the party's program, the KSČM has generally received well over ten percent of the vote in parliamentary elections (see Table 6.1).

Eight parties managed to gain seats in the 1992 elections to the Czech parliament. After the 1992 elections, a center-right coalition cabinet was formed by the ODS, the ODA, the KDU-ČSL and the Christian Democratic Party (KDS). Within two years after the 1992 elections, electoral support for the left-of-center Czech Social Democratic Party (ČSSD) increased from six to more then twenty percent (and as high as twenty-six percent in the 1996 elections). This was accompanied by decreasing support for

---

2   For more details on party development see, Petr Fiala, Miroslav Mareš, and Pavel Pšeja. 1999. "The Development of Political Parties and the Party System." In *Ten Years of Rebuilding Capitalism: Czech Society after 1989*, ed. Jiří Večerník and Petr Matějů. Prague: Academia, pp. 273–294; Tomáš Kostelecký. 2002. *Political Parties after Communism: Developments in East-Central Europe*. Washington, Baltimore: Woodrow Wilson Center/John Hopkins University; Zdenka Mansfeldová. 2004. "The Czech Republic." In *The Handbook of Political Change in Eastern Europe*, ed. Sven Berglund, Joakim Ekman, and Frank H. Aarebrot. Cheltenham: Edward Edgar, pp. 223–253.

3   The Czech Republic was constituted as a sovereign state on 1 January 1993. Previously, it operated as a member state of the Czechoslovak Federation. The Chamber of Deputies was established on the date of establishment of the Czech Republic through a transformation/re-naming of the former Czech parliament, the Czech National Council (CNC). The CNC was the legislature of a member state of the Czechoslovak Federation of the Czech Republic. It was constituted in 1968 after the establishment of the Federation and exercised legislative powers on topics that were not within the power of the federal bodies.

Table 6.1 Electoral gains and numbers of seats won by parties in the Czech National Council and in the Chamber of Deputies

Year of Election	1990 votes percent	1990 seats	1992 votes percent	1992 seats	1996 votes percent	1996 seats	1998 votes percent	1998 seats	2002 votes percent	2002 seats	2006 votes percent	2006 seats
OF	**49.5**	**127**	–	–	–	–	–	–	–	–	–	–
KSČM[1]	13.24	32	14.05	35	10.33	22	11.03	24	18.51	41	12.81	26
HSD-SMS[2]	**10.03**	**22**	5.87	14	–	–	–	–	–	–	–	–
KDU-ČSL[3]	**8.42**	**19**	6.28	15	8.08	18	9.00	20	–	21	**7.22**	**13**
ČSSD	4.11	0	6.53	16	26.44	61	**32.31**	**74**	**30.21**	**70**	32.32	74
SPR-RSČ[4]	1.00	0	5.98	14	8.01	18	3.90	0	0.97	0	–	–
ODS[5]	–	–	**29.73**	**76**	**29.62**	**68**	27.74	63	24.48	58	**35.38**	**81**
LSU	–	–	6.52	16	–	–	–	–	–	–	–	–
ODA	–	–	**5.93**	**14**	**6.36**	**13**	–	–	0.51	0	–	–
US-DEU[6]	–	–	–	–	–	–	8.60	19	–	10	–	–
Koalice[6]	–	–	–	–	–	–	–	–	**14.28**	**31**	–	–
SZ[7]	4.10	0	–	–		0	1.12	0	2.36	0	**6.29**	**6**
Others	13.70	0	19.11	0	11.16	0	6.30	0	8.68	0	5.98	0

[1] In 1992, the KSČM ran with the Democratic Left of the Czech-Slovak Federative Republic in the coalition Left Block.

[2] Between 1993 and 1995, the HSD-SMS changed its name several times and merged with the LSU (Liberal Social Union). They ran on a single list in 1996 under the name ČMUS, but they failed to enter the parliament.

[3] In 1990, the Czechoslovak People's Party (ČSL), the Christian-Democratic Party and the Christian-Democratic Movement ran together in a Christian-Democratic Union (KDU) coalition.

[4] In 1990, the SPR-RSČ (Association for Republic-Republican Party of Czechoslovakia) ran in coalition with the All People's Democratic Party. In 2000, the SPR-RSČ was succeeded by the RMS.

[5] In 1992, the ODS ran in coalition with the KDS.

[6] In 2002, the KDU-ČSL and the US-DEU ran together as Coalition (Koalice).

[7] The Green Party (SZ) ran in 1992 as part of an electoral coalition, LSU.

Source: Compiled by the authors from statistical yearbooks published by the Czech Statistics Office each year.

Notes: Party factions of governing parties are shown in bold.

parties which defined themselves as centrist (mainly the HSD-SMS and the Liberal Social Union and their successor parties). The 1996 Chamber elections ended with a victory for the right-of-center governing parties, but they were unable to form a majority cabinet. Thus, a minority cabinet of the ODS, the KDU-ČSL and the ODA was formed with the support of the main opposition party, the ČSSD. During 1997, the ruling parties faced not only a worsening economic situation in the country but also party finance scandals. Thus, the cabinet was dismissed at the end of 1997 after it was revealed that the ODS had been sponsored by a company involved in a state privatization bid. Almost half of the ODS deputies and almost twenty percent of ODS party members left and entered the new liberal Union of Freedom (the US and since 2002 the US-DEU).

After the 1998 elections, a majority cabinet was unable to form because of personal animosities among party leaders and party program differences. Finally, the two biggest parties (the ČSSD and the ODS) signed the so-called "Agreement on Creating a Stable Political Environment in the Czech Republic" which assisted in forming a minority cabinet as the ODS promised to neither initiate a vote of no confidence against the government nor support such a vote. For the ODS, the agreement guaranteed its involvement in the appointment to important political positions, consultations with the government prior to the government making important decisions, and above all, the consent of the ČSSD to electoral reform. Cooperation of the largest parties on electoral reform resulted in the close collaboration of smaller right-of-center parliamentary parties (the KDU-ČSL, the US and the ODA). The coalition of these parties gained more than thirty percent of vote in the 2000 regional and Senate elections and was thought to win the 2002 Chamber elections. With the defeat of electoral reform by the Constitutional Court in 2001, the main motivation for the cooperation of these parties disappeared followed by quarrels among them and the loss of support.

A one-vote majority cabinet was formed after the 2002 Chamber elections with the support of the ČSSD, the KDU-ČSL and the US-DEU. It survived until the next national elections in 2006, even though there were two changes at the post of prime minister. In the 2006 elections, the support for the US-DEU disappeared and instead, the Green Party (SZ) managed to pass the electoral threshold and gain seats. The right- and left-wing block of various parties received all of the parliamentary seats and after long negotiations, a right-wing cabinet was formed composed of the ODS, the KDU-ČSL and the SZ.

Each election since 1992 has brought a reduction in the number of parties represented in the Chamber of Deputies. In 1996, the number of parties in the Chamber dropped from eight to six and in 1998 to five and has remained the same since. With two exceptions, no new parties have appeared in the Chamber of Deputies since the 1992 elections. The only exceptions are the US established in 1998 as a splinter group from the ODS (the US disappeared after the 2006 elections) and the SZ elected for the first time to the Chamber of Deputies in 2006. At present, the party system is relatively stable with four main parties. The right-wing ODS and the left-of-center ČSSD, with electoral support between twenty-five and thirty-five percent, occupy a dominant position in the party system. The right-of-center KDU-ČSL and the left-wing KSČM play a supplementary role. The polarization of party competition is relatively weak despite the presence of the Communist Party. The gradual reduction in the number of parties does not mean, however, that there are no parties entering electoral competition at the regional and the local level or even at the national level. Around twenty parties compete in elections of all levels.[4]

The Electoral System

The electoral system for the Chamber of Deputies (in the years 1990 and 1992 for the Federal Assembly and the Czech National Council) has barely changed since 1990 even though there were various attempts to reform it.[5] Elections are based on a proportional representation electoral system. They are organized by the state and regulated by the Central Electoral Commission (CEC) at the national level and by regional and local electoral commissions. During the 1990s, these commissions were composed of party nominees, but since 2001, the CEC is headed by the minister of home affairs and composed of state bureaucrats. Local electoral commissions, which are responsible for counting votes at polling stations, are composed of party nominees and volunteers receiving wages from the state. Since 1990, no accusation has been lodged by any of the electoral commissions concerning the selective treatment of parties or candidates.

Only parties and political movements registered according to the "Law on Political Parties" or their coalitions may propose candidates. If a party stands for office as part of a coalition, it cannot at the same time stand for office individually. Moreover, coalitions have to be formed by the same parties in all electoral districts. In the 1990 and the 1992 elections, parties had to fulfill some organizational requirements to have the right to submit a ballot. In 1990, a party had to have registered 10,000 members. If party membership did not reach this number, the party had to gather enough signatures supporting the party candidacy in the election so as to reach the required limit. For the 1992 elections, this requirement did not apply to parties which were represented in the parliament or which gained at least 10,000 votes in the previous election. Since the 1996 elections, requirements for running in elections have been mainly financial. Previously, parties had to pay a deposit of 200,000 Czech koruna or CZK (approximately $7,500) in each electoral district they ran (in total 1.6 million CZK or $60,000).[6] If a party received more than five percent of the vote, the deposit was returned. After several critical statements and decisions made by the Constitutional

---

4   For more details on party system development see, Tomáš Kostelecký, *Political Parties after Communism: Developments in East-Central Europe*; Lukáš Linek and Petra Šalamounová, ed. 2001. *The Parliament of the Czech Republic 1993–1998: Factbook*. Prague: Institute of Sociology Czech Academy of Sciences.

5   For details of electoral system in the Czech Republic see, Tomáš Lebeda. N.d. "The Czech Republic." In *Elections in Europe*, ed. Dieter Nohlen. Oxford: Oxford University Press. Forthcoming.

6   The calculations in this chapter are done based on an exchange rate in a given year using the information of the Czech National Bank (obtained at www.cnb.cz). If the amount of dollars is given without a year, then the amount relates to the year of the introduction of the rule.

Court (among which the most important was the Court's recommendation published in 1999), the deposits were lowered to 15,000 CZK or $615 per district (in total 210,000 CZK or $8,600), but the deposits are not returned to parties.

Seats are divided among parties that manage to get above the five percent national threshold. Since 1992, there are limiting provisions for coalitions: a coalition of two parties has to gain seven percent of the vote, a coalition of three, nine percent of the vote and a coalition of four or more parties eleven percent. These thresholds increased for the 2002 elections. Seats are allocated to electoral districts according to the number of votes cast in the district (distribution is based on the Hare method with unassigned seats allocated according to the method of largest remainder).

The allocation of seats among the parties between 1990 and 1998 used a two-round system. At first, parties were given seats according to the Hagenbach-Bischoff electoral formula. All seats, which were not allocated in the first round, were re-allocated in a second round at the national level where all remaining votes from districts were re-allocated. Since the 2002, seats have been allocated based on a d'Hondt electoral divisor. Also since 1990, mandates have been distributed to candidates according to their position on the ballot. Voters are allowed to change the position of candidates on the ballot by using preferential voting, but the required level of votes for a candidate to move up the ballot is quite high. Thus, only a limited number of candidates are able to get enough votes to subvert party intentions.

The electoral system, especially the small number of electoral districts and the proportionality of the system, results in campaigns being organized nationally. In view of the fact that voters vote for a party list of candidates with only a limited use of preferential voting, parties play a primary role in the campaign, and the role of candidates is marginal. Campaigns usually concentrate on the district party list leader. Since voters can use preferential voting, individual parties have their internal rules addressing independent campaigns so that individual candidates do not damage or deviate from the party campaign. While the KDU-ČSL allows its candidates to have their own campaigns with the goal of persuading voters to use preferential voting, the other main parties place restrictions on this possibility. The main tool parties have instituted for this purpose is the possibility to recall an individual candidate from the party list before the beginning of an election.

The Senate's eighty-one members are elected in one-seat districts for a six-year term with a partial re-election of one-third of the Senate every two years. Parties and coalitions can nominate one candidate per district. Independent candidates nominate themselves but have to attach a petition of at least 1,000 eligible voters within a given electoral district supporting their candidacy. Candidates have to pay a deposit of 20,000 CZK (at the time the deposit was introduced it equaled $740). If a candidate gains at least six percent of the vote in an electoral district, the deposit is returned. The electoral system is a two-round majority system.

Party Finance Model Description

The legislation on public funding has undergone considerable changes since the beginning of the 1990s. The development of the legislation can be divided into three phases. The first phase entailed the initial passing of laws addressing the activities of parties and the organization of elections at the beginning of the 1990s. It was at this time that state subsidies for votes were instituted. The second phase from 1994 to 2000 is when the party finance model was established which basically continues today (although the amount of individual subsidies and the conditions governing their payment have changed). The period since 2001 is the third phase and is noted for introducing a significantly greater regulation of party funding than in the previous phases, stricter sanctions for breaching the rules and the expansion of state subsidies to include parties elected to district boards of representatives and those running in European parliamentary elections. This expansion of state subsidies has resulted in a transformation of the structure of public funding. Until 2000, parties received around half their income from non-governmental sources (in non-election years). However since 2001, all the main parties are funded mostly by the state.

The "Law on Political Parties" was adopted by the federal parliament at the end of January 1990 and contained only basic rules governing party registration.[7] A new law passed in October 1991 did not entail important changes in party finance.[8] It only prohibited gifts from the state and state bodies and introduced annual financial reports. A 1994 amendment broadened the extent of state subsidies and defined new categories of permissible types of party income including donations, public funding, membership fees and income from party activities. Since then, the sources of party income have not changed.

Party Donations

The first "Law on Political Parties" in 1990 stipulated in a single sentence that the same rules concerning the financial management that apply to other social organizations also apply to parties. Party donations were unregulated for the 1990 elections. Because there was practically no private capital in the country at that time, parties obtained most of their funds from members or from foreign donors.[9] The law passed in 1991 did not address party sponsorship sufficiently. On the one hand, it banned donations from the state and state bodies, but on the other hand it legalized donations (without limitation) from foreign donors and sponsorship by enterprises with a state-owned stake. There were no restrictions placed on the amount donated. Moreover, party members were not limited in any way in sponsoring their own party. Although the law stipulated that one-time individual donations exceeding 10,000 CZK ($360) or total annual donations of 50,000 CZK ($1,800) had to be registered, the manner in which this registration was to occur was never sufficiently specified. The annual financial reports of parties at that time were not public, and the law did not provide for any penalties for breaching the rules.

---

7   Act No. 15/1990 Coll. on Political Parties.
8   Act No. 424/1991 Coll. on the Association in Political Parties and Movements.
9   John K Glenn. 1999. *International Actors and Democratisation: US Assistance to New Political Parties in the Czech Republic and Slovakia.* EUI Working Papers, SPS No. 99/7. Badia Fiesolana, San Domenico: European University Institute.

One of the major changes brought by the 1994 amendment was the loosening of the obligation to register donations as the amendment increased the amount from 50,000 CZK to 100,000 (from $1,800 to $3,600) as the minimum amount which parties must keep records of. The new bill also gave power to the Supreme Audit Office to control, to some extent, the accuracy of the annual financial reports, but it did not introduce an automatic obligation to make these reports publicly available. Only if the Supreme Audit Office discovered errors in the accounting was a report published. However, the Supreme Audit Office lost its control powers that very same year based on a decision of the Constitutional Court which claimed that the state cannot interfere within the internal financial affairs of parties.

The main features of the current regulation of donations to parties were adopted in 2000 in reaction to a series of events which resulted in the fall of the Klaus cabinet in 1997. Since the adoption of new rules in 2000, there have been only minor changes in the regulation, targeted towards the liberalization of this stricter 2000 regime.[10] The law prohibits parties from receiving donations from foreign legal entities with the exception of donations from parties and foundations. Individuals may donate only if they have permanent residence in the Czech Republic. The law further stipulates that donations cannot come from the following: the state (with the exception of state subsidies), organizations financed by the state, municipalities and regions, state enterprises, legal entities with a publicly-owned stake over ten percent and non-governmental organizations.

There are no restrictions on the amount of donations or time limits (it is possible to give donations at any time). For all donations, parties have to publicize the name and the identification data of the donor. Between 2000 and 2006, donations above 50,000 CZK had to be verified by a donation note (a brief version of a donation agreement according to a template prepared by the Ministry of Finance furnished with the signature of the donor and a party representative). It is enough to verify donations via a copy of the donation agreement. The stricter regulation applies for party members who give a party fee above 50,000 CZK with the only difference that they have to be identified by their name and address (between 2000 and 2006, party members were not allowed to give more than 50,000 CZK).

The provision of donations to candidates (to both chambers of parliament) either by a party or other sponsors is not regulated in any way. Some parties contribute a certain amount to the personal campaign of the leader on their candidate list in the individual district and also to Senate candidates. Donations to candidates from companies and individuals are also quite wide-spread. Because the law does not regulate this in any way, these types of donations are beyond regulation.

---

10 In the 1990s, Václav Klaus was the chairman of the ODS, then the strongest ruling party and the prime minister. The largest wave of state property privatization took place when the ODS was in power. In 1997, it was discovered that among ODS donors, there were names of two non-existent foreign donors who contributed a total of 7.5 million CZK ($231,000). However, it was revealed that in fact the money came from a businessman who won a tender for the purchase of a prominent state-owned steel company. In reaction to the unwillingness of Klaus to accept personal responsibility for the scandal, the coalition parties of the ODS left the cabinet and the government fell.

Although the "Act on the Conflict of Interests" obligated members of parliament (both deputies and senators) to submit reports on their income, donations and newly acquired real estate, it was only necessary to declare incomes received while in-office.[11] Donations received during an election campaign, therefore, are not part of these reports. The rules regulating party funding can thus be evaded through the direct funding of candidates.

Direct Public Funding

Public subsidies have been given to parties since 1990 when the state started to reimburse electoral costs. In 1994, the system of reimbursement of electoral costs was replaced with a new system of public funding. These new subsidies were more generous to established parties. Since 1994, the types of state subsidies have remained the same and consist of the following: a permanent subsidy consisting of two components (a subsidy for regular activities and a subsidy for the seat of a deputy or a senator), and a subsidy for the payment of election costs.

The subsidy for regular activities is provided during the entire election term to parties which received at least three percent of the vote in the last national election. Since the introduction of the subsidy in 1994, and until 2001, a party that obtained three percent of the vote was entitled to three million CZK per year (this amounted to $104,000 in 1994). For each additional 0.1 percent of the vote, the subsidy increased by 100,000 CZK ($3,500 in 1994 dollars) and above five percent the subsidy amounted to five million CZK ($174,000 in 1994). Since 2001, the subsidy for activities has doubled. The law does not regulate how parties spend their money nor does it define a deadline by which the amount needs to be spent.

The subsidy for a parliamentary seat was set at 500,000 CZK in 1994, and this amount did not changed until 2001 (in 1994 it equaled $17,400). However, only parties are entitled to this subsidy, and consequently independent senators are disadvantaged and must cover many expenses from their own resources. Since 2001, the amount of the state subsidy per parliamentarian has been established at 900,000 CZK (in 2001, this amounted to $23,700). Since 2001, parties have received a subsidy for each seat acquired in the newly established district boards of representatives in the amount of 250,000 CZK (in 2001 it was $6,600).

The subsidy for the payment of election costs has been paid since 1990 when a party with more than two percent of the vote in an election was entitled to receive ten CZK (approximately thirty cents) for each vote. It applied to elections to all three legislatures (the two houses of the Federal Assembly and Czech National Council). Thus, the winner of the election, the Civic Forum, was given more then one hundred million CZK ($3 million) as a one-off payment. In 1992, the reimbursement increased to fifteen CZK per vote. Federal elections reimbursements were paid as a one-off payment; however, payment for votes in elections to the Czech National Council were paid annually (twenty-five percent of the total sum). In 1994, this annual payment was transformed into the above mentioned state subsidy for a seat.

---

11 Act No. 238/1992 Coll. on Some Measures Related to the Protection of Public Interest.

However, the 1995 "Law on Parliament Elections" re-introduced a one-off payment after the elections to the Chamber of Deputies.

At the time it was introduced in 1995, the subsidy was paid to parties with electoral gains in the elections to the Chamber of Deputies of at least three percent of the vote and amounted to ninety CZK per vote (a little over $3). As a result of the rulings of the Constitutional Court which twice addressed (in 1999 and in 2001) the complaints lodged by smaller parties, the criterion of relevance was reduced. Since 2002, the subsidy is paid to parties that gain at least 1.5 percent of the vote in the elections to the Chamber of Deputies, and it amounts to hundred CZK ($4) per vote. In 2003, this subsidy was expanded to include the elections to the European parliament. In these elections, it is necessary to receive one percent of the vote in order to be eligible for the subsidy, and the subsidy equals thirty CZK (approximately $1) per vote. The fact that the subsidy is paid after the elections based on election gains is often criticized by smaller parties, arguing that they cannot invest much in an election campaign, which further reduces their chance of success. However, the subsidies cover a large portion of the campaign costs of larger parties.

The legal regulation of state subsidies has been very stable. However in 1999 and in 2000, a major reform of state subsidies was carried out in connection with election reform. Both the election reform and the change in the state subsidies were eventually cancelled by the Constitutional Court but both reforms suggest a way in which elections and funding rules may be modified to the benefit larger parties. The two biggest parties (for example, the ČSSD and the ODS) agreed in 1998 on modifying the electoral rules and after nearly two years of discussions, the parliament approved an amendment to the electoral law in 2000. The Constitutional Court cancelled the election reform, and the bill was never implemented.

In this same reform package, state funding underwent changes as well. The state subsidy for a mandate was to double from 500,000 to one million CZK. At the same time, the state subsidy for votes received in elections to the Chamber of Deputies was to be reduced from ninety to thirty CZK. If the strong majority elements in the electoral system had not been cancelled by the Constitutional Court, the increases mentioned above would have largely benefited larger parties. The impact of the proposed reforms can be gleaned from a model calculation of state subsidies for parties that would be entitled to the subsidies in the 1998–2002 term when the reform was adopted (see Table 6.2). The data in column A are calculated based on the rules valid before the reform, and the calculations in column B are according to the proposed changes. It is clear from Table 6.2 that the two strongest parliamentary parties (for example, the ČSSD and the ODS) would receive the bulk of financing. At the same time, the subsidy for the remaining three parliamentary parties would significantly decrease, and non-parliamentary parties would have received approximately thirty-eight percent less. Analogously, the disproportion between the election gains and the state subsidy would have increased.

Table 6.2   **Model calculation of aggregated state subsidies during the 1998–2002 election term**

	Electoral Results 1998 (percent)	Seats 1998–2002		State Subsidies 1998–2002			
				A^1		B^2	
		A^1	B^2	mil. CZK	percent	mil. CZK	percent
ČSSD	32.31	74	103	342	32.79	490	44.56
ODS	27.74	63	83	295	28.32	402	36.54
KSČM	11.03	24	5	127	12.22	60	5.44
KDU-ČSL	9.00	20	6	108	10.40	60	5.47
US-DEU	8.60	19	3	104	10.00	47	4.31
Others	11.32	0	0	66	6.28	41	3.68
Total	100	200	200	1,042	100	1,100	100

[1] Calculated according to original rules.
[2] Calculated according to the electoral and party funding reforms proposed in 2000.

Source: Compiled by the authors.

Indirect Public Support

The Czech legal system specifies three forms of indirect state funding of parties (the indirect support of individual candidates is not possible). The first option is the exemption of sponsorship gifts from the tax on donations (since 1999), and the second option is for legal persons to deduct contributions donated to parties (since 2005). The second mechanism in particular is not yet an important impulse for sponsorship, and this will probably continue to hold in the future because donors can deduct only a small amount using this exemption. Since 1990, the state provides parties free air time on state television and radio shortly before the elections. This time is allocated evenly among all the parties and candidates running for office. At the same time, paid radio and television advertisement on both public and private channels is forbidden.

The state also funds the activities of parliamentary party groups or factions. This funding is not provided to parties as such but only to the parliamentary factions which are not established strictly on party lines (especially independent factions in the Senate). Funds are allocated from the internal budget of the Chamber of Deputies and the Senate. They are intended for the purchase of consumables, minor tangible assets, expenses for refreshments for working meetings, external evaluation and the leasing of meeting rooms outside the parliament. The contribution is not high, and in 2005, it was a fixed amount of 24,500 CZK ($1,000) and 3,400 CZK ($140) per member of a faction per month. Even though the contributions to factions are much less than state subsidies to parties, they are enough to cover the basic needs of factions. Requirements for the funding of factions also creates party discipline as new factions created in the parliament are not entitled to any funding.

Disclosure, Reporting and Enforcement

The main tool for controlling party funding in the Czech Republic is the annual financial report. Parties are obligated to provide these reports on an annual basis to the Chamber of Deputies. The fact that the supervisory body is the lower parliamentary chamber is its main problem: the controlling body consists of the same entities that are controlled. The law defines the mandatory content of the reports submitted by parties and the general framework according to which the Chamber of Deputies should proceed and set penalties if it discovers irregularities in the reports. In addition to accounting for profit and for losses, the annual report must also contain an overview of incomes, identify donors and include the total operating and salary expenditures and costs of elections (without specifying in greater detail individual cost items). All sponsors must be identified and in the case of donations exceeding 50,000 CZK, a donation note must be attached.

The law does not stipulate in what manner the completeness and the accuracy of the data should be verified. The Chamber of Deputies uses resolutions whereby it acknowledges receiving the reports. Although the law contains minor sanctions to penalize cases when data contained in a report are not in compliance with the law, their application depends on a decision of the Chamber of Deputies. Pragmatically, parties have no reason to submit accurate information on their management. Even if the Chamber of Deputies points to an irregularity in donations, parties have enough time to return such a donation without any sanction. However since 1994, sanctions have been possible for breaching the rules: state authorities could suspend party activities, and if the discovered problems were not eliminated, it is possible to submit a motion to a court to cancel the party. This measure was applied only against minor parties almost without any activity which did not submit the financial report repeatedly.

Another serious problem related to the Czech regulation of political funding is the absence of any regulation concerning the funding of individual candidate campaigns. This is particularly important in the case of candidates running for the Senate who run individually and not on a party list. The same is true about candidates to the Chamber of Deputies, even though the main expenditures are covered by parties which are the main vehicles of the campaign. Although it is possible for candidates to the Chamber of Deputies to have their own campaigns, the law does not introduce any rules to control them. The absence of control also concerns donations and loans of both new as well as re-elected deputies. The "Law on the Conflict of Interests" requires deputies to submit as of 1 July each year a report on incomes, gifts and newly acquired real estate to the speaker of the Senate.[12] However, only items must be declared that were accepted while in-office. Donations accepted during an election campaign are not necessarily included in these reports.

---

12 Senators submit the statement to the speaker of the Chamber of Deputies under the same conditions.

Trends in Party and Campaign Funding

Party Income

The rest of this chapter focuses on the party finance of the four main parties in the Czech Republic (the ČSSD, the KDU-ČSL, the KSČM and the ODS) with only a limited discussion of smaller parties. Patterns in party funding will be characterized based on the structure of categories which parties are obliged to use for their financial reports. In the outline that follows, we disregard loans and credits because they do not form a true income but only an accounting item.[13] Annual financial reports have been published since 1995, and therefore we start with this year. Table 6.3 and 6.4 present the income structure of the analyzed parties both in relative and in absolute terms. In the relative numbers, the main trend is the continuous increase in the share of state subsidies, limited growth of donations (concentrated mainly in election years) and the slow decrease of other sources of income.

Starting with state subsidies in relative terms, the percentage of state subsidies in party incomes fluctuated around fifty percent during the 1990s with the exception of election years when the share was higher as a result of the one-off contribution for the payment of election costs. However since 2001, the percentage of state subsidies has been above sixty-five percent, and in case of some parties, it has been above eighty percent. The reason for this change was the introduction of a new type of a state subsidy (for the seat of a regional representative). Finally, the growing role of state subsidies becomes even more apparent after the introduction of a subsidy for the payment of election costs for the European parliamentary elections in 2004. In absolute terms, the increase in state subsidies was caused both by the introduction of the new payments and by the increase of the sum paid for the seat and electoral costs. However, the increase in the sum mirrors a significant rise in inflation (between 1996 and 2006 almost fifty percent) and did not mean an increase in the real value. The increasing amount of state subsidies leads to the growing total income for parties. This makes established parties dependent on the state and vulnerable if they do not succeed in elections.

In addition to state subsidies, donations to parties are another source of their increasing total income. The stagnation or even decrease at the end of 1990s was caused mainly by the end of privatization and fears of potential donors after the 1997 financial scandal of the ODS. Moreover, the tightening of the rules for donations in 2000 also resulted in fewer and smaller donations. However since 2004, there is a huge growth in donations even in non-election years. The share of other sources of funding has been falling symmetrically in relative terms while in absolute terms it has been stagnating or growing little. Membership fees were not an important income for parties in the 1990s. While before 2001, membership fees accounted for approximately thirteen percent of the income on average (especially for the KSČM and the KDU-ČSL which have a large membership base), after 2001, their share fell

---

13 A loan may become party income if it is not paid back. In case of the parties in this chapter, this has never happened.

Table 6.3 · Income structure of major parties as percentage of income

	1995	1996[1]	1997	1998[1]	1999	2000	1995–2000	2001	2002[1]	2003	2004	2005	2006[1]	2001–2006
Public Funding	30	74	50	81	56	51	64	76	80	74	65	69	72	73
Membership	18	9	19	7	19	19	13	9	6	9	8	9	5	7
Donations	12	8	9	4	3	10	7	3	7	4	16	9	15	10
Party Activities	40	8	22	7	22	20	16	13	8	13	11	13	7	10
Total in CZK²	229	672	287	773	288	318	1,962	603	1,089	597	766	655	1,318	5,028
Total in USD²	8.7	22.7	8.3	21.4	8.2	8.0	77.3	15.2	32.8	21.2	29.0	26.4	58.6	183.2

¹Indicates a year when there were national elections.
²In millions.

Source: Compiled by authors based on financial reports of the major parties.

Table 6.4. Income structure of major parties 1995–2006

		1995	1996	1997	1998	1999	2000	2001	2002	2003	2004	2005	2006
Public Funds	CZK	69.8	497.6	144.0	629.6	161.6	161.0	456.4	869.4	441.7	500.1	455.2	953.6
	USD	2.6	16.7	4.2	17.4	4.6	4.0	11.5	26.1	15.7	18.9	18.0	41.4
Membership	CZK	42.1	63.8	53.6	57.7	54.3	60.0	52.9	60.7	52.3	59.3	56.3	66.5
	USD	1.6	2.1	1.6	1.6	1.5	1.5	1.4	1.8	1.9	2.2	2.2	2.9
Donations	CZK	26.5	53.6	26.6	31.8	9.7	32.5	16.5	72.4	22.5	125.7	61.1	200.3
	USD	1.0	1.8	0.8	0.9	0.3	0.9	0.4	2.2	0.8	4.8	2.4	8.7
Party Activities	CZK	90.8	57.1	62.7	54.2	62.2	64.6	77.2	86.5	80.6	80.9	82.4	97.8
	USD	3.4	1.9	1.8	1.5	1.8	1.6	1.9	2.6	2.9	3.1	3.3	4.2
Total	CZK	229.2	672.1	286.8	773.2	287.8	318.1	603.0	1,089.0	597.0	766.0	655.0	1,318.2
	USD	8.7	22.7	8.3	21.5	8.2	8.0	15.2	32.8	21.2	29.1	25.9	57.3

Source: Compiled by the authors based on financial reports of the parties.

Notes: Major parties were identified as the ČSSD, the KDU-ČSL, the KSČM, the ODS and the US-DEU (1998–2005) and the SZ (2006). All amounts in millions.

to half.[14] Moreover in absolute terms, the income from members in 2006 was the same as in 1996. Finally, a sharp fall in the importance of the party money-making activities is clearly visible.

Election Costs

Neither the expenditures of parties nor those of candidates are regulated in any way. In particular, there are no restrictions on their expenditures during elections. Candidates and parties can use their own money without any limit (only radio and television advertising is forbidden). However, parties have been obligated to publish election costs since 2000 as part of their financial reports. Before that time, we have to rely on statements of parties in the media. There are two main trends in election expenditures (for electoral expenditures see Table 6.5).

First, there is a gap between the two main parties (for example, the ČSSD and the ODS) and the rest of the parties in terms of expenditures. This is mainly caused by the structure of state subsidies for seat and electoral costs which rewards success. Second, there is a continuous increase in expenditures (in case of the KSČM since 1996). This reflects the growing financial reserves of the party as well as its changing strategy. Instead of relying only on party members and hard-core communist voters, it also tries to get voters from other segments of society via a marketing driven campaign

Table 6.5   Costs of Chamber of Deputies elections

		1996	1998	2002	2006
ČSSD	CZK	80	30	75	270
	USD	2.7	0.8	2.3	12
KDU-ČSL	CZK	55	30	72[1]	68
	USD	1.8	0.8	2.2[1]	3
KSČM	CZK	6	8	15	41
	USD	0.2	0.2	0.5	1.8
ODS	CZK	127	30	60	350
	USD	4.3	0.8	1.8	15.6
US-DEU /SZ[2]	CZK	–	20	72[1]	26
	USD	–	0.6	2.2[1]	1.2

[1] The KDU-ČSL and the US-DEU created a coalition with common costs totaling seventy-two million CZK ($2.2 million).
[2] The US-DEU for 1998 and 2002 and the SZ 2006.

Source: The years 1996 and 1998 reported by various media sources. The years 2002 and 2006 compiled by the authors from financial reports of the parties.

Notes: All amounts in millions.

---

14 The KSČM is the only party in the Czech Republic that has received a majority of its income from membership fees. In 1995, membership fees accounted for half its income, and forty percent in 1997, 1999 and 2000.

as seen in 2006. The former electoral strategy of the party was not very costly so the expenditures in 1996 and 1998 were extremely low compared to other parties. In addition to that, the expenditures of all parties (except the KSČM) in 1998 elections were less than those in 1996. This was caused by draining party finances in the 1996 election and calling for an early election in 1998. The costs of general elections for parties almost equal the money invested in their party organizations (staff salaries, rents, publications, communication and public opinion polling).

Distribution of Public Funding among Parties

An examination of the rules governing state subsidies, entitlements and payments reveals that they are in favor of established parliamentary parties. This is legitimized primarily by the interpretation of the term "representativity" employed by the Czech party funding regulatory bodies (the term is used by the government in the explanatory notes to the party finance bills and also by politicians). However, the Constitutional Court in its decisions uses a different interpretation. The entitlement for state subsidies is derived from the following. The basic criterion is electoral success and the other is the type of election in which a party runs. The electoral success criterion is used linearly (the more votes and seats a party receives, the more state money) for both main state payments (for example, the electoral reimbursement and the payment per seat). The criterion of electoral success denies the explicit purpose of this subsidy (that is, payment of part of the election costs to create conditions for a competitive campaign). It only rewards successful parties, and in the case of parties with parliamentary representation, it covers all electoral expenses. This has consequences for smaller parties, especially on their entry into electoral competition. In addition to that, state subsidies are paid for votes and seats in different types of elections so that it helps larger parties.

For example, an electoral reimbursement is paid only for Chamber of Deputies elections (and since 2004 for European parliament elections). This begs the question whether the mediatory role of parties in regional and in local elections is that much less important for the functioning of the political system so to exclude them. Moreover, subsidies for seats are paid for seats in national and regional parliaments (but not for seats in the European parliament). The inclusion of regional elections in the system of state subsidies for a seat has only one explanation: the number of seats is vast (675) which leads to high total payments to parties. The logic behind the division of payments among different types of elections is not clear and suggests that the legislation is not driven by a clear concept but rather *ad hoc* strategic considerations of profit and loss for parliamentary parties. This interpretation is supported also by the rules of the above mentioned electoral and party finance reform of 2000.

Effects of Public Finance on the Development of Parties and the Party System

There are several ways in which political finance has influenced Czech parties and the party system, and they include: first, the role of inherited resources at the start of party competition in early 1990s, second the growing and stabilizing role of state subsidies and third the "earthquake effect" of party finance scandals. The first factor contributed to the crystallization of the party system as all main parties inherited resources superior to their challengers. The second factor strengthened the role of established parties *vis-à-vis* the newcomers. On the other hand, the third factor points to the vulnerability of parties in the election arena when a financial (in this case meaning corruption) scandal emerges.

The initial financial sources of the current main Czech parties (the KSČM and the KDU-ČSL) had their roots in the communist period (both had well-developed organizational structures, owned several properties and had a large membership base that secured almost half of the party income before state subsidies were introduced). The ČSSD has an inter-war (and a short post-World War II) history and links to the social democratic parties of Austria and Germany. The party obtained important financial support from foreign social democratic parties and their foundations in the early 1990s. Finally, the ODS inherited significant financial and human resources from the Civic Forum which received a majority of its revenue from American foundations and after the 1990 elections from the state.[15] All four parties had large initial resources which might help them in party competition and organization-building (on the other hand, there existed one party with similarly high financial sources from the communist period which was not successful in elections after 1989).

Another party finance related factor that helped to stabilize the party system was that the public finance model emphasized state subsidies which were generous to successful parliamentary parties (see Table 6.6 for the structure of major party incomes). Both the model of reimbursement of electoral costs and subsidies for parliamentary seats are based on electoral success. The rewards are given to successful parties that have financially better positions in the following elections. Deposits which parties are required to pay before national elections have the same effect. We are not arguing that there is no level playing field but that there is a strong bias towards established parties in the way state subsidies are provided, and this bias might help to foster party system stability.

Table 6.6   The structure of party finance for major parties between 1995–2006

	Public Funds	**Members**	**Donations**	**Party Activities**
ČSSD	77	4	9	10
KDU-ČSL	63	9	4	23
KSČM	56	24	1	18
ODS	73	4	16	6
US-DEU	92	2	4	1

Source: Compiled by the authors based on the financial reports of parties.

Notes: Amounts represent percentage of total income. For the US-DEU, only the years 1998–2005.

---

15 Glenn, *International Actors and Democratisation: US Assistance to New Political Parties in the Czech Republic and Slovakia.*

Moreover, the ineffective disclosure and reporting procedures, mainly during the 1990s, were advantageous for the parties in the power. With the vague regulation of party donations and an absence of control, a massive privatization of state property was launched in the Czech Republic. Some toughening of the legislative framework came as late as 1994 (and then later in 2000) which meant that the 1992 elections were held in an atmosphere of vagueness pertaining to party funding regulation. The absence of a stricter regulation of party finance management at a time of economic transformation resulted in speculation about the links between parties and businesses.

The third factor is related to financial scandals involving illegal party donation practices and corrupt behavior during the privatization period. These factors in 1997 led to the split of the ODS and the collapse of the then junior governing party, the ODA. After the revelation of those scandals, support for the ODS decreased by fifty percent, and it seemed that the newly created US would become the main center-right party. Even though the ODS managed to secure its main position in the right-wing part of the political spectrum, the US was the only party for a decade since 1992 which entered the parliament as a newcomer (in 2006 the SZ managed to also overcome the electoral threshold).

Conclusions

The Czech party system is the one of the most stable in the post-communist region. There might be various reasons for this stability, mainly the one-dimensional structure of party competition based on class division, institutionalized parties, a stable electoral system and the five percent electoral threshold. Moreover, the public finance model, mainly state sponsorship of the major parties, creates a financial disadvantage for newcomers and potential challengers to the established parties. The amount of money given by the state to parties in the parliament exceeds those used in electoral campaigns. Electoral campaigns in the Czech Republic are relatively cheap as there is a ban on political advertisements on television and radio. From this perspective, the structure of campaign expenses of the Czech parties is unique among the post-communist countries. Thus, state subsidies provide parties with reasonable financial reserves and consequently, they assist parties in building their organizations and providing general stability to the party system.

Chapter 7

Moldova:
Party Institutionalization in a
Resource-Scarce Environment

Oleh Protsyk and Ion Osoian

Moldova represents an interesting case of relatively successful democratic development in the post-Soviet space. According to a number of quantitative and qualitative indicators, Moldova has performed better since the mid-1990s in terms of ensuring the provision of basic political rights and civil liberties than other post-Soviet republics (outside of the Baltic region).[1] It did so under adverse circumstances that traditionally hamper democratic development including a low level of urbanization, high levels of poverty and ethno-territorial conflicts.[2]

The party system is responsible, to a significant extent, for advances in institutionalizing democratic practices. Moldovan party development is impressive when compared with patterns of political competition in other Western Commonwealth of Independent States (CIS) countries such as Belarus and Ukraine. The Moldovan party system proved to be sufficiently robust to withstand the pressures of popularly elected presidents attempting to bypass parties and monopolize power during the 1990s. The party system also managed to preserve its competitive character under the lasting dominance of the Party of Communists of the Republic of Moldova (PCRM) whose full commitment to democratic values has been questionable throughout the 2000s.

Moldovan parties played a significantly more important role in politics than their counterparts in other Western CIS countries throughout the post-communist transition. Institutional choices made in the early years of the transition can be largely credited with helping to establish party politics at the center stage of the political process in Moldova. These institutional decisions proved to be more important than adverse communist legacies, the extreme hardships of economic transition and ethno-territorial tensions, all of which threatened to derail the process of Moldovan democratic transition. The choice of the electoral system as well as decisions about the constitutional powers of the presidency and the organization

---

1 On Freedom House's political rights score, Moldova consistently outperforms Belarus and Ukraine since the second half of the 1990s.

2 For socio-economic characteristics see individual chapters in Ann Lewis, ed. 2004. *The EU & Moldova: On a Fault Line of Europe*. London: Federal Trust for Education and Research; Igor Munteanu, ed. 2005. *Moldova on Its Way to Democracy and Stability*. Chisinau: Cartier.

of the executive government were among the institutional factors that had the most profound effect on the evolution of the party system and party politics. Choices made in all these institutional arenas were consistent with what the comparative politics literature generally considers as a party-friendly institutional design.[3] This design facilitated the process of the emancipation of newly established parties and contributed to their ability to establish themselves as central players in the political process in an independent Moldova.

While the decisions made with regard to the design of political institutions had a positive effect on party system development, choices of more specific rules and procedures regulating party finance proved to be more problematic in terms of their effect on the institutionalization of parties. The Moldovan party finance model exhibits an absence of direct state financial support for parties and weak enforcement of campaign contribution and expenditure rules which tends to undermine party independence from interest groups and the party's ability to foster programmatic rather than clientelistic linkages with their constituencies. An extremely high dependence on business and foreign funding, as the chapter argues, affects not only party linkage strategies with regard to either vote-rich or resource-rich constituencies but also the distribution of power inside the party structure. Rank-and-file party members and party professionals have only a very limited say in determining party strategies and policies compared to party members with business ties.

The Electoral System and Elections

From the very beginning of the post-communist transition, Moldova adopted a proportional representation (PR) electoral system. The first fully free and competitive parliamentary elections that were held in 1994 used the PR formula for seat allocation. This choice of electoral system was unusual in the post-Soviet context. All other Western CIS countries, as well as all other post-Soviet states excluding Estonia and Latvia, opted for a mixed-member or single-member district (SMD) system.[4] The political forces that dominated the transition in post-Soviet republics preferred the latter types of electoral system primarily due to the fact that these types build on personalistic ties and networks which characterized much of late Soviet politics.[5] At the same time, parties were at a very early stage of development and societal support for introducing a PR electoral system, which would have favored parties, was rather weak.

---

3   For a discussion of institutions favorable to party system institutionalization see, H. Kitschelt, Z. Mansfeldova, R. Markowski, and G. Toka. 1999. *Post-Communist Party Systems Competition, Representation and Inter-Party Cooperation*. Cambridge: Cambridge University Press.

4   For an excellent discussion of post-communist electoral systems, see Sarah Birch. 2002. *Embodying Democracy: Electoral System Design in Post-Communist Europe*. New York: Palgrave Macmillan.

5   John Willerton. 1992. *Patronage and Politics in the USSR*. Cambridge: Cambridge University Press.

These general circumstances of the post-Soviet transition were also applicable to Moldova. The record of this early period reveals heated debates about various draft laws favoring a mixed-member or pure PR electoral system.[6] The reason why PR was chosen was due to the political need to have an electoral formula that could give at least a possible option of electoral participation for citizens in the secessionist region of Transnistria.[7] This consideration was connected to the most salient issue on the political agenda of that period, the conflict in Transnistria. The authorities of this breakaway region had almost complete *de facto* control of the area by mid-1992 and would have been able to prevent parliamentary elections based on an SMD system. Introducing a PR system, with a single national district was thus seen by Moldovan politicians as a way of avoiding an explicit subvention of Moldova's sovereignty. PR was the electoral system which would allow citizens from the Transnistria region to participate in elections by casting their votes in locations controlled by the central government.[8]

The secessionist conflict shaped deliberations about the electoral law in another important way. By the time the drafts of the electoral law were debated in the Moldovan parliament in 1993, a large number of Transnistrian deputies had left. The preferences of a majority in this group, which included a large number of state enterprise directors, were in-line with those law drafters who favored a personalistic and candidate-centered electoral system. The passage of a PR electoral law was facilitated by the departure of these members of parliament (MPs).

The resulting October 1993 "Law on Parliamentary Elections" introduced a PR system with a single national district. A four percent threshold for entering the parliament was established both for individual parties and party blocs. After the first post-independence parliamentary elections were held in February 1994, the new parliament entrenched the same basic principles in the 1997 "Electoral Code." Parties thus became the central players in the electoral process. According to the law, which has only seen a limited number of procedural changes since 1997, all parties registered with the Ministry of Justice can participate in elections. Apart from this requirement, Article 79 states that "at least 51 registered candidates and at most the number of deputies in Parliament provided for in the Constitution, plus two deputy candidates, shall be included on a list."[9]

Independent candidates are also allowed to run in the elections, but their position is clearly disadvantaged. The law stipulates that "independent candidates shall be considered elected if they receive at least three percent of the valid votes cast in the election throughout the republic." The electoral threshold for individuals parties has reverted to four percent (it was six percent for the 2001 and 2005 parliamentary

---

6   Victor Popa. 1993. "V apparate palramenta uzhe obsuzhdayut proceduru dosrochnykh vyborov." *Nezavisimaya Moldova* 138: 11.

7   Ibid.

8   Alexander Khavronin. 1993. "Politicheskaya osen' obeshchaet byt' zharkoi." *Nezavisimaya Moldova* 137: 8.

9   Changes in the electoral threshold rate are presented in Table 7.1. An important discussion of electoral law changes and the role of the Council of Europe's pressure in this regard can be found in Cristian Untila. 2006. "Improvement of Electoral Legislation." *Moldova E-Journal* 68.

elections), and an eight percent threshold has been established for electoral blocs. In order to be registered, an independent candidate must collect signatures in support of their candidacy (at least 2,000 signatures) which is not the case for parties and electoral blocs. Although many independent candidates have run in the various parliamentary elections, none of them has ever been elected.

Overall, the passage of the first electoral law and the use of the same basic principles in the subsequent pieces of legislation were of critical importance for the institutionalization of the party system. Electoral system rules, which were combined with a constitutionally weak presidency and party participation in the cabinet formation process, provided incentives for parties to start investing in developing policy-making capacities and in constructing coherent public images. These rules also led to the dominance of the party rather than candidate-oriented campaigns throughout Moldova's entire post-communist period.

As Table 7.1 indicates, the identity of parties and party blocs was very unstable in the early period of the post-communist transition. Many parties and blocs represented in the first parliament elected in 1994 chose different organizational configurations and party labels to participate in the next parliamentary elections in 1998. The creation of new parties and coalitions was the response of politicians to failures in governance during the period from 1994–2001. The party system became somewhat more stable after the 2001 parliamentary elections. The PCRM has dominated the political process in the country since its parliamentary victory in the 2001 elections. This victory was magnified by the inability of several parties to clear the six percent threshold which enabled the PCRM to control the majority of parliamentary seats between 2001 and 2005. The party managed to retain power by winning the 2005 parliamentary elections, although with a significantly smaller margin than in 2001.[10]

Campaign Finance Model

There are two basic laws dealing with party finance issues: the 1991 "Law on Parties and Other Socio-Political Organizations"[11] and the 1997 "Electoral Code."[12] The first law regulates the financing of parties in general while the second focuses on campaign finance. The basic features of the campaign finance model have not changed over time. The legislation requires electoral contenders to establish an

---

10 On the evolution of the party system in Moldova see, William Crowther, and Yuri Josanu. 2004. "Moldova." In *The Handbook of Political Change in Eastern Europe*, eds. Sten Berglund, Joakim Ekman, and Frank H. Aarebrot. Cheltenham: Edward Elgar, pp. 549–593; Igor Botan. 2006. "Многопартийность в Республике Молдова: энтропия развития." *Политическая Наука* 1; Oleh Protsyk, Igor Bucataru, and Andrei Volentir. 2007. *Competiţia partidelor în Moldova: ideologie, organizare şi abordarea conflictelor etno-teritoriale.* Chisinau: Universitate de Stat din Moldova.

11 "Law on Parties and Other Socio-Political Organizations." 1991. No. 718-XII of 17 September 1991 Vestile No 11–12/106.

12 "Electoral Code." 1997. No 1381-XIII of 21 November 1997 *Monitorul oficial al Republica Moldova* No 81/667.

Table 7.1   Moldovan parliamentary election results, 1994–2005

Year	1994		1998		2001		2005	
Electoral threshold	4%		4%		6%		6%=1, 8%=2, 12%>2 parties	
Electoral contestants	V%	S%	V%	S%	V%	S%	V%	S%
Democratic Convention Electoral Bloc	–	–	19.42	25.7	–	–	–	–
For a Democratic and Prosperous Moldova Electoral Bloc	–	–	18.16	23.8	–	–	–	–
(Democratic) Agrarian Party	43.18	53.9	3.63	0	1.16	0	–	–
Alliance of the Popular Christian Democratic Front	7.53	8.65	–	–	–	–	–	–
Christian Democratic People's Front/Party[1]	–	–	–	–	8.24	10.9	9.07	10.89
Democratic Party of Moldova[2]	–	–	–	–	5.02	0	–	–
Electoral Bloc Braghis Alliance	–	–	–	–	13.36	18.8	–	–
Electoral Bloc *Moldova Democrata*	–	–	–	–	–	–	28.53	33.66
Electoral Bloc *Patria–Rodina*	–	–	–	–	–	–	4.97	0
Party for Rebirth and Conciliation of Moldova	–	–	–	–	5.79	0	–	–
Party of Communists of the Republic of Moldova	–	–	30.01	39.6	50.07	70.3	45.98	55.45
Party of Democratic Forces	–	–	8.84	10.9	–	–	–	–
Peasants and Intellectuals Bloc	9.21	10.6	–	–	–	–	–	–
Socialist Party and *Unitate-Edinstvo* Movement Bloc	22	26.9	–	–	–	–	–	–
Others (parties, blocs and independent candidates)	18.1	0	19.9	0	16.34	0	11.5	0
Total	**100**	**100**	**100**	**100**	**100**	**100**	**100**	**100**

[1] In 1994 in a coalition named the Alliance of the Popular Christian Democratic Front and in 1998 in the Democratic Convention Electoral Bloc.
[2] In 1998 in a coalition named For a Democratic and Prosperous Moldova Electoral Bloc and in 2005 in the Electoral Bloc *Moldova Democrata*.

Source: Data from www.e-democracy.md (accessed 4 April 2007).

Notes: Only the electoral contestants who obtained more than four percent in at least one election are listed.

electoral fund and provides the Central Electoral Commission (CEC) the authority to establish a ceiling on the size of the fund. The CEC does not regulate the limits of individual donations to the campaign but primarily monitors the compliance with the fund ceiling. The legislation requires that all types of campaign donations be made through the electoral fund. In addition, parties and independent candidates are obliged to disclose the names of their donors. However, there are no limits on donations between elections, and parties are not obliged to declare or to publish these types of donations. Some experts believe the amount of money spent by parties between elections is much more significant than officially reported by the parties.[13]

No donations are allowed from the following types of individuals and organizations: anonymous persons, state-funded organizations and charity/religious organizations. The 1997 "Electoral Code" explicitly prohibits direct or indirect funding or material support of any kind by foreign countries, foreign enterprises and foreign non-governmental organizations as well as individuals who are not Moldovan citizens. If such funds are found, the law requires them to be confiscated and added to the state budget. However, the law does not prohibit the use of foreign money for purposes of training party officials or electoral observers during the period before legal campaigning.

To date, there is no direct budget financing for parties, but some important modifications to the system are currently being debated. In 2005, the government approved a draft law on the financing of parties and electoral campaigns which was subsequently modified by the parliament due to draft amendments to the 2001 "Law on Political Parties." These amendments were adopted in the first reading, and the draft law was sent for expert evaluation to the Council of Europe in December 2006. These amendments envision for the first time that parties receive funding from the state budget. The amendments propose to divide 0.05 percent of the state budget as follows: one half goes to parties proportional to their number of mandates obtained in parliamentary elections while the other half goes to parties proportional to the number of votes obtained in local elections, with a requirement that they obtain at least twenty mandates in district-level councils.

Campaign loans are one form of public subsidy available under the current Moldovan legislation. The electoral campaign contestants (parties and individuals) are eligible to receive interest-free loans that have to be re-paid two months after the election in case a contestant fails to receive three percent of the nation-wide vote. Contestants that clear this threshold have four months to re-pay the loan. Since this legislation applies equally to parties and to individuals, this serves as one more indication of how Moldovan legislation favors parties over independent candidates. The legislation allows electoral candidates to use public transportation free of charge for the period of the campaign. Also, a paid leave for electoral candidates was once provided as a form of indirect public subsidy. Payments for the leave were provided in the past from the CEC's election fund. Payments were based on a candidate's salary. However in March 2007, the parliament cancelled this provision, and candidates who chose to take leave can no longer request compensation.

---

13 L. Caraşciuc, E. Obreja, V. Gâscă, N. Izdebschi, C. Lazăr, and M. Mazur. 2002. "Sistemul integrităţii naţionale: Republica Moldova." Transparency International Moldova.

The Moldovan legislation contains a quite elaborate provision regulating media access during campaign periods. Electoral contestants are given free air time for debates. The limits of free air time are established by the CEC. The legislation ensures that principle of equal access is maintained by requiring that all electoral contestants receive the same amount of time, participate in the same programs (or are divided in groups on criteria announced by the CEC to participate in different programs) and are informed on the time of the broadcast seven days prior. The 1997 law also limits the amount of paid air time that electoral contestants can purchase. Each contestant is limited to two hours of paid air time for the entire period of the campaign. The additional requirement is that paid air time should not exceed more than two minutes per day for each contestant. The law obliges electronic mass media to announce the conditions for booking air time and the relevant fees which are not allowed to exceed the commercial basis.

The existing legislation does not provide an explicit definition of a campaign expenditure. However from the text of the legal provisions, one can infer that a campaign expenditure is defined in very broad terms. For example Article 38 of the 1997 law, which specifies conditions and methods of support for campaigns, refers to direct and indirect financing and material support to the campaign in any form. The main form of expenditure control is a requirement that all campaign expenditures are made thorough the electoral fund. The existing legislation does not include restrictions on the type of spending. The requirement to establish an electoral fund as the only legal mechanism for the disbursement of campaign money, which is a common practice in most post-Soviet states, does not address the wide-spread problem of unaccounted cash transactions for campaign-related expenses. There is a general acceptance in society towards the use of cash transactions as a means of avoiding taxation. This social environment allows parties to rely on cash in financing different types of expenses. Given the weakness of monitoring and enforcement practices, which are discussed more specifically below, parties face few credible threats of being punished for using cash transactions.

Reacting to one form of vote buying that became widespread in the early years of the post-communist transition, the 1997 "Electoral Code" explicitly prohibits electoral contestants from offering voters money or gifts. It also prohibits the distribution of goods free of charge, including humanitarian aid or other forms of charity. Besides establishing the expenditure ceiling, the legislation does not attempt to impose any restrictions on personal spending (as opposed to money collected through donations) in campaigns. Campaign participants are required to submit bi-weekly financial reports throughout the campaign period to the CEC or, in case of local elections, to district electoral councils (DECs). These include data on their revenues and expenses. Parliamentary election contestants (for example, parties and independent candidates) are also obliged to publish data on their electoral fund revenues in one of the national newspapers within a month after the start of the campaign.

The campaign period was reduced from ninety to sixty days after the 2001 parliamentary elections. Candidates can only campaign after they are officially registered, and the registration period ends thirty days before the election date. The law imposes reporting requirements on banks in which campaign participants open electoral fund accounts. A bank has to notify the CEC about money transferred to an electoral fund within twenty-four hours after the transfer. The CEC is required to keep all data available for public purposes. In addition, the CEC and DECs are required to issue a weekly report on the amount and the source of contributions received by each electoral contestant. They also have to release their final pre-election report two days prior to the election. The law also requires these bodies to prepare a final report compiling all the information that they have received concerning the amount and the sources of contributions. A declaration of financial status is mandatory for a candidate to be registered to run either as an independent or on a party list. The financial declaration requirement for parties and independent candidates includes stating the amount and the source of real estate holdings, bank accounts, securities, inheritance and income received two years prior to the election.

The CEC is the agency responsible for the enforcement of campaign rules. The agency recently acquired some degree of autonomy from the government due to changes in how the agency is funded, and how the members are appointed. The CEC consists of nine members. Five out of the nine are nominated by parliamentary opposition parties, two by government parties, one member by the cabinet and one by the president. All appointments must be confirmed by the parliament. These appointment procedures were enacted under opposition pressure in November 2005. Prior to this, the parliament, the cabinet and the president each appointed three members of the CEC.

The CEC has a number of instruments for enforcing compliance with campaign rules. However, most of the sanctions against those who violate the rules cannot be applied unilaterally by the CEC. If the CEC's monitoring activities identifies violators, the CEC has the option of taking them to court or requesting the Ministry of Interior to investigate the matter further. Only weaker types of sanctions, such as issuing a warning, can be administered by the CEC on its own. In checking the sources of income or the accuracy of accounting records, the CEC and DECs may request the Court of Accounts or the Ministry of Finance to review the financial records.

The CEC's decision in the 2007 local elections to issue a warning to several parties about their lack of compliance with the various legal provisions serves as an example of the rather reserved approach that the organization has adopted on the issue of sanctions. The warning followed an investigation by the Ministry of Interior which found that several parties printed electoral posters without contracts with a publishing house and without printing the required publication details. However, another CEC decision in the 2007 local elections testified to the existence of a certain degree of independence of the CEC from the ruling PCRM. For example in a May 2007 decision, the agency asked the speaker of the parliament not to use the position for the purposes of campaigning on behalf of the PCRM.[14]

---

14 See the CEC's decision reported at: http://www.azi.md/news?ID=44497 (accessed 7 June 2007).

Trends in Campaign and Party Funding

The available data provides some indication that the costs of campaigning have significantly increased in Moldova. One way to make an approximate estimation of the increase in party campaign expenses is to look at changes in the electoral fund ceiling over time. Assuming that politicians are interested in making these ceilings realistic and related to the patterns and the practices of campaign competition, examining the dynamics of changes in the ceiling requirement provides a longer-term view on the evolution of political finance. This is especially the case in less-developed, post-communist countries where other types of longitudinal data on party finance issues are not available. Table 7.2 reports the ceiling requirements for electoral contestants in all parliamentary elections held in Moldova.

The ceilings for parties and for electoral blocs rose at least a hundred percent in local currency terms from one election to the next throughout the entire post-communist period. The increases in the ceilings for independent candidates showed a similar movement. While the size of the increases, especially during the first decade of transition, could be attributed to inflation, this is not the case in the 2000s. The average annual inflation rate since 2001 has been around ten percent. The increase in the ceiling in the recent parliamentary election far outpaced this rate of inflation. The cap for the size of electoral funds for parties and for blocs grew from $77,300 in 2001 to approximately $200,000 in 2005.[15] This suggests that even in political systems that introduce limits on electronic media advertising, which is one of the most expensive forms of political advertisement, the costs of campaigning can grow rapidly.

Table 7.2   The ceilings for the size of electoral fund of contestants in parliamentary elections

Year	1994		1998		2001		2005	
Currency[1]	MDL	USD	MDL	USD	MDL	USD	MDL	USD
Parties and Electoral Blocs	100	24.5	500	105.8	1000	77.3	2500	199.1
Independent Candidates	2.5	0.6	30	6.3	50	3.9	100	7.9

[1]All amounts in the thousands.

Source: Calculated on the basis of Central Electoral Commission decisions 47 from 30 November 2003, 28 from 5 January 1998, 672 from 14 January 2005 and a reply of the Central Electoral Commission 9/179 from 24 April 2007 to a MP information request 358 from 17 April 2007. The exchange rate is provided from the National Bank of Moldova: http://www.bnm.md/en/index.html (accessed 7 April 2007).

---

15 The higher-level reported for US dollars for the 1998 ceilings in comparison to the 2001 ceilings is due to a rapid depreciation of Moldovan currency after 1998. The 1998 exchange rate was approximately 4.5 MDL to $1 while the 2005 rate was around thirteen MDL to one $1.

The self-reported expenditures of parties in the last two parliamentary campaigns are listed in Table 7.3 which contains a summary of all campaign expenses reported in these two elections. The expenditures of individual parties and blocs are reported only if they obtained more than four percent of the vote in one of the two elections or had declared expenditures of more than one million lei or MDL (approximately $80,000). Several parties and blocs changed their party labels in these elections which explains the variation in reporting. In addition, some electoral contestants, parties and independent candidates, failed to submit reports on campaign expenditures. This, however, did not lead to any sanctions against these organizations and individuals.

The CEC's data on overall campaign expenditures by the campaign participants, which is reported in the last row of Table 7.3, indicates that the electoral contestants spent more than twice as much in the 2005 parliamentary campaign than in the 2001 campaign. The overall expenditures for the 2001 campaign were approximately 4.3 million MDL (approximately $339,000) while the 2005 campaign expenditures were about 9.7 million MDL ($770,400). Independent candidate campaigns accounted for only a very small portion of the expenditure providing further evidence for a thesis about party dominance in the Moldovan political process.

Table 7.3   Self-reported campaign expenditures in Moldova

	2001		2005	
Currency[1]	**MDL**	**USD**	**MDL**	**USD**
Party of Communists of the Republic of Moldova	516.4	40.9	1477.0	117.3
Christian Democratic People's Party	577.3	45.7	355.8	28.3
Social Democratic Party of Moldova	27.7	2.2	1020.5	81.0
Electoral Bloc *Moldova Democrata*	–	–	2135.7	169.6
Party for Rebirth and Conciliation of Moldova	498.6	39.4	–	–
Democratic Party of Moldova	394.8	31.2	–	–
Electoral Bloc Braghis Alliance	762.2	60.3	–	–
Electoral Bloc *Patria-Rodina*	–	–	418.2	33.2
Moldova Centrist Union	–	–	1059.9	84.2
Peasants Christian Democratic Party	44.0	3.5	1688.1	134.0
Other parties and electoral blocs	1371.8	108.5	1188.1	94.3
Independent candidates	92.1	7.3	358.2	28.4
Total	4284.9	339.0	9701.4	770.4

[1]Amounts in thousands.

Source: Reply of the Central Electoral Commission 9/179 from 24 April 2007 to a MP information request 358 from 17 April 2007. The exchange rate is from the National Bank of Moldova: http://www.bnm.md/en/index.html (accessed 29 April 2007).

Notes: Only the electoral competitors who obtained more than four percent in at least one election or have reported expenditures of more than one million MDL ($80,000) are listed. Some electoral competitors, both independent candidates and parties that did not pass the threshold, have not submitted reports on campaign expenditures (this did not result in punishments).

As Table 7.3 indicates, the expenditure patterns of individual parties and blocs varied quite substantially. The ruling PCRM spent almost three times as much in the 2005 campaign as in the 2001 campaign. At the same time, the Christian Democratic People's Party (CDPP), which received a similar share of the vote (around eight to nine percent in both elections), spent considerably less in the 2005 campaign than in the 2001 campaign. The center-right electoral alliance, *Moldova Democrata*, which received the second largest share of the vote in the 2005 elections, was a leader in terms of spending in this election. The ability of non-government parties, both those that had parliamentary representation and those that did not, to secure substantial amounts of funding testifies to the competitive nature of the Moldovan political process. The existence of opportunities for electorally less-successful parties to raise money can be inferred from the relatively wide and equal distribution of finances among a large number of electoral contestants in both of the elections listed in Table 7.3. Indeed, a detailed look at the data reveals no clear correlation between expenditure and electoral performance. Neither the second nor the fourth-largest spender in the 2005 elections gained enough votes to secure parliamentary representation.

While the incumbency status of government parties provided a strong advantage for political fundraising in Moldova, opposition parties have also been able to raise significant funds throughout the entire post-communist period, and the ruling PCRM has not changed this practice. Although the number of cases of government harassment against businesses supporting the opposition has increased after the PCRM gained full-control of government in 2001, the Party has abstained from the large-scale persecution of opposition business people practiced by the governments of most post-Soviet states.

Development of Parties and the Party System

The analysis undertaken in the previous section of this chapter allows us to list a small number of key characteristics of the Moldovan model of party and campaign finance. This model is characterized by the absence of direct public funding for parties and independent candidates, limited forms of indirect state subsidies (such as free air time and media space), legal limits on campaign expenditures, the importance of electoral funds and detailed reporting requirements as key mechanisms for ensuring the transparency of funding and the centrality of the CEC as the main monitoring body with partial enforcement powers.

While each of these characteristics has some implications for party system development, the absence of direct public funding has probably been the most consequential for the development of individual parties and the party system in general. The lack of public funding dramatically increased the need for parties to find other sources of financing. Business sponsorship and party dependence on businesses have become a major feature of party development in Moldova. Foreign financing, although officially prohibited, has also been an important factor in the development of the party system.

The importance of business and foreign sponsorship can be illustrated using data from a recent survey of the Moldovan party system.[16] While survey data are rarely used in the literature on political finance, such data can serve as an important source of information on party finance and can provide useful insights into the informal aspects of the functioning of party finance mechanisms. Table 7.4 summarizes expert responses to a survey concerning sources of party finance. The experts were asked to name the first and the second most important sources of income for each of Moldova's main parties. The experts had to choose from a list of nine potential sources of party finance listed in the first column of Table 7.4.

The case of the ruling PCRM highlights the advantages that incumbency has in terms of attracting political contributions from businesses. Eighty percent of experts designated "business sponsorship" as the most important source of finance for this party. The remaining twenty percent divided their opinion between "donations of party members" and "budget allocations for parliamentary faction" as the most important source of finance for the PCRM. With regards to the second most important source of finance for the PCRM, the expert opinions were more widely and equally distributed.

Business sponsorship was also defined by the experts as the most important source of funds for the party system in general. This is reflected in the column labeled as "average" which gives a mean distribution of expert opinions for all the parties included in Table 7.4. More than forty percent of experts named business sponsorship as the most important source of finance for the party system. The figure becomes even larger if one takes into account donations from party members who are business leaders. Overall, around sixty percent of experts named business contributions as the main source of party finance in Moldova.

The next largest percentage of experts named foreign donations as the most important source of finance for the party system. This is despite the fact that official regulations prohibit financing from abroad. Foreign donations were identified by a varying number of experts as the first most important source of finance in the case of three parties: the Social Liberal Party (SLP), Bloc of *Patria-Rodina-Ravnopravie* (BPRR) and the CDPP. While two of these parties represent the political right with a pro-Western orientation (for example, the SLP and the CDPP), the third one, the BPRR, is a bloc of pro-Russian leftist political organizations which are in the

---

16 This survey was conducted by the European Centre for Minority Issues in 2006 and drew on two types of respondents: mid-level party functionaries and members of the expert community. Party functionaries from each of the main parties were interviewed countrywide. Parties that received more than two percent of the vote in the 2005 parliamentary elections were included in the survey. Members of expert community were selected on the basis of their expertise in covering party politics. Experts represented leading Moldovan academic, policy and mass media institutions. Unlike surveys of public opinion, surveys of party functionaries and experts rely on a relatively small number of respondents. Cognitive skills of this type of respondents are generally considered to be a mitigating factor against error usually associated with mass surveys. For example, a frequently cited article on expert judgments of party position is based on an average of eight expert ratings per country. See, Jon Huber, and Ronald Inglehart. 1995. "Expert Interpretations of Party Space and Party Locations in 42 Societies." *Party Politics* 1: 73–111.

Table 7.4 Expert estimates of the most important sources of party finance

	PCRM		POMA		CDPP		DPM		SLP		SDPM		BPRR		Average	
	1	2	1	2	1	2	1	2	1	2	1	2	1	2	1	2
Membership fees		30[1]		11.1								22.2	10	11.1	1.4	10.6
Donations from party members	10	10	10	22.2	10		10	44.4	10	11.1	40	33.3	20	11.1	15.7	18.9
Foreign grants for non-partisan political projects					20		10		20	22.2			10	22.2	8.6	6.3
Contributions of candidates for a place on party's electoral lists		20	10	44.4		11.1	10	33.3			10	11.1			4.3	17.1
Business sponsorship	80		80	22.2	10	33.3	70			33.3	50	33.3		22.2	41.4	22.0
Publishing activities					30	11.1									4.3	1.6
Budget allocation for parliamentary faction	10	20													1.4	2.9
Foreign donations					30	44.4		33.3	70	33.3			60	33.3	22.9	20.6
State administrative resources		10														1.4
Total (%)	100	100	100	100	100	100	100	100	100	100	100	100	100	100	100	100

[1] The distribution of expert opinions in percentages.

Source: European Centre for Minority Issues Survey. Chisinau, February 2006 (N=10).

Notes: Calculations are based on a different number of expert responses to the question about the first and the second most important source for all parties, except the PCRM. This is due to the fact that one of the experts chose not to name the second most important source of finance for any of the parties except the PCRM. 1-The first most important source of finance; 2-the second most important source of finance PCRM–Party of Communists of the Republic of Moldova; POMA–Party Our Moldova Alliance; CDPP–Christian Democratic People's Party; DPM–Democratic Party of Moldova; SLP–Social Liberal Party; SDPM–Social Democratic Party of Moldova; BPRR–Bloc Patria-Rodina-Ravnopravie.

process of merging into a single party.[17] The fact that parties of opposite political orientations rely on foreign financing suggests that the party system's dependence on external funding has a wide scope. The role of foreign financing becomes even more significant if one includes the implementation of projects using foreign grants in this category. These two sources of funding, business sponsorship and foreign financing, also proved to be highly important in expert responses to the question about the second most important source of finance for the party system. Although expert opinions were more divided with respect to this question, business sponsorship and foreign financing were the two categories that were most frequently named by the experts in answering the question about the second most important source of finance (data in the last column of Table 7.4).

It is also important to note that a survey question about the most important sources of party finance included an option of adding additional sources if an expert believed some key sources were missing from the proposed list. The only additional source added by the experts was "state administrative resources" (the last item listed in Table 7.4). State administrative resources are frequently used to describe practices of using the state administrative apparatus and government funds for the purpose of securing an electoral advantage. Not surprisingly, this source was named to be important in the case of the ruling PCRM. The survey also polled party functionaries on the issue of funding sources. The functionaries of the main parties were presented with the same list of potential sources of funding as the experts. In the case of party functionaries, however, a closed-list form of question was used and a different structure of answer options was employed. The respondents were asked to rank the importance of each source of financing for their party. The results are presented in Table 7.5.

As the last column of this table indicates, donations from party members received the highest score in terms of importance for the party system in general. Membership fees and foreign grants were rated by party functionaries as the second and the third most important source of party finance. Business sponsorship and foreign donations were rated only as moderately important sources of finance for the party system. Payments for a place on a party list were rated as the least important source of finance.

These results, which suggest a somewhat different picture of party finance from the one presented by the experts, should be viewed with a certain degree of caution. It is likely that party functionaries in their responses about the sources of their party's finance tried to construct a positive image of their political organization. As highly sophisticated agents of their parties, they could have tried to downplay the importance of those sources of party finance which are considered unappealing and highlighted those that are traditionally associated with a mass party model such as membership fees and party member donations.

While taking this potential bias into consideration, the results of this survey are still of interest because of the variation in the responses about the importance of individual sources of finance across parties. Membership fees, for example, were rated as a much more important source of party finance by PCRM functionaries

---

17 These parties participated in the Bloc of *Patria-Rodina-Ravnopravie* in the elections for the position of Chisinau mayor held in 2005 and in the general local elections in 2007.

Table 7.5   Importance of sources of party finance: Party functionary responses

	PCRM	POMA	CDPP	DPM	SLP	SDPM	BPRR	Average
Membership fees	9.3	5.6	5.5	5.3	5.3	6.3	5.9	6.2
Donations from party members	6.7	8.5	7.3	5.5	7	7	8.2	7.2
Foreign grants for non-partisan political projects	2.8	7.3	7.5	7.2	8.6	6.3	2.1	6.0
Contributions of candidates for a place on party's electoral lists	1.3	5.3	2.6	4.5	3.9	3.6	2.3	3.4
Business sponsorship	4.5	6.1	7.3	5.5	5.9	4.9	5	5.6
Publishing activities	6.1	5.7	8.3	5.3	4.7	6.1	3.4	5.7
Budget allocation for parliamentary faction	3.5	5.7	5.1	4.8	4.3	3.1	3.2	4.2
Foreign donations	2.3	5.3	7	4.3	6.2	4.3	1.2	4.4

Source: European Centre for Minority Issues Survey. Chisinau, February 2006 (N=101).

Notes: Ten-point Likert-type scale: 1–not important; 10–very important. PCRM–Party of Communists of the Republic of Moldova; POMA–Party Our Moldova Alliance; CDPP–Christian Democratic People's Party; DPM–Democratic Party of Moldova; SLP–Social Liberal Party; SDPM–Social Democratic Party of Moldova; BPRR–Bloc Patria-Rodina-Ravnopravie.

than by respondents from other parties. The Communists, of course, have a strong tradition of collecting membership fees. PCRM regulations ask party members to donate two percent of their monthly income. Other Moldovan parties require a much more modest monthly sum, usually about one to five MDL. One could assume that sums obtained in this way constitute a considerable part of the party budget. At the same time, even the PCRM is not a mass-based party. It has only about 20,000 members, and sums obtained from membership fees are unlikely to cover even basic administrative expenses such as the maintenance of the party's numerous offices. Unlike membership fees, donations of party members received a score that was more uniformly high across parties. One way of interpreting this result is to treat it as a masked acknowledgement of the importance of business sponsorship since party donations are usually made by party members with a business background. Implementation of projects using foreign grants and direct foreign donations, with the latter being officially illegal under Moldovan legislation, were rated as important by some of the parties but not by others.

Neither the expert nor the functionary survey suggest that state funding for parliamentary factions was an important source of financing for parties other than for the ruling PCRM. Given the size of the majority that this party has enjoyed in parliament since 2001, it is somewhat surprising that party functionaries do not acknowledge that state funding of the parliamentary faction is an important source of PCRM financing. Parliamentary factions, according to parliamentary procedures, can be established by at least five MPs and only during the first ten days after the start of a new parliament's first working session. Each faction has an annual budget proportional to faction representation which can be spent according to faction needs (for example, personnel and equipment).

In general, the state funding of parliamentary factions does not have a strong influence on the behavior of faction members. This proposition is indirectly supported by the frequency with which parliamentary factions lose their members. While at the start of the parliamentary term in March 2005, every deputy had a factional affiliation, fifteen out of 101 parliamentary deputies left their factions and acquired the status of an unaffiliated deputy by the middle of 2007. Most of the departures were motivated by serious policy disagreements. The prospect of losing some financial benefits associated with membership in a faction does not seem to constrain the behavior of individual politicians when policy disagreements between them and their faction emerge.

Although business sponsorship in its direct and indirect (through party member donations) forms emerged as a factor that is critically important for party finance, it is incorrect to conceptualize the main Moldovan parties as being controlled by oligarchs or captured by business groups. There is a certain degree of autonomy between the political and the economic spheres that makes parties more than just an extension of business groups. This autonomy is, to a significant extent, a product of institutional rules that structure the political process. PR rules and the party leadership's control over nomination procedures led very early in the post-communist transition to parties holding a virtual monopoly over who enters the political process. Parties thus emerged as independent political actors who controlled recruitment in general and cabinet formation in particular prior to the consolidation of significant financial resources in the hands of private business persons by the late 1990s. This allowed parties to negotiate with the emerging business interest groups from a position of relative strength and to secure, as a rule, financing from more than one business source. Relationships between parties and businesses can thus be better described as contractual and mutually dependent.

The danger of state capture by a party, which is another issue that is frequently cited as a potential risk for transitional societies, has been largely avoided in Moldova. The major test came with the arrival of the PCRM in 2001. This party, which held a constitutional majority during the 2001–2005 period, has tried to bias the rules of the game in its favor by pursuing policies such as establishing a high level of government control over state media, politicizing the law enforcement apparatus and pressing criminal charges against opposition leaders. However, the Party refrained from a full overhaul of democratic rules and procedures. As the survey data earlier cited indicates, opposition parties continue to enjoy the financial support of private businesses. This is in contrast to other countries in the region (for example, Belarus) which have always actively sought to deny the opposition access to sources of private funding. Election monitoring reports also note that Moldovan opposition parties continue to have a fair amount of access to state media during campaigns and between election periods. They have also recently managed to acquire the majority of seats on the CEC and have other means of ensuring that their participation in the electoral process is effective. All this has led to the preservation of a competitive party system throughout Moldova's entire post-communist period which is in marked contrast to the experience of other former Soviet republics.

Conclusions

The party finance model created in Moldova has had a significant effect on the development of the party system. While party finance provisions *per se* cannot account for patterns of party system stability, they shape the internal organization and the recruitment strategies of Moldovan parties. In terms of internal organization, business donors have a greater say in party internal decision-making than party functionaries or party activists. In terms of recruitment, efforts to attract business representatives tend to be more highly valued by parties than efforts to recruit new activists or build a large base of rank-and-file members. The arrival or the departure from the party ranks of even a single important business person often has serious implications for party finance and for the distribution of decision-making authority inside the party.

While some of the developments in the Moldovan party system resemble patterns found in the Western European transition from a mass party to a professional or a cadre party system model, Moldovan parties have yet to become professional or cadre parties. There is little evidence that Moldovan party functionaries have become a distinct professional category that have significant resources at their disposal or a major say in determining party policies. The absence of public finance for parties, which is one of the key features of the Moldovan finance model, makes parties highly dependent on business and foreign financing. This dependence creates a number of risks for the party system in terms of fostering clientelistic rather than programmic linkages with the constituency and making political processes vulnerable to outside pressures. These risks, however, are mitigated by the nature of the electoral system that has been in place since the early 1990s and by such features of the party finance model as expenditure limits on electronic and print advertisements which tend to be the most expensive forms of campaign advertisement across political systems. The recent legislative initiatives in the form of draft legal provisions that advocate the introduction of public financing for parties also indicates that these risks are well-understood by party system actors. The passage of these drafts, which might prove to be politically unpopular, signify the willingness of parties to address these issues and lessen the risks of parties becoming more focused on catering to their business and foreign sponsors than on delivering public goods.

Chapter 8

Bulgaria:
Three Finance Regimes and Their
Implications

Tatiana Kostadinova

After the November 1989 collapse of the Zhivkov regime, multiple parties emerged in Bulgaria claiming representation of various group interests. Since then, the development of a multi-party system has been facilitated by the introduction of a proportional representation (PR) electoral system which enhanced electoral competition and encouraged newcomers. At present, there are over three hundred registered parties in the country. Only a few of them, however, have consistently won seats in parliament and many have not been politically active for years. Aside from the electoral system, another explanation that may cast light on how the party system in Bulgaria evolved in the last fifteen years can be drawn from arguments about the importance of party finance.[1] Among the various characteristics of a funding regime, the origin of the money supporting organizational campaigns is especially relevant to party development. Some would expect that public funding minimizes party dependence on large donors which enables parties to better serve the broader public interest. Skeptics argue, however, that even if public finance is available, party leaders continue to compete for additional funds which can be extracted from the corporate sector.[2] Therefore, regulation becomes important to set limits on both the amounts raised for and the sums spent in election campaigns. The above perspectives propose two mechanisms of state engagement: First, public money may (or may not) be made available to parties as private associations which provide a public service. Second, national legislation establishes (or may not) ceilings for the flow of money in and out of party coffers. These two instruments are combined to create a regime of public finance that is then expected to influence party organizational development and electoral fortunes.

1   Ingrid van Biezen, and Petr Kopecky. 2001. "On the Predominance of State Money: Reassessing Party Financing in the New Democracies of Southern and Eastern Europe." *Perspectives on European Politics and Society* 2, p. 401; Michael Pinto-Duschinsky. 2002. "Financing Politics: A Global View." *Journal of Democracy* 13, p. 69; Marcin Walecki. 2005. "Political Money and Corruption." IFES Political Finance White Paper Series.
2   Michael Pinto-Duschinsky, "Financing Politics"; Jānis Ikstens, Daniel Smilov, and Marcin Walecki. 2001. "Party and Campaign Funding in Eastern Europe: A Study of 18 Member Countries of the ACEEEO." Paper presented at the ACEEEO Conference. Brijuni, Croatia.

After 1989, a finance system began to emerge in Bulgaria which introduced public subsidies for the main parties. For this reason, observers have characterized the Bulgarian funding arrangements as "egalitarian."[3] While the choice of public finance has not met serious opposition from society, public opinion polls consistently show increasing disappointment among voters who blame party leaders for corruption and for a disregard of the interests of their constituents. This chapter addresses the problem of party financing in Bulgaria by analyzing the sources and the consequences of existing institutional instruments. The first section discusses the electoral system and the main actors in Bulgarian parliamentary elections in the last fifteen years. Then, I describe the specifics of public financing in Bulgaria by focusing on how provisions on sources of finance and conditions for spending have changed in a series of legislative acts. In this section, I distinguish and assess the institutional traits of three distinct regimes. Next, I evaluate patterns and trends in fundraising using data reported by parties from 2001 to 2005. The section elaborates on the consequences for party-building and party system consolidation, and I conclude with a discussion of the implications of this study.

The Electoral System and Elections

Post-communist electoral reform in Bulgaria has created two major transformations in the system of election of members of parliament (MPs). In 1990, one of the products of the national roundtable negotiations between representatives of the Communist Party and the Union of Democratic Forces (UDF) was an agreement over a new law for holding the upcoming elections for the Grand National Assembly. A change in the electoral rules was made one year later in the summer of 1991. Since then, the formula for election of MPs has remained basically intact. After long negotiations over the new electoral system in the spring of 1990, the national roundtable finally reached a compromise. Because the new Grand National Assembly was assigned to adopt a constitution for the country, the stakes were high and the confrontation over the rules was quite dramatic. The two sides of the debate had different visions about how the seats in the constituent assembly should be allocated. These contending ideas were formed not only by distinct political positions and uncertainty about the outcome of the election but also by the distribution of party resources.

The Communist Party, which in the course of the roundtable talks re-named itself the Bulgarian Socialist Party (BSP), supported a proposal for a majority-dominated system where at least seventy-five percent of the seats were allocated in single-member districts (SMDs).[4] The former communists realized that a party-labeled campaign would hurt them because the name of their party had been discredited. Therefore, competition in SMDs was perceived as a better option than running candidates on party lists in multi-member PR districts. Moreover, the former

---

3   Daniel Smilov. 2002. "Structural Corruption of Party Funding Models: Government Favoritism in Bulgaria and Russia." In *Political Corruption in Transition: A Skeptic's Handbook*, ed. Stephen Kotkin, and Andras Sajo. Budapest: CEU Press, p. 327.

4   *The Round Table (Kruglata Masa)*, stenographic notes. Sofia: Dr Zhelyu Zhelev Foundation, N. d. pp. 402–404.

Communist Party was in a position to nominate SMD candidates who would not necessarily be closely connected with the Party, including well-known intellectuals, experts and even dissidents who had opposed the Zhivkov regime in the past but remained committed to the ideas of socialism.[5] Finally, the BSP was the one party in Bulgaria that had the resources to run individual candidates in districts all over the country. Majoritarian contests would have given the party a significant advantage *vis-à-vis* the other parties which were building structures and lacked basic equipment and staff. In the rare instances where the BSP opponents had their own newspapers, they had a limited circulation.

In the camp of the opposition, the leaders of the UDF were divided over the issue of electoral reform. The small parties within the Union preferred pure PR for good reasons. Running an ideological, anti-communist party-labeled campaign was perceived as advantageous. Individual-centered competition was also not preferred because opposition leaders were not yet well-known to the public. Some of them had just recently been released from prison. Furthermore, the young parties did not have the organizational network, the resources, personnel and media access to run local campaigns. The older parties within the UDF, such as the Democratic Party and the Radical Democrats, were not opposed to SMD elections as they relied on their pre-communist past. In the end, the leaders of the UDF managed to unify the opposition around a common position of proportional rules and multi-member districts.

The roundtable decided to introduce a mixed electoral system in Bulgaria. The law provided for an even mixture of majoritarian and proportional seats with 200 seats elected in SMDs through majority run-off and 200 seats allocated in twenty-eight multi-member districts through party lists. A four percent threshold was installed in the PR part to reduce parliamentary fragmentation and facilitate the consolidation of the emerging multi-party system. By combining these two methods of election, the mixed system of 1990 allowed for both individual candidates and party-list candidates to run in the contest. In the SMDs, independents and party-nominated individuals competed but the latter, using party resources, prevailed. Not surprisingly, the PR races were dominated by parties—their campaigns were organized by the central leadership with themes promoting democratic reform and re-discovering the communist past. While the BSP had to carefully choose and rank candidates in order to avoid association with the crimes of the Zhivkov regime, the opposition faced different challenges. The UDF had no time to prepare for the election, and as a consequence, the nomination process was chaotic.

The roundtable also agreed upon the first law on political organizations, the 1990 "Political Parties Act" which was promulgated before the campaign for the June elections. The main role of this legislation was to legitimize the formation of non-communist parties and to establish a legal basis for the emerging multi-party system. With several amendments, the 1990 "Political Parties Act" remained in force until

---

5   There is evidence that the BSP leadership seriously considered the idea of running independent candidates. In a speech given to the Congress of the Party in February 1990, Alexander Lilov, soon to become the Party's first secretary, spoke about the adequacy of such a nomination strategy, see Tatiana Kostadinova. 2000. *Mixed Electoral Systems: Determinants and Political Consequences*. PhD Dissertation. (Florida State University).

2001, much longer than its engineers envisaged. In July 1991 before its dissolution, the Grand National Assembly adopted a new constitution and a new electoral law. The decision to switch to pure PR was affected by the unfolding of the transitional process and the development of the party system in particular. By the summer of 1991, the BSP had suffered a significant withdrawal of party members, further decline in public support due to a disclosure of human rights violations committed by the communist regime and a weakening of the party's previous institutional and financial strength. Massive demonstrations in the streets of Sofia had led to opposition demands for the reburial of Georgi Dimitrov and the closure of the Mausoleum, and forced President Petar Mladenov, former foreign minister under Zhivkov and leader of the BSP, to resign the presidency. The Socialists were not certain how many votes they would be able to receive in the fall elections. For many BSP members, competing in SMDs seemed too risky, and much of the opposition also insisted on pure PR. However, serious splits over the adoption of the new constitution deepened within the UDF. The Bulgarian Social Democratic Party, the Green Party, the Liberals and part of the Bulgarian Agrarian Union-Nikola Petkov left the Union. There was uncertainty about the votes each of these parties would receive, and therefore, they all opted for proportionality.

The new election law of 1991 established a closed-list, pure PR system where 240 parliamentary seats are allocated in thirty-one electoral districts. The previous provision for a four percent nationwide threshold of representation was retained. Parties became the central players in the electoral game. Party leaders were offered the role of gate-keepers who would exercise total control over the nomination process and hence, the distribution of party resources for the campaign. While nomination procedures remained generally the same, the rules for the registration of parties and candidates to run in elections to the National Assembly underwent some changes. In general, parties and coalitions of parties registered with the courts have been given a central role in nominating candidates for parliamentary seats. Independents have rarely run (only if nominated by initiative committees and if they managed to gather a certain number of voter signatures). This voter signature requirement evolved over time from 500 in 1990 to between 1,100 and 2,000 in 2005 (depending on the size of the electoral district). The issue of monetary deposits taken from election participants upon registration has been raised on different occasions but until the last election in 2005, it failed to gather sufficient political support. The current election law requires that in order to register candidates in parliamentary elections, parties need to make no-interest deposits into an account within the Bulgarian National Bank. The amounts vary from 5,000 leva ($3,185) for initiative committees nominating independent candidates to 20,000 leva ($12,740) for single parties and 40,000 leva ($25,480) for coalitions.[6]

---

6   "Law on the Election of People's Representatives." 2005, available (in Bulgarian) at: http://www.bta.bg/site/izbori2005 (accessed 12 November 2006).

The Campaign Finance Model

The first rules of party campaign finance in Bulgaria were drafted in 1990, and since then, have undergone two major changes in 2001 and in 2005. The initial model came as a result of the national roundtable talks between the BSP and the UDF. As temporary as it might have been intended to be, those rules governed the campaign finance process for over a decade. The 2001 "Law on Political Parties" had been expected to correct for the vagueness and the deficiencies of the initial regulations, but it failed to deliver. Four years later, a new law was passed aimed at facilitating greater transparency and accountability. Table 8.1 summarizes the main characteristics of the three party finance regimes in Bulgaria.

The "Political Parties Act" of 1990 provides for four main sources of party finance: Membership fees, donations and inheritance, business activity and the state budget.[7] According to the law, parties in Bulgaria were not allowed to receive "aid, donations and testaments from foreign states and organizations, as well as from anonymous sources." At the same time, the legislation allowed for donations from individual citizens from foreign countries of up to 380 leva ($500) and for group contributions up to 1,520 leva ($2,000). The legislation further restrained parties from receiving multiple donations from the same foreign individuals or groups. In addition, parties in Bulgaria were not allowed to receive financing from "enterprises, offices, and organizations." It was believed at the time that most of those restrictions, especially those related to contributions from abroad, were imposed by the incumbent BSP to hurt the opposition as the UDF was expected to benefit the most from foreign aid.

The rather incomplete 1990 regulation of party financing was replaced in 2001 by a new law on parties which introduced more specific rules about property, incomes and finance mechanisms. In some ways, this law was more liberal than the preceding one. It allowed for anonymous donations, if amounts did not exceed twenty-five percent of the annual state subsidy allocated to a party and for parties who were not eligible for support from the state budget, up to twenty-five percent of the smallest annual party subsidy. Donations were restricted to a maximum of 30,000 leva ($13,732) from individuals or legal entities, and enterprises with fifty percent or more state participation were not allowed to donate to parties. Donations from foreign governments and foreign organizations were also forbidden.

The 2001 law met severe criticism for allowing too much financial freedom to parties seeking donations. Soon after its introduction and after the coming of the National Movement Simeon II (NMSII) to power, drafts for a new law were submitted for consideration to the National Assembly. A third law was passed in late 2004, vetoed by the president, and passed again by parliament in the spring of 2005. The new legislation prohibited anonymous donations of any kind, and specified that donations from individuals should not exceed 10,000 leva ($6,370). The 2005 law further prohibited party financing from religious institutions and from the gaming industry.

---

7 "Political Parties Act." 1990. Republic of Bulgaria, National Assembly, available at: http://www2.essex.ac.uk/elect/electjp/bg_pp19098.htm (accessed 24 September 2005).

Table 8.1   Rules on party financing in Bulgaria, 1990–2005

Laws on Parties			
Indicators	**1990**	**2001**	**2005**
Donations			
Individual	no limit	up to BGL 30,000	up to BGL 10,000
Corporate	no limit	up to BGL 30,000	up to BGL 30,000
Foreign countries	No	No	No
Foreign firms	No	No for state firms	No
Foreign citizens	up to $500 individually	up to BGL 30,000[1]	up to BGL 10,000[1] & $2,000 for groups
Firms w/ foreign share	–	–	–
State firms	No	No	No
Firms w/ state participation	No	up to 50% state part	up to 5% state part
Anonymous	No	up to 25% of annual state subsidy	No
State subsidy	No	Yes	Yes
Parliamentary parties	–	basis: #MPs	basis: #MPs
Parties w/ over 1% vote	–	basis: votes	basis: votes
Public disclosure	Yes, but not well specified	Yes	Yes
Sanctions for no reporting	No	loss of subsidy	loss of subsidy fees
Campaign spending limits	No	BGL 1,000,000[2]	BGL 1,000,000[2]
		BGL 2,000,000[3]	BGL 2,000,000[3]
		BGL 200,000[4]	BGL 200,000[4]

[1] Not for election campaigns.
[2] For parties.
[3] For coalitions.
[4] For initiative committees nominating individual candidates.

Sources: Election laws 1990, 1991, 2001, and 2005; "Political Parties Act" 1990, and laws on political parties 2001 and 2005.

On the eve of the first multi-party competitive elections in 1990, party access to state resources was very unequal. The incumbent Communist Party had at its disposal offices, equipment, state paid apparatus and unlimited access to the media. The "Political Parties Act" of 1990 established that subsidies from the state budget could be used as one source of financial support for party activities. However, the amount of public financing which was not well-specified was available mainly for campaigning. Throughout the 1990s, parties received funding in the form of loans from the state with preferential terms if they ran candidates in the elections (that is, interest-free loans). Those parties which failed to win seats in the parliament were supposed to return the borrowed money. This condition in practice gave an advantage to parliamentary parties.[8] Many parties which did not cross the four percent threshold but had taken state loans failed to re-pay the loans.

The shortcoming of this system soon became obvious: The size of state funding was not specified by the law, and funds would become available too late in the electoral process. In 1991, funds were not released until eleven days before the election, and parties had to rely on their own sources for the first phase of the electoral campaign. This imposed a burden on parties whose actions had already been constrained by the 2,000 leva ($111) limit on individual donations and the prohibition on campaign donations from abroad. In this situation, one solution found by party leaders was to start foundations which would get financing from abroad to organize civic educational activities supporting party electoral campaigns.[9]

A serious attempt to regulate public funding for parties in Bulgaria was made with the 2001 law which for the first time defined in more detail the mechanism of state support. This legislative act specifies public funding for party functions in general, not exclusively for election campaigns. According to its provisions, parliamentary parties (that is, parties with over four percent voter support) become eligible for state funding which is distributed on the basis of party seats.[10] The amounts are determined from the budget annually, and parties receive them in four installments throughout the year. Parties which remain out-of-parliament but won at least one percent of the total valid votes in the preceding election are also eligible for a state subsidy. The new 2005 "Law on Political Parties" retains these provisions in general but also specifies the amount of support (for one vote received in the last election, a party receives funds equal to one percent of the minimum wage).[11]

During election campaigns, parties have been provided with free air time on the national radio and television depending on their parliamentary representation. Equal access was given only for the first election in 1990, as agreed to at the national roundtable talks, including the opportunity to present their platforms at the beginning

---

8   For example, Decision 317 of the Council of Ministers, passed on 16 September 1991, specified the amount for gratuitous allocation from the state budget at 7,200,000 leva ($400,000). Half of it was available for immediate distribution to parties which had received more than 50,000 votes in the 1990 elections to the Grand National Assembly. In practice, those were parliamentary parties. The other participants were presented with the option for short-term, interest-rate loans up to 300,000 leva ($16,667) for a party or coalition. The total allowable amount that a party could obtain gratuitously from the state budget was calculated by the formula number of seats won multiplied by 30,000 leva ($1,667). See, *The 13 October 1991 Legislative & Municipal Elections in Bulgaria*. 1992. Washington, DC: National Democratic Institute for International Affairs, p. 45.

9   Ibid., p. 46.

10   "Law on Political Parties." 2001, available at: http://www.paragraf2.com/pravo/ zakoni/otm/16474.html (accessed 30 September 2005).

11   "Law on Political Parties." 2005, available at: http://www.paragraf2.com/pravo/ zakoni/zakoni-d/3919.html (accessed 5 November 2006).

and the end of the campaign. After that, time for thematic debates and statements was also available but on a commercial basis. Participation in debates broadcast by the Bulgarian National State Television and the Bulgarian National Radio was regulated according to party representation in the National Assembly.[12] In addition, parliamentary parties and coalitions were given the opportunity to participate in television and radio debates more often and were offered more time to present their positions than non-parliamentary parties.[13] Television time for advertisements has also been available for purchase at non-market rates.

Spending on electoral campaigns has been regulated by clauses in the laws for parliamentary elections. In 1990, total campaign spending was constrained to 20,000 leva ($26,316) per candidate, and that amount was changed in 1991 to 30,000 leva ($1,667). Since 2001, the campaign financing ceiling has been set to one million leva ($457,730) for parties and two million for coalitions. The 1990 law provided that by the end of March every year, parties should submit their written reports to an expert commission. The law specifies that those reports should provide information about the size and the sources of party income and outlays from the preceding year. The reports must be published in the *State Gazette*. A similar document from each party was also to be submitted no later than two weeks prior to each election.[14] In the absence of control mechanisms, however, compliance remained weak. Observers note that because finance reporting was only recommended and not enforced, some parties only submitted incomplete, if any, reports.[15]

Some requirements for public reporting were introduced first in the 2001 legislation. Under this law, parties are required to submit financial reports to the National Audit Office (NAO) by 15 March each year. Since then, reports have been made available to the public through Internet (www.bulnao.government.bg). Within a month after the election, parties must also submit reports on funds raised and spent during the campaign. This requirement was further tightened in the new 2005 election law, and now parties are required to report on their campaign related incomes and expenses within five days after registration with the Central Election Commission (CEC).[16]

Enforcement procedures in the respective legislation acts have been rather vague and lacking "teeth" to ensure proper implementation. For example, according to the 1990 legislation, "a permanent parliamentary and public body with the National Assembly" was supposed to monitor and control acquisition and management of

---

12 *Decision on the Access to the National Mass Media during Election Campaign.* 1991, available at: http://www2.essex.ac.uk/elect/database (accessed 1 October 2005).

13 Not all non-parliamentary parties would choose to use even this limited opportunity. Another requirement for receiving free media access was that parties register lists in at least one third of the thirty-one electoral districts.

14 "Political Parties Act," Art. 21.

15 Dobrin Kanev. 2003. "Party Funding and Political Corruption in Bulgaria: The Legal Aspects." In *Political Party and Election Campaign Financing in Southeastern Europe: Avoiding Corruption and Strengthening Financial Control.* Sofia: Transparency International Bulgaria, available at: www.transparency-bg.org/publications_files/publication_2_1.pdf (accessed 9 October 2005).

16 "Law on the Election of People's Representatives," Art. 71.

party property. The legislation, however, failed to specify the composition of that body as well as the procedures in cases of non-compliance and the range of possible punishments. The 2001 law assigns powers to the NAO to control the process of party finance reporting and to check the incomes and the expenditures indicated in the submitted reports. In practice, however, the NAO controls only the deadlines and the calculations but not the validity of sources and supporting documents.

Both the 2001 and the 2005 "Laws on Political Parties" contain a section (Chapter 4) that establishes measures for financial control. The former legislation only provided for the cancellation of state funding for one year in cases where parties do not meet the deadline for the submission of their reports.[17] This measure was not considered very effective mainly because of its narrow scope (not all parties are eligible for public financial support). The current law includes several sanctions as instruments to punish non-compliance. Parties which do not submit their reports, or submit late, loose their right to a state subsidy until the next election.[18] If the NAO finds violations in the way parties managed their finances, a report should be sent to the Sofia district attorney's office. Moreover upon registration for participation in elections, parties have to submit to the CEC certifications for filed financial reports issued by the NAO. A failure to do this causes a loss of the right to run candidates in the election.

Trends in Party and Campaign Funding

A comparison across categories of income would help to establish the relative importance of the main sources of party finance. As reported in Table 8.2, contributions based on membership fees are relatively small. Party reports reveal a wide range of membership money. The average share of all revenues is about fourteen percent in 2001 and eleven percent in 2003. Slightly higher is the relative weight of fees collected by the leftist BSP and the People's Union (PU) which specify the size of payments in their statutes. For the rightist parties (the UDF and the Democrats for a Strong Bulgaria or DSB), membership fees have been less important. These different shares could be attributed to the varying number of members, different fees and most likely, different distributions across categories.

A second observation is that the two largest categories of income are donations and state subsidies. These categories combine for about eighty-four percent of parliamentary party revenues in 2005. In election years, parties have been significantly more successful in raising donations from individuals and corporations. Larger parties, especially if incumbent, received huge sums of money from donors. In 2001 while most of the donations made to the UDF came from individuals, the lion's share of the contributions made to NMSII was of corporate origin. State subsidies have been crucial for the functioning and the electoral participation of smaller parties including the PU and the Movement for Rights and Freedoms (MRF). In both 2002 and 2003, these two parties relied on money from the state which accounted for

---

17 "Law on Political Parties," 2001, Art. 28.
18 "Law on Political Parties," 2005, Art. 36.

Table 8.2   Shares of selected income and expenditure indicators by party and by year

Party/Indicator[1]	2001	2002	2003	2004	2005
BSP					
Membership	21.2	26.7	19.1	27.6	15.8
Donations	66.3	29.1	52.5	32.6	54.8[2]
State subsidy	n/a	32.7	21.5	29.6	25.1
Total income	2,663,730	2,508,135	3,733,516	2,705,198	5,432,000
Total expenses	2,633,162	2,070,324	3,496,285	2.595,533	4,872,000
UDF					
Membership	11.1	13.1	10.8	10.4	13.0
Donations	69.9	23.6	35.0	28.7	72.7
State subsidy	n/a	41.7	38.0	50.2	13.5
Total income	3,464,99	1,935,700	2,114,734	1,600,790	2,323,651
Total expenses	3,353,454	1,893,500	2,320,763	1,394086	2,315,494
MRF					
Membership	0	0	29.6	32.9	12.6
Donations	78.4	10.0	1.2	0.3	50.7
State subsidy	n/a	89.9	69.1	66.0	36.6
Total income	346,221	435,931	565,913	593,240	1,668,000
Total expenses	322,827	232,501	639,725	522,561	1,507,000
PU[3]					
Membership	53.8	16.9	22.3	17.2	10.2
Donations	44.0	6.1	17.3	6.9	2.5
State subsidy	n/a	71.9	49.2	62.2	69.0
Total income	159,544	130,475	192,126	233,366	212,725
Total expenses	159,863	126,589	194,737	266,496	203,279
NMSII					
Membership	–	0.8	6.3	4.7	7.9
Donations	–	99.2	86.0	22.5	22.5
State subsidy	–	0	7.6	72.5	62.0
Total income	–	122,794	2,143,164	2,977,182	2,486,000
Total expenses	–	57,968	1,851,928	1,346,846	2,312,000
DSB					
Membership	–	–	–	–	6.0
Donations	–	–	–	–	41.9
State subsidy	–	–	–	–	52.1
Total income	–	–	–	–	1,422,000
Total expenses	–	–	–	–	1,340,000
Filed reports w/n deadline (%)	27.8	22.3	11.4	29.8	26.1
Inflation (%)	7	6	2	6	5

[1] Membership, donations and state subsidy are percentages of total income. Total income and total expenses are in leva.
[2] Including income from fundraising events organized by the BSP.
[3] Numbers for 2005 are for the Bulgarian Agrarian People's Union–PU.

Source: Author's calculations based on party reported finances (National Audit Office of Republic of Bulgaria, Report on the Results from the Auditing of Political Parties (2001–2004) and Report for the Audit of the Financial Activities and Management of the Property of Political Parties in 2005 available at: http://www.bulnao.government.bg.

Notes: Inflation is annual, consumer prices available at: http://www.worldbank.org.

between fifty and ninety percent of all their income. In 2005, public finance helped the NMSII spend more on campaigning than it raised through private means. Taken together, the money received by parliamentary parties from membership, donations and rents almost equaled the sum allocated to them as state subsidies.

Third, there is suggestive evidence that election years have a special effect on the size of Bulgarian party finance. In three of the years in Table 8.2, elections were held for the parliament (2001 and 2005) and for local government (2003). The total income numbers show that the revenues of most parties increased in those years. More data should be analyzed to see whether donors continue to be more generous in the months before elections than in interim years. Election campaign spending has been on the rise over the last fifteen years. According to some recent publications in the press during the period between 2001 and 2005, party campaign advertising costs increased four-fold.[19] Comparable numbers for election campaign expenditures, as reported by parties, are available for only 2005. They reveal that the MRF, the NMSII and the UDF spent about a million leva ($636,943). These amounts constitute a significant portion of their total expenses which vary from forty percent (the BSP) to sixty-six percent (the MRF).[20]

There is no doubt that incumbent parties are better positioned in terms of resources than other election participants in Bulgaria. The examples of governing parties benefiting from their positions in power are numerous. Starting with the 1990 election, the BSP enjoyed a significant advantage over the UDF with regard to access to all kinds of material resources, such as money, technical equipment and office space (this despite it being compromised by the years of communist rule).[21] This advantage had an important political consequence. Many people believe, both in Bulgaria and abroad, that the victory of the BSP in the first multi-party competitive parliamentary election was pre-determined by the capacity of the incumbent party to send its message to large groups within the electorate who were not reached by the less resourceful opposition.[22]

Throughout the post-communist period, the system has awarded incumbents. First, holding a majority of parliamentary seats allowed for a larger amount of state subsidy. The second advantage of incumbency is that it provides easier access to the mass media and increases the visibility of public officials during the inter-election period. Visibility has certainly two sides, reflecting the glory of success and exposing the humiliation of failure, but Bulgarian politicians have learned how

---

19 The price of one cast vote was inflated at a higher rate (seven times) because of decreasing voter turnout. See Marina Chertova. 2005. "The Expensive Campaigns Are with the Fewest Voters" *Vsekiden* available at: http://www.vsekiden.com (accessed 25 November 2005).

20 National Audit Office, *Report for the Audit of the Financial Activities and Management of the Property of Political Parties in 2005,* No. 400001006, Sofia, available at: http://www.bulnao.government.bg (accessed 20 April 2007).

21 Observers note that current BSP ministers used state-owned vehicles including helicopters to attend campaign rallies in the countryside. See, *Report on the Parliamentary Elections in Bulgaria, June 1990.* 1990. Commission for Security and Cooperation in Europe. Washington, DC.

22 Ibid.

to take advantage of being in power. For example in the aftermath of the 1996–1997 economic and government crisis, the UDF declined to take a public subsidy to finance its campaign declaring that the party could not take money from the state in difficult times and that people were already familiar with their program and that resources should instead be focused on helping the poor.[23] At the same time, rival parties accused UDF leaders of gaining disproportionately from leading the caretaker government which was allegedly providing them with daily access to print and electronic media.

From the position of control over the executive branch, the NMSII made innovative efforts to win another legislative mandate in 2005. Financial resources were re-directed from the state budget in the form of extra-revenues which were then allocated to municipalities which NMSII mayors spent on local projects. Those "unplanned" amounts were denounced by the opposition which accused the ruling party of deliberate budgetary miscalculations in the previous year with the intent to support its electoral campaign later. The second invention was, again using the extra-revenues to finance an "election lottery" aimed at increasing the turnout, broadly expected to benefit the NMSII. While the former mechanism perhaps did assist the electoral performance of incumbents, the lottery turned out to be a big failure with the lowest post-communist turnout rate of just under fifty-four percent, and the NMSII losing seats.

Deficiencies in the 2001 "Law on Political Parties," mainly the lack of effective mechanisms for sanctioning non-compliance, hindered the achievement of a more transparent process of party financing in Bulgaria. While the punishment for non-reporting within the established deadlines is significant (losing the annual state subsidy), the implementation of this penalty has been too weak in the absence of an independent agency to enforce it. Many parties have not met the deadline to submit their statements, and even a larger number have never filed a statement. In its 2003 yearly documents, the NAO points at a troubling trend with regard to the rate of party compliance with the requirement to report finances. Between 2001 and 2005, the relative number of parties submitting reports within the established deadlines never reached even thirty percent (see Table 8.2). The absence of reliable information and the resistance of party leaders to disclose organizational finances just added to the already existing high level of mistrust among the population towards parties as being corrupt and representing private rather than societal interests.

By allowing for some anonymous donations, the 2001 legislation opened the door to the illegal funding of party activities and to corruption. The use of anonymous donations has been controversial. In early 2001, President Stoyanov vetoed the draft bill passed by the Assembly, arguing that the term "anonymous" was not in use in the Bulgarian constitutional practices.[24] However, the MPs over-rode the veto. It took another four years for the parliament to prohibit anonymous donations. Another institutional feature that facilitated corruption was the lack of an effective

---

23 *Report on Bulgaria's Parliamentary Election: Veliko Turnovo, Gabrovo, and Surrounding Environs, 19 April 1997.* 1997. Commission for Security and Co-operation in Europe. Washington, DC.

24 "Bulgaria: Constitutional Watch." 2001. *East European Constitutional Review* 10.

regulatory measure to control and to sanction irregular foreign donations. The observer delegation of the Organization for Security and Co-operation in Europe sent to monitor the 1997 parliamentary elections reported accusations that several parties had received larger amounts of foreign donations than legally allowed.[25]

Development of Parties and the Party System

Pure proportional rules for the election of MPs introduce a party-centered nomination and competition process, and the adoption of PR in Bulgaria should be assessed from this perspective. The closed-list version of the system facilitated the formation of centralized organizations in which the influence of rank-and-file members declined progressively. Central party leaderships became responsible for raising candidacies, ranking names on district lists and financing the campaign process. Independent candidates have been disadvantaged by the lack of sufficient resources to compete against the emerging strong party campaign machines. As argued in previous research, assuring regular party support strengthens the parties which run in elections governed by a party-centered system.[26] For some of the smaller parties such as the PU, the state subsidy has been a major source of financial support. Providing Bulgarian parties with public finance only consolidated the dominant role already assigned to them and their leaderships through the electoral system.

The 2001 transition towards annual subsidies for parties which won more than one percent of the vote in parliamentary elections may have multiple consequences for the consolidation of the party system. There are good reasons to believe that the eligibility requirement for public finance has an independent effect on the number of parties and coalitions running in elections (different from what one would expect as a result from the electoral system alone). Two effective thresholds emerge: A four percent hurdle to win parliamentary seats (electoral), and a one percent minimum requirement to receive a state subsidy (financial). To win seats, office-seeking parties will either prefer to run alone or in coalition to surpass the higher threshold. The goal of smaller parties is to achieve a share of public funding in order to survive.[27] In theory, this latter type of incentive should have affected the size of the party system which emerged between 1990 and 2001 by pushing it towards more fractionalization. However in the absence of legal provisions for regular state support in the 1990s, the political arena was dominated by two big parties, the BSP and the UDF, and a third smaller ethnic-based party, the MRF. Benefiting from parliamentary representation since the first post-communist elections, those parties receive election campaign financing from the state while others had to return loans if they did not succeed. This situation changed somewhat after annual subsidies were introduced for parties winning more than one percent of the vote. The institutional change coincided with the appearance of an external player to the system, Simeon II (see Table 8.3).

---

25 *Report on Bulgaria's Parliamentary Election: Veliko Turnovo, Gabrovo, and Surrounding Environs, 19 April 1997*, p. 5.

26 Ikstens et al., "Party and Campaign Funding."

27 Staying in the game, hoping for future invitations to run in coalitions with "big" parties or winning offices in local government elections.

Table 8.3   **Electoral gains of main Bulgarian parties at parliamentary elections, 1990–2005 (% of total)**

Party	1990[1]	1991	1994	1997	2001	2005
BSP						
% vote	47.2	33.1	43.5	22.0	17.1	31.0
% seats	52.3	44.2	52.1	24.2	20.0	34.2
UDF						
% vote	36.2	34.4	24.2	52.3[2]	18.2[2]	7.7[3]
% seats	36.0	45.8	28.8	51.3	16.3	8.3
MRF						
% vote	6.0	7.6	5.4	7.6[4]	7.5[5]	12.7
% seats	5.8	10.0	6.3	7.9	8.8	14.2
PU						
% vote	–	–	6.5	[2]	[2]	5.2[6]
% seats	–	–	7.5	5.8	5.0	5.4
BE						
% vote	–	–	–	5.5	1.0	–
% seats	–	–	–	5.8	0.0	–
BBB						
% vote	–	1.3	4.7	4.9	–	–
% seats	–	0.0	5.4	5.0	–	–
NMSII						
% vote	–	–	–	–	42.7[7]	19.9
% seats	–	–	–	–	50.0	22.1
DSB						
% vote	–	–	–	–	–	6.5
% seats	–	–	–	–	–	7.1
ATAKA						
% vote	–	–	–	–	–	8.2
% seats	–	–	–	–	–	8.8
# running part.	41	38	48	39	54	22
# part. 1%+	n/a	10	10	7	7	10
# elected part.	7	3	5	5	4	7
eff.# parl.part.	2.40	2.41	2.73	2.52	2.92	4.81

[1] In the 1990 election, half of the mandates were allocated in single-member districts and half on proportional representation lists.
[2] The vote total for the UDF and the PU which in 1997 and 2001 ran in a coalition.
[3] In coalition with the Democratic Party, the St. George's Day Movement and others.
[4] In coalition with the Bulgarian Agrarian Union Nikola Petkov, the Green Party, Party of the Democratic Center, the Union New Choice and Federation Kingdom Bulgaria.
[5] In coalition with the Liberal Union and Euroroma.
[6] In coalition with the Party of Free Democrats and the Internal Macedonian Revolutionary Organization.
[7] In coalition with the Bulgarian Women's Party and the Movement for National Revival.

Source: Parties and elections available at: http://www.parties-and-elections.de/bulgaria.html (accessed 1 October 2005).

Despite concerns that public finance may hinder party competition and lead to "cartelization," it has not been impossible for newcomers to enter the political system and even win a significant number of seats. In 2001, Simeon II's Movement won half the seats in parliament and formed a governing cabinet. More recently a new organization, the Citizens for European Development of Bulgaria, received a plurality of the vote in the first country elections for representatives to the European parliament. In both cases, organizations with no state funding succeeded in communicating their message to voters, and this message was a promise for a new morality in politics. At the same time, parties that were long-time recipients of subsidies, such as the BSP and especially the rightist UDF, have lost much of their electoral support.

Experts also note that the amount of the public subsidy in Bulgaria is "symbolic" and considered by parties too small so that they are tempted to accept more donations, including anonymous ones, from corporations.[28] Survey data from 2003 show that almost fifty percent of interviewed politicians thought that the financial resources allowed by the law were insufficient and that about seventy percent of the entrepreneurs knew about instances when business leaders bought political protection by offering financial support to parties.[29] The 2005 prohibition of anonymous donations and the provision for strengthened public control over party reports were intended to minimize this effect. Whether this combination of enabling (state subsidies) and controlling (abuse preventing) policy instruments is effective in making Bulgarian parties less dependent is a question with implications for the representational capacity of the entire political system.

In general, the move towards regular state subsidies has been considered a mixed success in the process of party development. On the one hand, direct public subsidies have been available not just for election campaigns but also to maintain party activities and development during inter-election years. On the other hand, state subsidies have been assessed as uncertain and insufficient, and therefore, parties cannot rely solely on those funds in order to win elections. Searching for alternative sources, party leaders have increased the demand for donations from both individuals and corporations. When in power, Bulgarian parties have allegedly used the privatization and the economic restructuring of big state enterprises such as the Bulgarian Telecommunication Company, the Bulgarian Airlines company, the metallurgy plant Kremikovzi and Bulgartabak to extract material benefits.[30] Paradoxically, those who receive subsidies are also in better positions to attract private donations.

It has become public knowledge that party elites have been financially supported by private corporate interests in improper ways. In a television interview given on the eve of the June 2005 election, the leader of MRF, Ahmed Dogan, admitted

---

28 Ikstens et al., "Party and Campaign Funding"; Kanev, "Party Funding and Political Corruption in Bulgaria."

29 Ibid.

30 Andrei Prumov. 2005. "A Samurai Sword for the Party Finances: Privatization Is a Challenge to the Cabinet Stanishev as Well." *Standar* 10 September.

that a "ring of firms" supports his organization.[31] By staying in power and deciding on privatization and the distribution of European Union pre-accession funds, the party leadership governs in favor of these firms. As a result, private interests have been favored over public interests, and serious concerns exist that Bulgarian parties are increasingly failing to express the demands of the people which they claim to represent. For many, there is a crisis of representation in Bulgaria, and the low participation rates show it. The recent strong push for electoral reform also supported by the public, however, failed with parliamentary parties withdrawing their support at the final stage of passing a new election law re-introducing a mixed system.

Conclusions

This study started with an acknowledgement that a comprehensive explanation for the formation of the party system in post-1989 Bulgaria needs to include the newly established rules for party finance of organizational activities and election campaigns. The funding system evolved in three phases, moving towards instituting annual state subsidies and more rigorous regulation on donations and reporting. In response to the changing rules, party elites had to make important decisions on how to balance income from various sources. The rules for funding, and the absence of clear regulations has had an impact on the number of parties which have survived and run in elections, and how parties raise and spend resources in the competition for power. A need for public funding was approved by the major players in the political game from the very beginning, but access to public funding has been unequal. Parliamentary parties, and especially ruling parties, have been the main beneficiaries of this system. However, donations continue to be a dominant source of financing, often not transparent, which raises serious concerns about illegal interactions and corruption. Stricter regulation of party reporting and instruments sanctioning violators have increased but proved insufficient. As the case of Bulgaria suggests, regulation may be tightened but if not enforced, citizen trust in parties as representatives of the public interest continues to decline.

---

31 "Honest and Personal, Dogan: We Have a Ring of Firms—They Finance Us, We Help Them." 2005. *Mediapool* 26 June, available at: http:www.mediapool.bg/show/ ?storyid=106410 (accessed 28 June 2005).

Chapter 9

Hungary:
Rules, Norms and Stability Undermined

Gabriella Ilonszki

In 2006 after Hungary's fifth democratic election, party and campaign finance issues became highly controversial. In the face of public discontent about the role of money in campaigning and perceived compromised legal regulations, one of the first bills introduced after the new government was formed targeted party and campaign finance. While there seemed to be general support both from the government and the opposition, at the time of this writing, the bill has not become law, and the issue is still on the legislative agenda.[1] The main argument of this chapter is that the stability of the party and the campaign finance framework in its legal and constitutional sense is in sharp contrast with its actual implementation. I argue that the implementation of public finance laws undermines not only the rules but contributes to the increasing vulnerability of the political system as has been demonstrated by developments since 2006.[2]

Within the party finance regime, one can witness the weaknesses of Hungarian democracy. Indeed, party and campaign finance issues cannot be separated from some fundamental Hungarian regime features: early party consolidation, fragile mass-elite linkages and frozen elite. Despite the existing upper-limit on campaign spending, parties spend more than allowed, and older and more established parties have a better chance to win thus leading to the view that the party system is frozen and that public finance has played a role. These finance issues also touch on the legitimacy of politicians as they have been involved in several controversial money-related campaign practices. In terms of the consolidation of the party system, the question remains whether the finance regime is a cause or an effect or both. In this chapter, Hungarian public finance regulations will be placed within a broader political perspective to show the possible connections between the political needs of parties and their legal regulation. First, I will describe the regulations and then address political explanations for the development of the Hungarian party system and conclude by noting the connection between systemic and campaign finance problems.

---

1 This law requires a two thirds majority vote in the parliament.

2 See Gabriella Ilonszki and Sándor Kurtán. 2007. "Hungary." *European Journal of Political Research* 46: 960–967.

The Political and Legal Background of the Public Finance Regime

Since the 1970s, several European countries have introduced direct state funding to parties.[3] Therefore, the experience of Hungary fits within this general European pattern. The 1989 "Law on the Working and Financing of Parties" was an outcome of the roundtable negotiations which took place in Hungary between June and September 1989 and was based particularly on the German experience. This law's regulations are still in force, and this early date for the establishment of public finance demonstrates the early political attention to party formation in Hungary. In fact, the law was the creation of the newly-born parties and the last communist-dominated parliament. Thus in Hungary, when decisions were made on public finance in the environment of the roundtable talks between the old and the new elite groups, the decision was made to borrow from the prevalent European model. No public discourse or open political debate supported the creation of a system of public finance.

Although the law was explicit in several financial (and organizational) matters, the regulations were not implemented for the simple reason that no free elections were yet held. Thus until the first elections in April and May 1990, a kind of interim financial situation prevailed: parties were subsidized according to their claimed party membership figures which allegedly was one of the reasons for the mushrooming of parties since only ten persons were required to register a party. During this interim period, some parties which soon disappeared received a larger subsidy than those that still exist. Campaign costs were also covered on a provisional basis. Despite the unclear and unfair distribution of funding, the financial support had no major impact on the election results. Things changed fast, most developments were *ad hoc*, and the public voted either as an anti-communist protest or in sympathy for those who were visible during and after the roundtable discussion.

All in all, the 1989 regulations were implemented only after the first elections. The law was explicit with respect to the direct state funding of parties, and stated that in addition to public finance, party income could include membership fees, donations both from local and foreign entities (either individuals or legal persons) and from the party's own revenue. The origin of donations was strictly determined: neither a foreign state nor a Hungarian state-owned company were allowed to donate, and the name of the legal entity or the private individual who donated more than 500,000 forints ($2,500) had to be made public in the annual financial report of the party.[4]

Parties are entitled to public finance in accordance with their national election results. The amount of the state subsidy is determined by the budget law, and the amount is divided into two parts. Twenty-five percent is divided in equal proportion among all parliamentary parties while seventy-five percent is distributed according to election results among all parties in accordance with the proportion of the vote that the party (or its candidates) received in the first round of the election. However,

---

    3   See among others for example, Arthur B. Gunlicks, ed. 1993. *Campaign and Party Finance in North America and Western Europe.* Lincoln: University of Nebraska Press; Klaus H. Nassmacher, ed. 2001. *Foundations of Democracy. Approaches to Comparative Political Finance.* Baden-Baden: Nomos Verlag.
    4   Throughout the chapter, the forint/dollar exchange rate is 200 to 1.

a party that does not reach at least one percent of the vote is not entitled to a subsidy. Thus, the parliamentary parties are entitled to public finance on two grounds: as parliamentary parties and as parties that are above the one percent threshold. The drafters of the regulations sought to create a fair balance. On the one hand, they wanted to give some preferential treatment to parliamentary parties, but they also wanted to support smaller parties (however imposing the one percent threshold limited party fragmentation). At this time, the electoral threshold was four percent (later raised to five percent). With the diminishing number of parliamentary and extra-parliamentary parties, public funds eventually were concentrated in only a few parties. The law includes an appendix with the form that parties must complete for their yearly report and make public in the national press but concrete control measures were not specified at that time.

Similar to general European practices, access to media was also regulated. The parties were provided some broadcast time in the national and regional media, and individual candidates in the local media as well. Interestingly at the time the law was passed, there was no private media in Hungary. Members of parliament (MPs) could not have foreseen the extra media burdens which would later appear in an increasingly market-oriented media environment, not to mention the rapid increase in the use of new technologies. In the public media, time and advertisement opportunities have been provided to parties ever since, and the costs of this public media access is very close to that of public finance. Thus, the state both directly and indirectly (by ensuring access to public media) contributes to parties.

Direct state funding was complemented from the start by public campaign finance. In fact, campaign finance issues are more in the forefront of political and public discussion because the importance of money and the problems of party finance become more obvious during an election year. Nevertheless, campaign finance was more modestly regulated. The campaign financial conditions are determined by the "Law on the Electoral System." This law states that each party that runs candidates is entitled to have a campaign subsidy in proportion to the number of its candidates. It is important to note that non-party candidates are also eligible for this funding. The amount provided for candidates is very small, however, and this amount in itself would not have a major impact on the campaign chances of candidates or parties. In contrast to public party finance which is regulated by the budget law on a yearly basis, the amount for campaign spending is determined by the parliament for each election. The amount of the state campaign contribution was the same in 2002 and in 2006 (one hundred million forints or approximately $500,000). Overall, each candidate gains access to about only $200.

The Three Phases of Campaign Finance Development

In this section, I shall discuss how campaign finance and party development have interacted. In the background of the static legal framework, the real campaign world substantially transformed, and some legal adjustments also took place. The first election environment in 1990 can be called the transition campaign. Dozens of parties existed, and money did not seem to matter much. The only affluent party, the post-communist Hungarian Socialist Party (MSZP), could not turn its inherited financial advantage into an electoral advantage at that time. Many volunteered as party campaign activists, particularly in the conservative umbrella party, the Hungarian Democratic Forum (MDF), which eventually won the elections and in the main party of the genuine opposition, the Alliance of Free Democrats (SZDSZ). It is claimed that in the 1990 elections, the parties remained below 100 million forints in combined campaign spending.[5] The second election campaign in 1994 was the first real one and demonstrates that more democracy requires more money. An upward spending spiral began not the least because both the governing parties and the opposition parties sought to mobilize more extensively—one in face of their diminishing popularity and the other in the hope to ascend to power for the first time under democratic conditions.

In this early period of party formation, all parties (with the exception of the successor party, the MSZP) were poor in the sense that they did not have their own property. Initially, all parties were provided public buildings to use as party offices and party headquarters. This temporary regulation was changed by the modification of the party law in 1991 when these estates became real party property and became a source for campaign spending and a major reason for later campaign-related controversy. In the face of increasing campaign costs, the parties looked for loans and mortgaged their often highly valuable former public buildings, palaces and the like hoping to return the money after an electoral victory which would provide them access to public party financing and other benefits that governing parties can enjoy in the form of patronage.

Some parties went virtually bankrupt during the 1994 campaign, and they used their property to overcome financial difficulties. Ever since then, the selling of party properties has been an issue because parties, in the case of a shortage of campaign funding, tend to turn to this part of their resources and sell them, contract them out or use them as deposits. For example in 2002, the Smallholders Party (FKGP) not only lost the elections and was eliminated from parliament but also lost its party headquarters. It is revealing that the seven parties that were in parliament at one or more point since 1990, with the exception of the MSZP, all sold or exchanged their original headquarters in an attempt to generate revenue.

These developments draw attention to the fact that the control regulations in the "Law on the Electoral System" were vague. Although the law stipulated that parties should publicize their campaign costs in the national press, no deadlines and no precise places were mentioned. These considerations became particularly serious in the environment of the first real campaign. At that time, private donations arrived in much lower proportions to parties than during and after the first elections (a sign of the loss of public confidence) and even foreign support diminished (and has remained low ever since). In face of the overspending and the lack of transparency (most parties did not fulfill the vaguely prescribed declaration requirements), a new law was enacted in 1997 to ensure oversight.

---

5 Due to lack of clear control mechanism, information about this first year of democracy is uncertain and limited. See Gábor Juhász. 2001. *Pártpénzügyek*. Budapest: Aula.

According to the 1997 law, campaign expenditures have to be declared officially in the *Magyar Közlöny* (the official national gazette) by a certain date, and the State Audit Office audits every party budget within one year. The parties also have to declare their campaign-related spending within sixty days after the elections. It was also the intention of the MPs to put upper-limits on party campaign spending. It was ruled that the upper-limit should not exceed 386 million forints ($193,000) for each party. Since the Hungarian parliament has 386 members, this means in principle that if a party runs candidates in all places, the campaign spending should not be higher than one million forints per candidate. Whenever a party or a candidate is proven to have overspent during the campaign, it is obliged to pay double the sum to the state budget (this has never occurred). Thus, the new law concentrated on control issues and did not change the method of subsidizing parties or candidates.

In the third phase of campaign developments for the 1998, the 2002 and the 2006 elections, it seems that at least the winning parliamentary parties learned how to apply financial regulations to their advantage and to spend as much as possible on the campaign without revealing all the details. Parties clearly spent more than their public finance subsidy and membership resources provided, and parties increasingly asked for credits from banks and mortgaged their property. While bank loans and mortgages are legal instruments, the intensive and extensive campaigns hint at the presence of other sources which is an increasing concern that contravenes democratic norms.

The established parties found one additional instrument to legally increase their income. Law "XLVI" passed in 2003 modified the existing party law in one crucial area. The modification regulates the creation and the working of party foundations. A party foundation is entitled to a state subsidy if the party has representatives in parliament at least throughout two terms (which serves the interest of stable parliamentary parties). The state support is quite substantial and consists of a lump sum which is twenty-five times the amount of a yearly honorarium of an MP, an eighty-five percent payment based on the combined party MP honorarium and additional funding not specified. All in all, these foundations receive an additional one billion forints ($5 million) from public money. The current head of state, when he was not yet in this post, declared this new form of funding unconstitutional on the grounds that parliamentary parties received further advantages. All the issues previously discussed lead to the question as to why the original party finance regime does not fit the system any longer.

Explanations for Change: The Electoral System and Political Transformation

While the range of campaign spending is closely related to the electoral system, more politically sensitive issues like voting behavior and the party framework also have to be examined. As for the electoral system, multiple campaign levels increase the costs of campaigning. Hungary has a mixed-member electoral system.[6] Thus, parties

---

6 For a detailed analysis of the Hungarian electoral system see, Kenneth Benoit. 2005. "Hungary: Holding Back the Tiers." In *The Politics of Electoral Systems.* ed. Michael Gallagher, and Paul Mitchell. Oxford: Oxford University Press, pp. 213–252.

focus on two dimensions: on the national party campaign and, even if on a more modest level, the local constituency campaign. Voters cast their first ballot on party lists in twenty electoral districts. In addition in 176 single-member districts (SMDs) using a majoritarian formula, parties field candidates in a similarly party-centered environment. Only those parties are entitled to create a list which are able to field a candidate in twenty-five percent of the SMDs in that region, an obstacle for smaller parties. The twenty regional lists represent different sizes, the district magnitude ranges between four and twenty-eight. On average, 6.5 mandates are distributed on each regional list.

In addition to SMD mandates and regional list mandates, a third type of mandate is created, although not by the vote. The remaining votes from the SMDs and the regional lists are added-up and transferred to national lists. At the formation of the national list, parties face a further obstacle: they can only create a national list (and thus have a chance to get a mandate with the help of the remaining votes) if they established a regional list in at least a third of the regions. This electoral system creates a stable parliamentary framework and has a majoritarian bias. Table 9.1 shows the party and the parliamentary consequences of the electoral system. It demonstrates surprising stability for a new democracy. The two big parties (for example, the MSZP and the Alliance of Young Democrats or Fidesz) have a balanced strength. Altogether, only seven parties managed to get into parliament since 1990, and the number of parliamentary parties diminished to four by 2002 and only increased to five after the 2006 elections because the Christian Democratic Peoples Party, which was in an electoral coalition with the Fidesz, chose to establish its own parliamentary faction. Also, a five percent threshold is a strong inhibiting factor on smaller parties and the fragmentation of the party system. The party profiles have also become established: the MSZP occupies the center-left, the SZDSZ the center while the other parties share the right of the political spectrum.

The exceptional stability of the electoral system does not explain the transformation of the campaign, particularly the increase in campaign costs, but an important, personal dimension of the electoral environment has changed campaigning. The local basis of candidates has broadened. While in 1990 the local political background of candidates was completely absent, by 2006, more than sixty percent of MPs also had a local political post (for example, being a mayor or a member of a local or a regional council). This has an impact on campaigning and campaign finance: local resources are available at least for the sitting candidates. This gives an advantage to the incumbent and also provides additional resources and campaign tools (for example, local media and local businesses) and from another perspective it increases campaign spending. By the fifth national election in 2006, personality had increased in importance. For example, the Hungarian parliamentary incumbency rate by 2006 was the highest among all post-communist countries (approximately seventy percent).[7] Moreover, even personal electoral continuity can be observed as

---

7   Gabriella Ilonszki, and Michael Edinger. 2007. "MPs in Post-Communist and Post-Soviet Nations: A Parliamentary Elite in the Making." *Journal of Legislative Studies* 13: 142–163.

Table 9.1   Seats in the Hungarian Parliament after the first five elections

Year Party	1990		1994		1998		2002		2006	
	N	%	N	%	N	%	N	%	N	%
MDF	**164**	**42.5**	38	9.8	**17**	**4.4**	24	6.2	11	2.8
SZDSZ	92	23.8	**69**	**17.8**	24	6.2	**20**	**5.2**	**20**	**5.2**
FKGP	**44**	**11.4**	26	6.7	**48**	**12.4**	–		–	
MSZP	33	8.5	**209**	**54.1**	134	34.7	**178**	**46.1**	**190**	**49.2**
Fidesz	21	5.4	20	5.1	**148**	**38.3**	164	42.5	141	36.5
KDNP	**21**	**5.4**	22	5.7	–	–	–	–	23	6.0
MIÉP	–	–	–	–	14	3.6	–	–	–	
Others	11	2.8	1	0.2	1	0.2	–	–	1	0.3
Total	386	100.0	386	100.0	386	100	386	100	386	100.0

MDF: Hungarian Democratic Forum, SZDSZ: Alliance of Free Democrats (since 2005 the party's name is officially SZDSZ or the Hungarian Liberal Party), FKGP: Independent Smallholders Party, MSZP: Hungarian Socialist Party, Fidesz: Alliance of Young Democrats (the party was renamed Fidesz-MPP and later still Fidesz-MPSZ or the Fidesz-Hungarian Civic Association), KDNP: Christian Democratic People's Party and MIÉP: Party of Hungarian Justice and Life.

Note: Party of the government in boldface.

candidates ran in the same constituency.[8] Safe constituencies emerged, and more recently even the phenomenon of a personal vote could be detected.[9]

The party-level campaign (often nationally orchestrated) and the constituency campaigns are inter-related in financial respects as well. Obviously, the small party or non-party candidates who are entitled to very limited public campaign funds are in a less favorable position than the candidates of larger parties that also have national party money (from public finance). Nevertheless, this situation often puts even the candidates of the large parties in a difficult situation because an expectation prevails that a proper party candidate should be able to mobilize ample financial resources on the local level or preferably even nationally. This raises two issues: first, the candidate selection process might be influenced by this consideration, and second the need for resource mobilization might necessitate the use of local public resources for party electoral purposes which contributes to a lack of transparency. By 2006, some candidates complained publicly that the party headquarters expected them to mobilize their own resources during the campaign.

The parties and their candidates depend on each other in a complex way. Of course, there are considerably many more party-dependent candidates than

---

8   András Schwarcz. 2004. "The Central Core in the Hungarian Parliament." In *Central European Parliaments: First Decade of Democratic Experience and Future Perspectives,* ed. Zdenka Mansfeldova, David M. Olson, and Petra Rakusanova. Prague: Institute of Sociology, Academy of Sciences, pp. 200–215.

9   Zsófia Papp. 2007. "Pár(t)harc. Hogyan befolyásolja az egyéni választókerületek választási eredményeit a jelölt személye?" MA thesis. Corvinus University Budapest.

non-party-dependent candidates (for example, those who have their own resources), and a candidate-dependent party is really exceptional in Hungary. Indeed, party finance in Hungary means just that—it is not candidate campaign finance. Still, we can rightly assume from different reports that parties finance their candidates in SMDs well-above the levels indicated by official provisions. On the other hand, we know that there are candidates who, due to their status in the constituency, are able to manage their campaign or even contribute to the national party campaign and income. The two levels and the overlap between the two levels makes the campaign in principle more costly and increasingly less financially transparent. Overall, it is not the electoral system but the transformation of the electoral environment in personal terms, the accumulation of mandates and its consequences that explain increasing costs.

In terms of voting, a volatile electorate or an electorate that is not mobilized could be indicators of a more costly campaign. Electoral mobilization has remained relatively stable with a slight decrease in 1998. Turnout in the first round of the elections has been consistent in the five national elections (sixty-five, sixty-nine, fifty-eight, seventy-one and sixty-eight percent). Second round turnout shows some clearer increases in electoral participation. Also, electoral volatility substantially decreased from approximately twenty-six percent in 1994 to nine percent in 2006.[10] The number of parties clearly diminished, both in the electoral and in the parliamentary arena (see Table 9.1). In addition, we can observe a decrease in the number of candidates (from 3,507 in 1990 to 2,840 in 2006). This decrease in parties and candidates clearly cannot explain the increasing costs of campaigning.

The number of candidates has decreased not only because fewer parties exist but also because the parties increasingly use the same candidate pool at every electoral level. A candidate will run in a SMD and is placed on the regional and the national list of their party as well. In principle, a candidate can run in all three elections (for example, SMD, regional party list and national list), and the candidates of the two major parties have often been placed on more than two candidate places on average (MSZP candidates from 1.6 to 1.9 places and Fidesz candidates from 2.1 to 2.3 places by 2006).[11] Overall in this electoral context, I cannot identify a logical explanation for the increasing campaign costs. More indirectly, the party framework can have an impact on campaign costs. The more extensive and confrontational the campaign, the longer and more expensive the campaign. As shown in Table 9.2, the finance regime is related to party member characteristics. Behind these numbers, three broader issues can be identified that explain why the finance regime is undermined including party system bipolarization, party organization and the frozen elite phenomenon.

---

10 Electoral volatility is the share of voters who vote for different parties in two consecutive elections see, Gergely Karácsony. 2006. "Árkok és légvárak. A választói viselkedés stabilizálódása Magyarországon." In *Parlamenti választás 2006*, ed. Gergely Karácsony. Budapest: Demokrácia Kutatások magyar Központja Alapítvány, pp. 59–104.

11 Gabriella Ilonszki and Réka Várnagy. 2007. "Vegyes választási rendszer és női képvi selet."*Politikatudományi Szemle* 16: 93–109.

Table 9.2   Income sources of the major Hungarian parties, 1991–2006

Year Party	1991		1994[1]		1997		1998		2001		2002		2006	
	MF[2]	DSF[3]	MF	DSF	MF	DSF	MF	DSF	MF	DSF	MF	DSF	MF	DSF
MSZP	2.7	11.7	2.3	26.0	2.0	51.0	1.7	48.2	3.6	73.0	3.4	72.3	3.3	55.7
Fidesz	0.8	91.2	0.07	12.4	0.5	96.7	0.1	51.2	6.1	80.8	2.5	41.7	3.4	30.4
SZDSZ	3.3	56.4	0.7	37.3	0.8	91.9	0.4	37.3	2.2	84.9	1.6	46.8	1.8	30.5
MDF	4.3	69.4	0.8	19.6	2.1	58.5	3.1	71.6	8.0	72.6	3.7	86.8	0.8	40.1
KDNP	4.2	83.7	3.1	69.7	3.6	89.5	1.2	92.6	na	68.3	na	na	1.1	76.2
FKGP	na	94.4	na	na	na	61.4	na	78.0	na	92.9	na	na	na	na
MIÉP	na	na	na	na	na	na	3.9	90.2	2.5	93.8	na	na	na	-na

[1] Election year in boldface.
[2] Membership fee.
[3] Direct state funding.

Source: Data collected by author based on issues of Magyar Közlöny available at: http://
www.magyarközlony.hu/nkonline/index.php.

Notes: All figures in percentages.

Bipolarization of the Party System

Although the number of parties has diminished, they have become more confrontational in style with fundamental and growing hostilities between the left and the right. An examination of Table 9.1 reveals the tendencies of bipolarization. In 1990, Hungary can be regarded as a multi-party system, but by 1998, it is a two-plus party system with two major parties having almost equal strength. The combined share of seats of the two largest parties has increased ever since. In 1998, the combined seat share was seventy-five percent, and, in 2002, it was close to ninety percent only barely decreasing in 2006 to eighty-five percent. As for the list vote of the two largest parties, the trend continues—the combined vote in 1990 was forty-six percent and by 2006 eighty-five percent which is higher than at the peak of two-partism in British politics. Bipolarization can partially explain why parties run a highly intensive and more recently even a party leadership-centered campaign.

However, this is only a partial explanation. The two sides confront each other not only on policy but on more symbolic grounds as well. Symbolic messages about the nation and general values seem to require a more intensive campaign than a policy-oriented campaign. The electorate is highly divided between the two largest parties, and the majority of the electorate votes on symbolic messages that these two parties present. In a way, this is a vicious circle: division seems to be more the creation of the parties than the genuine intention of the public, but voting reinforces this division which requires an intensive campaign. Before 1998, campaigns were conducted within the party and through the national media. However since then, more attention is placed on constituencies with the help of local/national politicians. Party leaders and their staff pursue a nation-wide campaign, visiting as many constituencies as they can. The campaign is not limited to the time frame of the actual election which is costly and time consuming.

When the financial regulations were invented and introduced, nobody knew that the parties in Hungary would follow a more election-centered understanding of politics than most parties in established democracies. This follows not only from deep party animosities and bipolarization but also from the organizational and representative weakness of parties. In this vein, parties soon began to adopt more modern (or for that matter post-modern) campaign techniques that are also expensive. Indeed, "the coterie of professional consultants on advertising, public opinion, marketing and strategic news management become more co-equal with politicians" in a kind of permanent campaign.[12] This became the case to some degree in 1998, to a larger degree in 2002, and then fully in the 2006 elections. From a campaign organizational perspective, Hungarian parties clearly fit the cartel party category.[13] Since 1990, the media market has been thoroughly transformed. It is obviously much more market-driven now which requires additional resources from parties to pay for political advertisements placed either in the electronic or print media. New personalized campaign techniques using the Internet and mobile phones have been introduced, and political advertising is now widely used by all parties.

Party Organization and Finance

The organizational composition of parties, particularly their level of centralization and size, has been found to account for the structure of their income and expenditures.[14] The extent of party finance and contributions clearly demonstrate some party characteristics as well as the problems of the finance regime. The Hungarian polity is often described as a party-centered system.[15] Party elite decision-making, a weak civil society and fragile representative linkages prove the validity of this concept. Party centeredness is in sharp contrast with the fact that party membership levels remained low. While this is a general systemic problem, some finance related questions emerge. Parties cannot rely on substantial membership income. They cannot expect party activists to work for them during the election period, and in face of vague social linkages, they seek to rely on an intensive campaign. The MSZP is the only party that has demonstrated relatively stable membership figures, but even their membership fee, as a percentage of party income, is very small. Table 9.2 shows the proportion of membership fees and party finance in the party income for selected election and non-election years. These figures have to be analyzed in the

---

12 Pippa Norris. 2002. "Campaign Communications." In *Comparing Democracies: Elections and Voting in Global* Perspective, ed. Lawrence LeDuc, Richard G. Niemi, and Pippa Norris. London: Sage, p. 134.

13 Richard S. Katz, and Peter Mair. 1995. "Changing Models of Party Organization and Party Democracy: The Emergence of the Cartel Party." *Party Politics* 1: 5–28.

14 Zsolt Enyedi. 2006. "Accounting for Organisation and Finance. A Contrast of Four Hungarian Parties." *Europe-Asia Studies* 58: 1101–1117.

15 Attila Ágh. 1999. "The Parliamentarization of the East Central European Parties: Party Discipline in the Hungarian Parliament, 1990–1996." In *Party Discipline and Parliamentary Government*, ed. Shaunw Bowler, David Farrel, and Richard S. Katz. Columbus: Ohio State University Press.

context that party income figures have changed throughout the entire period, and they have increased for all parties without exception. The two extremes are the two major parties, the MSZP and the Fidesz. The MSZP's income has increased only 2.5-fold, mainly because they were "inheritedly" rich. For example, they were able to privatize all the regional party papers and the estates which they did not want to use any longer contributing to their income at the beginning. On the other side, the income of the Fidesz has increased by thirty-fold, from eighty-four million forints ($420,000) in 1991 to 2.7 billion forints ($13.5 million) in 2006 (although more than half of the income and campaign spending originated as loans).

This increase is also connected to the organizational development of the Fidesz from a small, opposition group to government party and a viable challenger to the MSZP. Indeed, the Fidesz introduced several institutional changes to spread and to strengthen the party organization. The proportion of membership fees in the party grew spectacularly from less than one to six percent in 2001 (and then to 3.4 percent in 2006). The differences in the latter years can be explained by the changing sum of the overall party income. In 2001, a non-election year, party income was lower than in the most excessively financed election year (2006). As a result comparatively speaking, the proportion of membership fees was larger in the former year.

The political fate of the parties can be seen from these figures. For example, the MDF, the first government party after systemic change, diminished in size. Thus, its membership dues decreased first, and their proportion only began to grow again when the party income also decreased because the party's overall electoral strength diminished. The smaller parties equally show very low membership fee income. Small parties clearly have and spend less; although in this respect, the SZDSZ is better-off than the MDF. In 2006, twenty-five percent of the MDF's income came from loans. Smaller parties can rarely use this financial instrument. If the party's election result does not improve, everything might be lost as was the case of the FKGP as previously mentioned. These statistics also point out that money does not solve everything. SZDSZ income in 2006 was 930 million forints ($4.65 million) while MDF income was 660 million forints ($3.3 million), and MSZP income was 1.7 billion forints ($8.5 million).

With these qualifications and comparisons in mind, membership fees do not contribute to party income to any considerable degree. As a contrast, the proportion of public finance within each party is relatively high; although, differences and trends have to be noted. The obvious outlier again was the MSZP due to their inherited wealth in 1991. For example, only ten percent of their income originated in public money compared to a party average of over seventy-five percent. If we add up the proportion of membership dues and direct public funding, the figure is not close to one hundred percent. This demonstrates that parties often take advantage of loans and credits because donations hardly ever count in the party budget. In election years, public finance represents a much lower proportion of all party income. Lastly, it is instructive to examine the 2006 national elections to understand the connection between the finance regime and party organization. By 2006, it is interesting to note how similar party financial figures had become, with the possible exception of the Christian Democratic People's Party.

The Elite Explanation of Party Finance and Party System Development

The accumulation of mandates makes the finance system less transparent but also assists in the stabilization of an elite group (equally true of the two largest parliamentary parties) which is supported by early party consolidation. These elites are now increasingly blamed for establishing a kind of simulated democracy where the legal norms are not observed.[16] This seems to be true for the finance regime as well as the responsibility of the parliamentary parties' leadership is unquestionable. In some cases, even "kickback" money has been identified leading to questions concerning transparency and control. While there is an upper-limit for campaign spending, the financial reports of parties clearly hide much larger amounts. Of course, parties need money for other purposes not only for the elections. They have to maintain the party in terms of staff and offices between elections, and they have to be present nationally as well as locally. These responsibilities appear in the so-called "political activity" column of the reports. However, this column hides some campaign spending, particularly in election years. Occasionally, it represents a ten-fold increase in election years when compared to non-election years.

It is not unreasonable to assume that some of the excessive and illegal campaign spending is hidden in this "other expenditure" category. However, political elites assume that high campaign expenditures will win elections, and they act accordingly. We have seen this in the declared income of parties, particularly in cases of the biggest parties. If we add up the different forms of finance that originate in public money, the overall sum by 2006 is close to six billion forints ($30 million). About half of this figure is public finance based on election results, thirty percent is the public media contribution to parties, and the remaining is the contribution to parliamentary party foundations. Public finance has not been increased by the budget law since 2000, but the amounts are substantial.

Conclusions and Concerns

These aforementioned phenomena confirm the view that the party system, the campaign environment and campaign finance issues are inter-related in a complex way and in some respects work differently than in established democracies. The experience of established democracies suggests that the finance regime should not change the party system. Some qualifications and concerns should be added to this view on the basis of the Hungarian experience. First in the starting years of democracy, public finance had an impact on the stabilization of new parties and gave them some opportunities to challenge the communist successor party. During the transition, a vibrant party system was created and was helped by a liberal yet inexpensive finance regime. At this time, the MSZP was in a more advantageous position than the newly created parties. The MSZP had three to ten times more income than any of the other parliamentary parties. As a relatively small parliamentary party at that time, the

---

16 Gabriella Ilonszki, and György Lengyel. N.d. "A Simulated Democracy? Democratic Elitism in Hungary." In *Democracy without Illusion: Democratic Elitism Reconsidered*, ed. John Higley, and Heinrich Best. Forthcoming.

level of their public finance was moderate (the same level as other parties of similar electoral strength). These features demonstrate that the strength of the successor party lied elsewhere, and public finance indeed helped the other parties to compete with the MSZP. The economic, social network and bureaucratic potentials of the party were rejuvenated after the initial years. After the second free election, there has been a re-appearance of the party's advantages: increasing public finance as a result of electoral success was complemented by relatively high membership fees and by the economic potential and old networks of the candidates. Paradoxically, the richest entrepreneurs and *nouveau riche* can be found in the ranks of the MSZP while the old working class and the upper social layers also belong to the party.[17]

Second, while the finance regime might influence party developments in other countries, in Hungary, it is rather the characteristics of parties and the party system that have had an impact on the campaign environment and as a result on campaign spending.[18] Party-centeredness, party and political bipolarization and frozen elites all point to the same conclusion: Hungarian elections are now more intensive and extensive and campaign money matters. From another perspective, a more indirect connection between campaign spending and party system development prevails tied to the money mobilization potential of parties and not to public finance.

In addition, another issue which is widely discussed in the public finance literature concerns whether parliamentary parties enjoy a more advantageous position than out-of-parliament parties. In the local Hungarian campaigns, the candidates of smaller parties can rarely compete financially with the candidates of larger parties. Hungary began systemic change with relatively well-developed parties (as compared to other post-communist countries) with the effect that a party-centered polity developed. Moreover, their early arrival helped the parties to stabilize themselves. New parties or split-away parties could not compete financially in the electoral market with the old ones. More than ninety percent of the amount defined by the budget law for public finance is at the disposal of the five parliamentary parties. Public finance does not serve to initiate or give newcomers a chance but helps those who are in a winning position. On the other hand, the one percent threshold that gives entitlement for state subsidy is lower than the parliamentary threshold, and thus it helps to maintain smaller parties. After all, it is not the finance regime itself but the identified political phenomena which explains the disappearance and the fragility of smaller parties.

Hungary adopted the prevalent European model by giving preference to public money in party finance, but the finance regime has not developed legitimacy and is looked upon with suspicion by the public. Public finance constantly raises concerns in established West European democracies as well because irrespective of the regulation, state subsidies do not stop parties from raising additional resources. Some particular conditions further increased this tendency in Hungary. In the post-communist transition, several transformations occurred at the same time

---

17 Attila Ágh. 2002. "The Dual Challenge and the Reform of the Hungarian Socialist Party." *Communist and Post-Communist Studies* 3: 269–288.

18 Richard S. Katz. 1996. "Party Organization and Finance." In *Comparing Democracies: Elections and Voting in Global Perspective*, ed. Lawrence LeDuc, Richard G. Niemi, and Pippa Norris. London: Sage, pp. 107–133.

(for example, economic as well as political) which overwhelmed party finance issues.[19] Entrepreneurs and politicians were bound, and business and politics was often generated by the same group of individuals. Conflict of interest issues were only belatedly legislated upon and from a broader political perspective, a situation developed in which a strong connection between politics and business gave rise to suspicions that parties are channeling public money for their own purposes, and in campaigns, they use this money without control.

We have seen some evidence, particularly around the period of systemic change, that the political finance regime influences the political opportunity structure of parties. This is a conclusion we can draw from the Southern European experience as well.[20] However in the Hungarian case, party system development had a major impact on the campaign environment which in turn set the standard for creating and applying the finance regime. Lasting tensions between real politics and formal rules do not serve democratic norms or the interests of the political class in the medium run.

---

19 Gabriella Ilonszki, and Gábor Iván. 2006. "Campaign–Parties–Money: Old Questions in New Democracies." *The Analyst* 2: 41–62.

20 Ingrid van Biezen. 2000. "Party Financing in New Democracies: Portugal and Spain." *Party Politics* 6: 329–342.

Chapter 10

Romania:
The Secondary Influence of Public
Finance on the Party System

Steven D. Roper, Adrian Moraru and Elena Iorga

Since 1996, Romania has had a system of direct party and campaign finance which exhibits many of the characteristics found among other post-communist countries. The funding scheme favors parliamentary parties, and the lack of financial controls has lead to repeated charges of corruption. Moreover, the use of public finance has become part of the larger debate over party registration and party patronage activities before and during campaigns. The Romanian case calls into question how state finance influences the party system and the role of money in politics. While considerable funding is necessary during the election campaign, party spending does not automatically translate into electoral success.

In addition, the provision of public funding has not decreased the costs of campaigns. As the costs and the necessity of purchasing media have increased, campaigns have become more expensive, and public finance has not alleviated the need of parties to seek additional funding sources. While public party and campaign finance has had a modest influence on the Romanian party system, other factors such as party registration, electoral thresholds and generally low levels of transparency in party internal structures have contributed to the fluidity and the relative stability of the party system. In this chapter, we discuss the development of the Romanian system of party and campaign finance and analyze issues surrounding party development including threshold and membership requirements. We analyze the various sources of party income, reporting requirements and generally level of transparency in the system. The last section of the chapter explores the impact that state finance has had on the Romanian party system by examining the entry and the exit of parties throughout the period between 1990 and 2004. More specifically, we analyze how public finance influences the party system by focusing on the number of parties that gain representation in the parliament as well as the composition of party revenues during the 1990s and the 2000s.

We analyze the influence of public finance on the party system and employ two measures for examining the effect. First, we use the "effective number of parties" index developed by Laakso and Taagepera to calculate the number of parties represented in the Romanian parliament as an indicator of the overall party system.[1] If public finance provides a more level playing field, then one would expect that the number of parties represented in the parliament would increase with the use of public finance. On the other hand if larger parties reap the lion-share of party and campaign finance, then state finance leads to the stability of larger parties and the party system. While the effective number of parties measure provides a comparative statistic over elections to determine whether the party system is fragmenting or consolidating, it does not allow us to see changes in the actual parties which enter parliament and form government.

Therefore, we also examine the relative change in the composition of parliamentary parties over time to determine the development of the party system. We calculate a party incumbency rate for each parliamentary term which is the percentage of parties and coalitions which were retained from the previous parliament. A high incumbency rate indicates party consolidation as the same parties are re-elected. However, a low incumbency rate indicates a fluid party system in which party identification and loyalties change between elections. If public finance produces a more level playing field among parties and does not freeze the party system, then we would expect a lower incumbency rate when finance is provided.

Calculating the incumbency rate among Romanian parties is difficult as they have splintered, re-formed and coalesced into new parties and associations, often several times. Therefore to simplify the process, we did not count new coalitions and alliances as incumbent even if they contained a party returning to parliament because the nature of alliance politics, especially in Romania, makes it difficult to discern whether in some cases the party would have been re-elected on its own. Overall, we find that public finance has had a limited influence on the party system as a whole but has been influential for specific parties, especially during non-election years.

The Electoral System

The Romanian electoral system has changed little since the 1990 parliamentary elections. The system of elections to both the Chamber of Deputies and the Senate are based on proportional representation with closed party lists. At the county district level, votes are translated into seats using a Hare quota, and the remaining seats which are not allocated at the district level are aggregated nationally and distributed based on the *d'Hondt* formula. For the 1990 elections, there was no electoral threshold for a party or a party electoral coalition while a three percent threshold for an individual party and up to eight percent threshold for party electoral coalitions was imposed for the 1992 and the 1996 parliamentary elections.[2] For the 2000 and the 2004 elections,

---

1   The Laakso and Taagepera effective number of parties index has been widely used in the literature. It is based on the idea that determining the number of parties should be based on their relative strength. See, Markku Laakso and Rein Taagepera. 1979. "'Effective' Number of Parties: A Measure with Application to Western Europe." *Comparative Political Studies* 12: 3–27.

2   Significantly, there was no change to the party registration requirement of 251 members.

the threshold was raised to five percent for an individual party and up to ten percent for a party electoral coalition.

These changes in the electoral threshold over time have had an important effect on party system consolidation. While there were eighteen parties and coalitions in the 1990 parliament, the number decreased to four by the 2004 elections. In addition, the raising of the threshold has also forced parties into electoral coalitions so that by 2004, fifty percent of the seats in the lower house were awarded to coalitions. Changes in the threshold have also been accompanied by changes in party registration requirements. The 1990 party registration law only required a party to have 251 members.[3] The number of members required for registration was raised to 10,000 in 1996 and further increased to 25,000 in 2003 (in addition, party membership must be drawn from at least eighteen counties, including Bucharest, with no less than 700 persons per county).

The Development of the Romanian Public Finance Model

Similar to the case of Hungary (discussed in Chapter 9), parties had access to limited campaign finance for the founding election in 1990. Article 53 of the 1990 election law provided all parties that participated in the election a state subsidy.[4] In addition, the law stipulated that contributions from foreign sources were not permitted. Article 51 provided parties free access to radio and to television during the campaign. In 1990, the ruling National Salvation Front (FSN) controlled the financial resources of the former Romanian Communist Party. Therefore the FSN, as the communist successor party, had substantial funding for the 1990 campaign while the state subsidy provide under the law amounted to only $500.[5] Therefore, the subsidy which was provided did not create a more level playing field. Moreover, the prohibition against foreign contributions was not motivated by a desire to minimize corruption. Instead, this prohibition was specifically designed to prevent Ion Ratiu (the opposition presidential candidate of the National Peasants Party Christian Democratic or PNTCD) from using his fortune amassed in Great Britain during the campaign.

In addition, the electronic media did not provide equal access to parties. In the early 1990s, there was only one national television station which was state controlled and a handful of state and independent radio stations. While the FSN was prominently featured in every broadcast, the opposition "suffered from limited access to programming, unpredictable placement and uneven access to recording studios and equipment."[6] This phenomenon is not unusual as Katz and Mair find that "although new parties may get access to the state media if they nominate a

---

3   *Monitorul Oficial al Romaniei.* 1989. 30 December.

4   *Monitorul Oficial al Romaniei.* 1990. 18 March.

5   Carothers argues that few, if any, opposition parties actually received the state subsidy. See, Thomas Carothers. 1992. "Romania." In *The New Democratic Frontier*, ed. Larry Garber, and Eric Bjorn. Washington, DC: National Democratic Institute for International Affairs.

6   Ibid.

sufficiently large number of candidates, that access is sometimes minimal, or is available only at the least attractive times."[7]

The first Romanian local elections were held in March 1992. In late 1991, a draft law supported by the opposition was debated in parliament which would have provided campaign finance to all parties.[8] Campaign finance was not only important to the opposition, including the PNTCD and the newly formed Democratic Convention of Romania (CDR), but also to certain members of the FSN. Prime Minister Petre Roman had been forced to resign by President Ion Iliescu in September 1991, and the pro-Roman wing of the FSN felt that public finance was necessary to be able to compete. Ultimately, pro-Iliescu MPs were successful in blocking the passage of the law which affected not only the pro-Roman wing of the FSN but all opposition parties. While there was no campaign finance for the 1992 local elections, the electoral law provided free television and radio coverage to parties. Even though there was no system of campaign finance, the opposition did extremely well, winning the mayoral contests in many of Romania's largest cities. The lack of a public finance did not undermine the competitiveness of the opposition; however, these were local elections in which candidates had a greater opportunity to interact with their constituency. As a consequence, media exposure and financing were not as critical. The real test for the opposition came in the following 1992 national elections.

While in principle public finance was available, no party actually received campaign finance for the 1992 national elections because parliament never passed the required enabling legislation. Once again, party finances were addressed in the election law which forbade parties from accepting funds from foreigners, public institutions or public authorities. Extra-parliamentary parties and independent candidates had media access on the basis of state negotiated contracts in which parties and independent candidates had reduced charges. In addition, the law stated that parliamentary parties were allotted at least twice as much broadcast time as extra-parliamentary parties and in proportion to their number of parliamentary seats.[9] Unlike the 1990 law, there was a contribution reporting requirement to the Ministry of Economics and Finance; although, a ceiling was never imposed for contributions for either individuals or corporations.[10] The 1992 national elections were conducted without campaign finance or a specific legislative framework for parties which addressed organizational and financial matters.

Between 1992 and 1996, there was no system of public party finance. As accusations of party financial corruption increased, parliament finally decided to

---

7   Richard S. Katz, and Peter Mair. 1996. "Cadre, Catch-All or Cartel? A Rejoinder." *Party Politics* 2, pp. 529–530.

8   The bill stipulated, however, that eighty-five percent of party finance was reserved for parliamentary parties.

9   The law made a distinction between pre- and post-nomination broadcast time. After the nominating period, a new allotment of time was issued in proportion to the number of candidate lists a party had throughout the country. If parties did not have lists in at least ten districts (there are forty-one districts and the city of Bucharest), they forfeited their right to broadcast time. See, *Monitorul Oficial al Romaniei.* 15 July 1992.

10   Each party had to designate a specific fiscal agent who registered with the Ministry of Economics and Finance.

implement a full-scale system of public party finance shortly before the 1996 national elections. At the same time, the parliament also decided to provide greater clarity regarding the regulation of parties. The 1996 "Law on Political Parties" comprised the first specific framework for the regulation of parties outside of the electoral process. Until 1996, parties, as organizations, operated based on a decree dating back to December 1989.[11] The 1996 law addressed the registration procedure and membership of parties as well as the system of public party and campaign finance. The law was adopted in April 1996 only months before the fall parliamentary elections. Various amendments to the law have been proposed to increase the amount of transparency in reporting, but no amendments to the legislation were passed until December 2002 (later modified in July 2006).

Sources of Party Income

The 1996 law addresses issues involving party registration, organization, finances and reporting. Generally, the three major categories of party revenue addressed in the legislation include public finance, membership fees and individual and corporate contributions. During non-election years, public finance, for many parties, is the single largest source of revenue; however, this is due to the fact that membership fees and contributions are generally under-reported. If these fees and contributions were better reported, they would be, for almost all parties, the most significant part of the total party income. Indeed, official statistics show that during election years, membership and contributions, for most parties, constitute the greatest sources of party revenue. Therefore public finance is not a *substitute* for private contributions but a *supplement* to party fundraising activity.

The current law provides parliamentary and extra-parliamentary parties public finance. Article 39 states that parties at the beginning of the yearly legislative session that are represented by a parliamentary faction in at least one of the chambers receive a base subsidy. The total of the base subsidy is one-third of the total state subsidy allocated to all parties. Parliamentary parties also receive a subsidy in proportion to their number of seats. The amount awarded per seat is established by dividing the remaining two-thirds of the total state subsidy by the total number of MPs (for the Chamber of Deputies and the Senate). The total amount allocated to extra-parliamentary parties cannot exceed one base subsidy.

Because the allocation is based on the party's vote share in the last election, the system of public finance freezes the party system for four years.[12] In other words, parties receive four years of financing even if by the third year the party no longer has significant electoral support. Starting in 1996, fifteen parties were awarded some form of state subsidy. As shown in Table 10.1 between 1997 and 2000, the two largest parties, the Party of Social Democracy in Romania (PDSR) and the PNTCD (as part of the CDR), not surprisingly received the largest amount of state finance.

---

11 *Monitorul Oficial al Romaniei*. 31 December 1989.
12 Unless there are early elections, parliamentary elections occur every four years.

Table 10.1   Subsidy for Romanian parliamentary groups, 1997–2000

Parties/ Coalitions	Democratic Convention of Romania[1]	Party of Social Democracy in Romania	Union of Social Democracy	Party of Romanian National Unity	Hungarian Democratic Union of Romania	Party of Greater Romania
1997	584,431[2]	420,770	301,417	155,622	187,068	161,339
1998	723,823	521,126	373,307	192,739	231,685	199,820
1999	655,367	471,841	338,002	174,511	209,773	180,992
2000	741,111	533,573	382,223	197,342	237,218	204,592

[1] The subsidy for all CDR parties has been combined into a single Convention total.
[2] Amounts reported in USD.

Source: These data were computed by Steven D. Roper based on budget revenues reported by the International Monetary Fund.

Unlike other post-communist countries, a special formula is used to calculate the subsidy for those parties which promote female candidate. For parties with female candidates on the party list, the amount assigned from the state budget is to be increased *pro rata* to the number of mandates obtained in the election by female candidates. This provision, although based on the principle of gender equality, has limited application as it does not stipulate a clear algorithm to perform the assignment. The subsidy from the state budget is paid monthly in the account of each party through the budget of the Permanent Electoral Authority, and it is to be recorded separately in party accounts.[13]

The current legislation limits yearly membership fees paid by a party member to a maximum of forty-eight times the minimum gross salary (approximately $8,800). Total contributions received by a party during a fiscal year may not exceed 0.025 percent of the state budget, except in years when parliamentary, presidential or European parliamentary elections take place when it is adjusted to 0.050 percent. The contribution limit a party may receive from an individual during the year is 200 times the minimum basic gross salary ($36,600), and the limit from legal entities such as corporations is 500 times the minimum gross salary ($91,000). The fair value of movable and immovable goods donated to a party and services supplied free of charge are also included in these limits. In particular, any donation to a party which represents a twenty percent price reduction from the value of the good or the service must be registered separately as a contribution. It is illegal for parties to receive contributions from legal entities that have outstanding debts to the state budget, the social security budget or a local government budget older than sixty days. Also prohibited are contributions and services supplied free of charge from public institutions or authorities, *regies autonomes*, trading companies or banks with at least a majority of state capital, labor unions and religious organizations.

Table 10.2 reports income from membership fees for the major parties from 1997 through 2000. It is interesting to note that there is a different pattern of finance

---

13 As of 1 July 2007, the authority in charge with the control of financing parties and electoral campaigns in Romania.

Table 10.2   Romanian Party income from membership fees, 1997–2000

Parties/ Coalitions	Democratic Convention of Romania[1]	Party of Social Democracy in Romania	Union of Social Democracy	Party of Romanian National Unity	Hungarian Democratic Union of Romania	Party of Greater Romania
1997	550.3[2]	315.8	109.4	7.3	654.6	149.9
1998	1,170.6	624.6	67.2	5.6	587.3	251.6
1999	2,086.3	1,546.4	33.8	14.0	1,092.6	395.5
2000	509.7	0	70.6	44.7	2,328.7	690.1

[1] The subsidy for all CDR parties has been combined into a single Convention total.
[2] Amounts reported in billions of lei.

Source: These data were computed by Adrian Moraru and Elena Iorga based on revenues reported by the Romanian Court of Accounts.

among the parties reported in Table 10.1 and 10.2. While the Democratic Party (PD) of the Union of Social Democracy received the third highest amount of public finance in 1999, it had one of the lowest levels of membership fees of all major Romanian parties. Moreover for all the parties, public finance as a percentage of total income was more important than membership fees during the 1990s. This pattern changes throughout the 2000s as membership fees and contributions become more important. Besides the traditional sources of private financing, Romanian parties may also obtain income from a series of activities including editing and publishing publications, organizing meetings and seminars with political, economic or social themes, cultural, sport and entertainment activities, leasing party buildings and interest paid by banks.

Spending Ceilings

The Romanian legislation is very strict in regards to the types of expenses that parties and candidates may incur and the amount of the expenses. From income originating from the state budget, parties may incur expenses for the following: the enhancement and the operating of the central office, personnel, media, the organization of activities of a political nature, travel in-country and overseas, telecommunications, fees owed to international political organizations to which the party is affiliated, investments in movable and immovable goods necessary for the activity of the party, protocol and campaigning. In regards to the expense ceiling which parties and candidates may incur during campaigns, the amount varies from twenty times the minimum gross national salary for candidates in local elections ($3,660) to 25,000 times the minimum gross national salary for presidential candidates (over $4.5 million).

Reporting and Measures of Transparency

Parties are obliged to declare and to publish revenues and expenses as follows: first, parties must report the total amount of income obtained from membership fees by 31 March of the following year as well as a list of party members who paid membership fees valued over ten times the minimum gross national salary ($1,800). Second, the list of individual and corporate members who made, during one fiscal year, contributions which exceeded ten times the minimum gross national salary ($1,800), and third, the amount of the financial contribution of any political formation which the party is associated.

The main institution charged with controlling party finances and election campaigns is the Permanent Electoral Authority (PEA) and more specifically the Department for the Control of Financing Parties and Electoral Campaigns. This Department works in conjunction with the Court of Accounts which is the agency tasked to audit and to oversee funding from the state budget. The results of these audits are published in the Official Gazette of Romania. From 1996 until the 2006, all financial oversight was provided by the Court of Accounts, but authority for supervising party finances was transferred to the PEA in 2006. However, the reforms implemented which created this electoral management body were plagued with problems. With the transfer of the control liabilities to the PEA (starting initially in January 2007), it was determined that due to certain failures of the institution, the PEA could not fully assume the complete supervision of parties. Only since July 2007 has the PEA taken over all authority related to party financing and campaigns, and the first test of this institution occurred during the European parliamentary elections in November 2007.

Deficiencies in the Regulation of Party Finance

The 2006 party finance reform legislation contained certain measures which were designed to increase the level of transparency in party funding. There are, however, a number of deficiencies in the actual implementation of the law. The local party structures developed a parallel system of financing through the underground economy which has not significantly changed. Record keeping has been spotty at best, and few parties at the local level have maintained good accounting practices. The lack of transparency has led in certain cases to the transformation of the party's finances into a private business. This mechanism starts with the charging of "fees" for candidates that are not reported, the obtaining of contributions that remain undeclared and the conclusion of contracts with companies owned by party members resulting in exaggerated settlements. Therefore, there is a concern that there is too much money in the political process. However, this fear is not justified as estimates indicate that Romanian elections, as a percentage of the state budget, are relatively modest. Instead, the problem is the manner in which the money is used, often in the form of covert advertising (for example, street publicity and publicity in the print media). Moreover, the use of the public resources in campaigns by incumbents is a frequent problem, and the current legislation does not adequately address the issue of patronage sufficiently.

The Influence of Public Finance on Party Development

Aside from the issue of financial transparency and corruption, the other major issue within the party finance literature is how the system of public finance influences the development of the party system. Given that so many factors influence the development of individual parties and the party system as a whole, it is empirically difficult to measure the singular impact of public finance. As discussed above, party membership requirements, the use of electoral thresholds and even the formation of parliamentary factions influence the broader party system. That said, the Romanian case provides evidence that public finance does not alleviate the need for private funding nor does it have as much of an influence on party electoral success as might be expected.

The 1990 election provides a baseline for examining party system development in Romania. In 1990, the FSN won over sixty-eight percent of the lower house seats and FSN presidential candidate Iliescu won over eighty-five percent of the vote. While the FSN held an absolute majority of parliamentary seats, seventeen other parties gained seats.[14] The large number of parties represented in the parliament was a direct consequence of the party registration law and the lack of an electoral threshold. However, most of these parties held few seats, and because of the overwhelming dominance of the FSN, the effective number of parliamentary parties was actually quite low (2.11) which indicates a relatively consolidated party system centered on the FSN (see Table 10.3).

Table 10.3   Romanian Party incumbency and effective number of parties, 1990–2004

Parliament Term	Incumbency Rate (%)	Number of Parliamentary Parties
1990–1992	–	2.11
1992–1996	18	4.49
1996–2000	83	3.98
2000–2004	60	3.54
2004–Present	50	3.83

Source: Data compiled by Steven D. Roper. The incumbency rate was calculated for all parties and coalitions which were re-elected to parliament.

By the 1992 parliamentary elections, the new threshold requirement had a significant impact on the number of parties represented in parliament (see Table 10.3). The number of parties elected to the lower house (Chamber of Deputies) was less than

---

14 This number does not include ethnic minority parties which are guaranteed a seat in the lower house. Of the ethnic-based parties, only the Hungarian Democratic Union of Romania and the German Democratic Forum received enough votes to win an outright seat in 1990.

half the total from 1990.[15] While the number of parties which entered parliament decreased, the actual size of these parliamentary parties increased so that the effective number of parties index more than doubled for this election (4.49). Therefore even in an election with no public finance, there was an actual increase in the number of seats which non-governing parliamentary parties gained, at the expense of the old FSN. Perhaps because of the dominance of the FSN in the 1990 parliament, it is not surprising that the effective number of parties would increase as parties chipped away at the FSN seat total. Moreover by 1992, many parties consolidated into larger party organizations. In addition, the incumbency rate for the second parliament (1992–1996) was eighteen percent demonstrating considerable fluidity in the actual parties which passed the newly imposed threshold. Indeed, many of the 1990 couch parties simply vanished or merged with other parties.

Since the introduction of party finance in 1996, there have been three parliamentary elections in which we can specifically assess the impact of state finance on party electoral performance. However because the changes in public finance occurred only a few months before the national elections in 1996, it is doubtful that the finance had any meaningful impact on the electoral fortunes of smaller parties. Indeed as seen in Table 10.3, the party system further consolidated after the 1996 election, and the number of incumbent parties returned to parliament increased to almost eighty-five percent. Given that state finance occurred so late in the electoral cycle, it is not surprising that smaller and new parties had a difficult time entering parliament.

By the time of the 2000 national elections, the trend towards party consolidation continued as the number of parties which passed the newly installed five percent threshold fell from six to five. Indeed what is most striking is that the ruling coalition, the CDR, which received the greatest amount of state subsidy during the period from 1996–2000 failed to pass the threshold for the 2000 national elections. Significantly, few parties which entered the parliament were a pre-electoral coalition of parties and organizations which demonstrates the increasing maturity of the Romanian party system. While the system consolidated in terms of the number of parties, there was still considerable fluidity in terms of the types of parties which entered and exited out of the parliament (see Table 10.3).

Approximately forty percent of the parties from the 1996–2000 parliament failed to pass the threshold in the 2000 national elections (most significantly the ruling coalition), and the National Liberal Party (PNL) re-entered the parliament for the first time since the 1990 national elections. It is difficult, however, to establish that the consolidation and the fluidity of the party system by 2000 were directly related to the system of public finance. As the number of private television and radio channels proliferated by 2000, free media access and other benefits of public finance proved less important. The failure of the ruling CDR to pass the threshold in the 2000 elections indicates that this was a party coalition that was out-of-touch with voters throughout the country, and no amount of finance would assist the coalition in re-capturing votes.

---

15 Interestingly, the number of parties represented in the upper house actually increased from seven to eight.

The 2000 election marked the return of the PDSR to government as well as former President Iliescu, and the largest parties enjoyed substantial state finance compared to smaller parliamentary and especially non-parliamentary parties throughout the early 2000s. By the time of the 2004 national elections, the two leading parties entered into coalitions. The PDSR renamed itself the Social Democratic Party (PSD) and entered a coalition with the Humanist Party of Romania (PUR) labeled the National Union PSD + PUR while the PNL and the PD entered into the Justice and Truth Alliance. Once again, the Romanian party system was both fluid and consolidating at the same time. While the number of parties and coalitions which entered the parliament was reduced to four, a new party, the PUR, was elected. In addition, incumbent parties were re-elected at a slightly lower level than previously.[16]

Public finance neither froze the party system nor led to a more level playing field for smaller parties. While state finance can be an asset to party performance, the case of the Greater Romania Party (PRM) is instructive. This party received substantial party finance between the 2000 and the 2004 elections (see Table 10.4). However, the performance of the party suffered considerably as it lost almost fifty percent of its seats. This demonstrates that parties which are personalistic (the PRM is an election vehicle for the nationalist Corneliu Vadim Tudor) can suffer a reversal of fortune no matter how much money is at the party's disposal.

The importance of the party subsidy varies—for some parties, the subsidy forms the vast majority of its yearly income. However over the last few years, the importance of the subsidy as a percentage of total party income has actually decreased for all parliamentary parties. In Table 10.4, we calculate the percentage of income that the party subsidy represents for all parliamentary groups. In every case,

Table 10.4   Romanian Parliamentary group subsidy as a percentage of income, 2001–2003

Parties/Coalitions	Social Democratic Pole of Romania[1]	Democratic Party	National Liberal Party	Hungarian Democratic Union of Romania	Party of Greater Romania
2001	53	46	–	50	78
2002	31	43	64	22	83
2003	23	35	47	26	70
2004	5	15	13	16	32

[1] The Social Democratic Pole of Romania includes the Party of Social Democracy in Romania, the Romanian Social Democratic Party and the Humanist Party of Romania.

Source: These data were computed by Steven D. Roper based on subsidy and income reported by the Ministry of Finance and the Court of Accounts.

---

16 The incumbency rate for the 2004 election is a reflection of the new coalitions which emerged before the election. The actual retention rate of parties was higher than fifty percent, but these parties were part of new coalitions (often with newly created parties).

the percentage of income that the subsidy represents has decreased since 2001. In some cases such as the PSD and the PUR coalition, the importance of public finance as a percentage of party revenue has decreased by almost fifty percent. Interestingly, only the extremist PRM continues to rely heavily on the public finance.

Because of changes in coalitions and factions, it is more difficult to calculate these figures prior to 2001; however for the Hungarian Democratic Union of Romania (UDMR) and the PRM, the pre-2001 pattern is largely the same. In 1999, the party subsidy represented fifty percent of UDMR income while it represented eighty-four percent for the PRM. By 2003, the reliance on the subsidy decreased for both parties. Also as reported in Table 10.4, the reliance on the state subsidy as a percentage of party income during an election year diminishes significantly. During the 2004 election, the state subsidy for the PRM represented approximately thirty percent of the party's income while for the PSD, the subsidy constituted only five percent of the party's total income.

Conclusions

The relationship between pubic finance and party development is complex. On the one hand, finance laws can be designed by politicians to exclude the entrance of new parties. However as Katz and Mair argue, the attempt to use public finance to suppress new parties can actually backfire and provide these parties a rallying cry against the political establishment.[17] In the Romanian case, we have seen considerable fluidity in the type of parties that have entered parliament. Governing parties have failed to re-enter parliament (for example, CDR in 2000) while other parties re-appeared after not having achieved electoral success for many years. Indeed during the period from 1992–2004, the average incumbency rate in Romania was approximately fifty percent. While this figure is partially an artifact of coalition-building before elections, we have witnessed parties come and go and come back again.

The discussion of the impact of party and campaign finance on the party system must also be broadened to include such issues as party membership requirements and the electoral threshold. By raising the parliamentary threshold requirements in 1992 and again in 2000, Romanian politicians placed party system consolidation as their primary goal rather than providing a level playing field. State finance was seen as tangential to this overriding concern. Politicians and parties have devised finance laws in order to promote partisan or intra-party factional advantage, and the Romanian case shows that the effect of state finance on the electoral fortunes of parties varies widely and that the use of public finance does not guarantee electoral success for a party. Moreover while the larger Romanian parties have attempted to create a cartel party system, they have been unsuccessful in preventing the establishment of new parties and ultimately maintaining their political power. In isolation, public finance has a marginal influence on the party system as a whole but can be important to the electoral performance of individual parties. For Romanian parties, access to finance is necessary, although not sufficient, to guarantee electoral success.

---

17 Richard S. Katz and Peter Mair. 1995. "Changing Models of Party Organization and Party Democracy." *Party Politics* 1: 5–28.

Index

For Product Safety Concerns and Information please contact our EU
representative GPSR@taylorandfrancis.com
Taylor & Francis Verlag GmbH, Kaufingerstraße 24, 80331 München, Germany

www.ingramcontent.com/pod-product-compliance
Lightning Source LLC
Chambersburg PA
CBHW050716280326
41926CB00088B/3060